M CI

Boom Cities is the first published history of the profound transformations of British city centres in the 1960s. It has often been said that urban planners did more damage to Britain's cities than even the Luftwaffe had managed, but this study details the rise and fall of modernist urban planning, revealing its origins and the dissolution of the cross-party consensus, before the ideological smearing that has ever since characterized the high-rise towers, dizzying ring roads, and concrete precincts that were left behind.

The rebuilding of British city centres during the 1960s drastically affected the built form of urban Britain, from traditional cathedral cities through to the decaying towns of the Industrial Revolution. *Boom Cities* uncovers both the planning philosophy and the political, cultural, and legislative background that created the conditions for these processes to occur across the country.

Boom Cities reveals the role of architect-planners in these transformations. The volume also provides an unconventional account of the end of modernist approaches to the built environment, showing it from the perspective of planning and policy elites, rather than through the emergence of public opposition to planning.

Otto Saumarez Smith is an Architectural and Urban Historian, and is an Assistant Professor in Art History at the University of Warwick.

Praise for *Boom Cities*

'*Boom Cities* is much more than a book about buildings. It is instead a study about town planning, welfare and the politics of affluence, and hence central to the history of mid-20th century Britain. *Boom Cities* may be a slim volume but it is packed with insights which make it an essential reference point for the new urban social history that is rapidly—and excitingly—emerging.'

Professor Simon Gunn, *Reviews in History*

'The strength of *Boom Cities* lies in its insistence that blaming individuals for the failures of a whole political and economic system is too easy. It makes us see the things that should have been different, and the ways in which they could still be.'

Lynsey Hanley, *New Statesman*

'Saumarez Smith demonstrates that the urban plans of the 1960s were shaped by forces that are still central to contemporary practice: the need to use urban renewal to reduce inequalities and yet serve an affluent citizenry; the requirement to balance the needs of a local community against the developer's profit motive; and the desire to insert new forms into the historic cityscape thoughtfully. The resonances with contemporary practice are clear throughout this book: *Boom Cities* is therefore essential reading not just for historians of 20th century architecture and urbanism, but also for anyone seeking a deeper understanding of the development of the contemporary planning profession.'

Ewan Harrison, *The RIBA Journal*

Boom Cities

Architect-Planners and the Politics of Radical Urban Renewal in 1960s Britain

OTTO SAUMAREZ SMITH

OXFORD
UNIVERSITY PRESS

OXFORD
UNIVERSITY PRESS

Great Clarendon Street, Oxford, OX2 6DP,
United Kingdom

Oxford University Press is a department of the University of Oxford.
It furthers the University's objective of excellence in research, scholarship,
and education by publishing worldwide. Oxford is a registered trade mark of
Oxford University Press in the UK and in certain other countries

First published 2019
First published in paperback 2020

Published in the United States of America by Oxford University Press
198 Madison Avenue, New York, NY 10016, United States of America

British Library Cataloguing in Publication Data
Data available

Library of Congress Cataloging in Publication Data
Data available

ISBN 978–0–19–883640–7 (Hbk.)
ISBN 978–0–19–886519–3 (Pbk.)

Acknowledgements

I have been very fortunate to have received the encouragement, enthusiasm, and guidance of Nick Bullock and Peter Mandler. Simon Gunn, William Whyte, and Guy Ortolano have also been immensely generous and galvanizing. Others who have provided the buttresses of intellectual community and practical support in countless ways include Samuel Bibby, Paul Binski, Megan Boulton, Pat Boyd, Simon Bradley, Emma Bridgewater, Susan Brigden, Max Bryant, Anya Burgon, Richard Butler, Barnabas Calder, James Campbell, Gillian Darley, Francé Davies, John Davis, Julien Domercq, Louise Durning, Alistair Fair, Adrian Forty, Roy Foster, John Gold, Emily Guerry, the late Peter Hall, Erika Hanna, Fuchsia Hart, Elain Harwood, Aaron Helfand, Peter Hennessy, Alistair Kefford, Alastair Langlands, Peter McCollough, Hannah Malone, Gillian Malpass, Melanie Marshall, Helen Meller, Alan Powers, Juliet Ramsden, Matthew Rice, Lucian Robinson, Peter Ruback, Frank Salmon, Charles Saumarez Smith, Richard Sennett, Neal Shasore, the late Gavin Stamp, Sam Wetherell, Ellis Woodman, Henry Woudhuysen, and George Younge. My thanks to the Master and Fellows of St John's College, Cambridge, where I completed a PhD funded by the Kemp Scholarship. Also thanks to the Rector and Fellows of Lincoln College, Oxford, where I was Shuffrey Junior Research Fellow.

My thanks to the staff at the University Library, Cambridge; the Architecture and History of Art Library, Cambridge; St John's College Library, Cambridge; the Bodleian; Lincoln College Library, Oxford; the Sackler Library, Oxford; the British Library, London; the RIBA Library, London; the National Archives, Kew; the London Library; Bolton Archives History Centre; Haringey Archive Centre; Hertfordshire Archives and Local Studies; The Huntington Library, San Marino; Lancashire Archives, Preston; London Metropolitan Archives; Portsmouth Record Office; the Record Office for Leicestershire, Leicester and Rutland; RIBA Drawings and Archive Collection; Colin Buchanan Papers at Imperial College; and the London School of Economics Archive.

Contents

List of Figures

Introduction

> Morris took the newly opened section of the Inner Ring, an exhilarating complex of tunnels and flyovers . . . From here you got a panorama of the whole city and the sun came out at that moment, shining like floodlighting on the pale concrete facades of the recent construction work, tower blocks and freeways, throwing them into relief against the sombre mass of nineteenth-century slums and decayed factories. Seen from this perspective, it looked as though the seeds of the whole twentieth-century city had been planted under the ground a long time ago and were now beginning to shoot up into the light, bursting through the caked, exhausted topsoil of Victorian architecture.
>
> David Lodge, *Changing Places* (1975)

This book covers a constellation of ideas about the radical renewal of the central areas of British cities in the 1960s. It is devoted to exploring the changes wrought on British city centres during that decade—a process with lasting repercussions for the built environment and for society more generally. In contrast to related areas such as new towns or council housing, city-centre redevelopment has received very little scholarly attention, despite its obvious importance, manifest in towns and cities throughout the country.

In the early 1960s there was a short-lived but deep-rooted consensus about the need to radically remake cities for a changing Britain. The year 1963 marked the high point in the trajectory of an ambitious set of ideas. It saw the publication of the official report *Traffic in Towns,* which proposed the rebuilding of cities for the automobile. It was also the year that geographer Peter Hall gave a vision of London by the year 2000, in which the city was surrounded by twenty-five new towns and interlaced with motorways, so that residents would live an ultramobile life, while the centre would become a patchwork of precinctual traditional areas and new neighbourhoods on multiple levels.[1] The year saw the publication of

[1] Peter Hall, *London 2000* (London, 1963).

the planner Wilfred Burns's plan for Newcastle upon Tyne, which gave expression to the politician T. Dan Smith's ideal of a 'Tyneside Renaissance', a city centre to which people would come not just to shop, but merely to 'stand and stare'.[2] The year 1963 represents the high point of what Christopher Booker described as the 'neophilia' of the 1960s, with both the Conservative and Labour parties appropriating the rhetoric of rebuilding cities as part of their efforts to present themselves as capable of refashioning Britain along new modern lines, through a re-emphasis on Keynesian government stimulus.[3] The conjuncture of these two modernizing impulses, architectural and political, created a holistic approach to cities, which connected architecture to everyday life, the state, and political elites.

The history of British modernism, let alone of urban modernization, covers a much longer span than the years covered by this book.[4] The years surrounding 1963, however, are a peak point in the actual physical changes to cities and of sheer bloody-minded ambition—an ambition driving not just the paper architecture of an ineffectual avant-garde, but also propelling those at every level of the urban decision-making process, both inside and outside the architectural and planning professions. This was a period with its own distinctive flavour, when post-Blitz 'reconstruction' was overtaken by a distinct set of concepts clustered around the labels 'redevelopment' or 'renewal'. The 1960s was the decade of the new universities, of the second generation of new towns, and of prefabricated tower blocks. But it was also the decade of the rebuilding of city centres. As built, these city-centre schemes tend to be made up of a gimcrack modernism of tacky pedestrian precincts, grim underpasses, budget megastructures, and gargantuan car parks: an architecture which was the product of public–private partnership and often designed by anonymous firms. So much of the invisible everyday building that makes up a part of every British city was built in this decade, creating the cityscapes chronicled and denigrated in books such as *Britain's Crap Towns* and Martin Parr's *Boring Postcards*. Whether or not the cityscape of the 1960s is *crap*, it is not *boring*, as it articulated British hopes and fears about the future.

The planning philosophy of the 1960s had its own flavour as opposed to that of the 1950s. More *radical* solutions were seen as necessary in the

[2] T. Dan Smith, *Autobiography* (Newcastle upon Tyne, 1970), p. 47.

[3] Christopher Booker, *The Neophiliacs* (London, 1970).

[4] John Gold, for example, starts his multivolume history in 1928, has brought it up to 1972, and a further volume will bring modernism's 'legacy' even further forward. John R. Gold, *Experience of Modernism, Modern Architects and the Future City, 1928–53* (London, 1997); John R. Gold, *The Practice of Modernism: Modern Architects and Urban Transformation 1954–1972* (London, 2007).

face of new problems thrown up by a changing society. 'Radical' was a word frequently deployed by architects and planners, and had a meaning which echoed and allied it with contemporary political ambitions (see, for example, Labour politician Roy Jenkins's frequent and pointed use of the word from the late 1950s).[5] What is extraordinary about the 1960s is that *radical* solutions were not only proposed by members of a self-confessed avant-garde, but gained widespread traction among political elites.

This book shows how, around and about the pivotal date of 1963, various political cultures informed and interacted with the widespread ambition to totally reshape British city centres. Among advocates for radical reconstruction in the 1960s we find a motley cast of architecture and planning professionals, one-nation Tories, Labourite expansionists, members of the Establishment, earnest civil servants, local-authority bigwigs, and grafting developers. The book focuses on the political motivations behind planning decisions. *Boom Cities* uncovers the variety of, at times fractious, alliances that came together to produce city-centre redevelopment. The protean nature of 1960s planning is a reflection of something of the way architectural ideas operate within a culture. For architectural ideas to gain traction they need to be able to appeal to a shared set of aspirations—but this cuts both ways, as they are easily made malleable towards various people's purposes. The planning images of the period were invested with a sliding range of positive meanings for different people. The redevelopment of the 1960s emerged out of a point of junction between various architectural and political cultures.

The rebuilding of British city centres during the 1960s is arguably among the single most dramatic moments in British urban history. It is certainly one of the most controversial. This moment drastically affected the built form of urban Britain, including places ranging from traditional cathedral cities through to the decaying towns of the Industrial Revolution. Instead of focusing on the experience of any single city, or attempting to make a survey of all cities affected, this book instead uncovers both the planning philosophy and the political, cultural, and legislative background that created the conditions for these processes to occur across the country.[6] In the course of the book many cities, both big and small, are

[5] John Campbell, *Roy Jenkins* (London, 2014), p. 192–3.

[6] Most previous scholarship has started from locally oriented case studies: See Simon Gunn 'The Rise and Fall of British Urban Modernism: Planning Bradford 1945–1970', *Journal of British Studies,* 48:3 (2010), pp. 849–69; Peter Shapely, 'Civic Pride and Redevelopment in the Post-War British City', *Urban History,* 39:02 (2012), pp. 310–28; John Pendlebury, 'Alas Smith and Burns? Conservation in Newcastle upon Tyne City Centre 1959–68', *Planning Perspectives,* 16 (2001), pp. 115–41.

visited, both briefly and for more extended periods.[7] Many of the cities covered are places where a twentieth-century historiography has barely begun to be written, in large part because they are principally understood as products of the nineteenth century.[8] As will be seen, the rebuilding of British cities was in large part a response to the continuing legacy of the Industrial Revolution.

Philip Larkin's famous poem *Annus Mirabilis* picks 1963 as the date 'sexual intercourse began', an event he links with the Beatles' first LP.[9] In turn, the architecture critic Ian Nairn saw the replanning of central Liverpool as 'drawing its vitality from some common resurgence' with the Mersey Sound, finding in both Liverpool and in *Twist and Shout* an 'exuberance and defiant grandeur'.[10] The early 1960s were a period of uneasy optimism for provincial cities like Liverpool.[11] Although *Boom Cities* looks to a variety of types of city, and to a degree all cities faced the pressures that led to city-centre redevelopment, my emphasis is disproportionately on the north-west of England, where these pressures were especially acute—not least in Blackburn, the focus of Chapter 3. The north-west is a region sorely under-represented in the historiography of modern Britain, but it was a locus for deindustrialization, arguably *the* overarching process for understanding historical change, not least urban change, over the whole post-war period.[12] The north-west is a particularly good place from which to appreciate that city-centre redevelopment was part of an attempt by cities to construct a new role in the face of the decline of their nineteenth-century industrial primary purpose. This, then, is a book with provincial foci, but also a book that tracks how large-scale abstract historical processes were manifested, made concrete, in particular places.

Architectural culture is central to the story. The 1960s saw a high point in the belief that the form of the built environment could be used to

[7] I have made a survey of all British plans of the period, conveniently held in the Cambridge University Library under the class mark Atlas 0.29. Non-English British cities are under-represented, and there were regional differences in how similar processes played out in Scotland, Wales, and Northern Ireland. See A. G. McClelland, 'Inventorying Armagh: Max Lock, civil society, and the diffusion of planning ideas into Northern Ireland in the 1960s', *Planning Perspectives* (2017); Andrew G. McClelland, 'A "ghastly interregnum": the struggle for architectural heritage conservation in Belfast before 1972', *Urban History* (2017); Miles Glendinning, *Rebuilding Scotland: The Postwar Vision, 1945–1975* (Edinburgh, 1997).

[8] Gunn, 'The Rise and Fall of British Urban Modernism', p. 850.

[9] Philip Larkin, *High Windows* (London, 1974).

[10] Ian Nairn, 'Liverpool', *The Listener*, 11 June 1964, p. 949.

[11] Geoffrey Moorehouse, *The Other England* (London, 1964).

[12] Jim Tomlinson, 'De-industrialisation not decline: A new meta-narrative for post-war British history', *Twentieth Century British History*, 27.1 (2016), pp. 76–99.

mould society.[13] Architecture, although by no means the only discipline to have a role in redevelopment, was therefore in a historically unparalleled period of ascendency. The book highlights a relatively new breed of professional, architect-planners: men (it was a very male profession) who combined architecture and planning qualifications and suggested architectural solutions over vast areas. To use the vocabulary of the period, architect-planners were interested as much in 'town design' or 'civic design' as in 'town planning'. They set out to create three-dimensional plans with a vision that, as Anthony Goss put it in a report calling for more architect-planners, 'rose above the kerb level'.[14] None of them had much sympathy for the Corbusian ideal of towers in parkland; instead, they proposed distinctly urban visions.

Architect-planners were by no means in the majority amongst planners, accounting for only 41.5 per cent of the membership of the Town Planning Institute in 1965. Many authorities did not employ any architect-planners at all.[15] The majority of plans produced in the post-war period were statutory development plans, the principal vehicle for the implementation of the 1947 Town and Country Planning Act. These plans focused on establishing the quantities and distribution of land use, and might be written by a borough engineer such as Bradford's Stanley Wardley, or a borough architect like West Ham's Tom North.[16] Typically, these plans had a typewritten appearance, their covers embossed with the heraldic crest of the town in question, and were devoid of the kind of rhetoric and three-dimensional architectural visions that are found in the plans of architect-planners. These architect-planners pioneered a visually bold, literate, and accessible approach to the publication of town plans, with high production values.[17] Because these plans operate within a field of design and self-justification, they offer an insight into the ideas behind decisions. *Boom Cities* uses plans as sources to illuminate the culture that produced them. Although plans provide only a partial account of outcomes, they are an excellent source for understanding the culture,

[13] For an early sociological critique of this so called 'physical fallacy' see Herbert Gans, 'City planning and urban realities', *Commentary*, 33:2 (1962).

[14] Anthony Goss, *Architect and Town Planning: a Report Presented to the Council of the RIBA* (London, 1965), p. 9.

[15] Ibid., p. 22.

[16] Gunn, 'The Rise and Fall of British Urban Modernism', pp. 849–69; Nicholas Bullock, 'West Ham and the Welfare State 1945–1970: a suitable case for treatment', in *Architecture and the Welfare State*, ed. Mark Swenarton, Tom Avermaete, and Dirk van den Heuvel (2014).

[17] Although they have much in common with the 1940s plans of Thomas Sharp.

assumptions, and ambitions that provided the contours for how cities were thought about in the period.[18]

Even if architect-planners only account for a proportion of the profession at large, they had an inordinate influence because the plans they produced for cities received wide coverage and could be taken as blueprints to be emulated by those facing similar challenges in neighbouring cities. In the course of the 1960s many became adept at ventriloquizing the concerns, aesthetic, and general approach of architect-planners, but often shorn of the redemptive aspects. *Boom Cities* includes detailed biographical case studies of two typical architect-planners of the period—Graeme Shankland and Lionel Brett—chosen because they both combined their planning work with much proselytizing and self-reflective writing. Shankland and Brett are representative of others covered more briefly in this book, including Walter Bor, Wilfred Burns, Arthur Ling, Gordon Logie, Percy Johnson Marshall, Konrad Smigielski, Hugh Wilson, and Lewis Womersley. These architect-planners share a common biographical trajectory. Their planning philosophy was often shaped during the post-war years in one of the more adventurous public architects' departments, especially in a new town corporation or at the London County Council, Sheffield, or Coventry, where they absorbed a spirit of optimism and experimentation. Many of them were members of the SPUR group, the Society for the Promotion of Urban Renewal, which ran from 1958 to 1963 and advocated a shift of attention from population dispersal and new town development towards the renewal of existing centres.[19] They were intensely influenced by the philosophy and aesthetic advocated by the monthly journal *The Architectural Review*, especially through the concept of 'Townscape', which advocated a picturesque approach to planning, the weaving together of old and new, and enclosed urban forms that privileged the pedestrian. Townscape looked beyond the design of individual buildings, towards the whole composition of a city. The architectural illustrator Gordon Cullen, a key proponent of the Townscape movement, frequently contributed drawings and analysis to plans by architect-planners. Tropes from Cullen's approach, as well as drawings in his style, became an almost ubiquitous feature of planning documents, even when he was not directly involved.

[18] I have been influenced by the approach of Guy Ortolano, 'Planning the Urban Future in 1960s Britain', *The Historical Journal*, 54.2 (2011), pp. 477–507.

[19] John Gold, 'A SPUR to action: the Society for the Promotion of Urban Renewal, "anti-scatter" and the crisis of reconstruction', *Planning Perspectives*, 27.2 (2012), pp. 199–223.

The publication of Colin Buchanan's 1963 government report, *Traffic in Towns*, which argued that the growth in car ownership threatened 'the whole familiar form of towns', was a seminal and galvanizing moment for architect-planners, as it gave official endorsement to the kind of philosophy and approach that they had been developing throughout the 1950s.[20] On publication, *Traffic in Towns* received remarkable publicity for a civil-service report, and was glowingly written up by publications ranging from *The Tablet* to the *Daily Worker*.[21] It would go through multiple printings, and was republished as a shortened Penguin Special. Buchanan devised his own terminology and presented the case with exceptional rhetorical power, but the design solutions Buchanan proposed (as he is generous in admitting) were not original but came from an engagement with current ideas and practice, both in Britain and internationally.[22] *Traffic in Towns* was summative rather than innovative in terms of current planning practice. The book is nevertheless key to understanding what happened in city centres because of the way it energized discourse, giving planners both added clarity of purpose and a rhetorical bolstering. Its reverberating influence will be a theme running throughout this book.

The redevelopment of the 1960s is often treated as epiphenomenal to the thinking of the 1930s and 1940s, which have been granted significantly more attention. Historians, when they do grant the architectural production of the 1960s a distinctive flavour, tend to see it in opposition to an earlier modernism, characterized as 'a *soft*, relatively humanist modernism', and instead distinguish it as standing 'for something starker, harder, more ruthless'.[23] Undoubtedly something of this happened in the way buildings looked, in the penchant for heavy and robust forms, and in the use of exposed concrete. Such a progression is illustrated by the oeuvre of the architects Chamberlin, Powell, and Bon—from the jubilant colours of their early projects, such as the Golden Lane estate and Bousfield School, to the concrete gigantism of the Barbican and Leeds University. The vital question is whether this hardening of style was paralleled by a coarsening in the general approach to cities; whether *brutalism* as a look is

[20] Buchanan, *Traffic in Towns*, p. 17.

[21] 'Cities and Cars', *The Tablet*, 7 December 1963, p. 3; and James Sutton, 'Is the Buchanan Report too late?', *Daily Worker*, 29 November 1963, p. 2.

[22] On Buchanan's admiration for West Germany and aversion to the United States see Stephen V. Ward, 'What did the Germans ever do for us? A century of British learning about and imagining modern town planning', *Planning Perspectives*, 25.2 (2010), pp. 117–40.

[23] David Kynaston, *Austerity Britain, 1945–51* (London, 2007), p. 613; Peter Mandler, 'John Summerson (1904–1992): the Architectural Critic and the Quest for the Modern', in *After the Victorians: Private Conscience and Public Duty in Modern Britain*, ed. Susan Pedersen and Peter Mandler (London, 1994), p. 240.

synonymous with *brutality* of urban approach. Certainly we do not have to look very hard to find *brutality* in much of the disregard for the historic cityscape, the belligerent application of inner-city motorways, and the overbearing scale of developments. But these outcomes were not often driven by a blind adherence to a philosophy of *tabula rasa* planning, Corbusian or otherwise.

The 1960s holds a curious dual role as the decade saw both a high point in the history of urban renewal and the beginning of the end of a very long consensus, going back at least as far as the nineteenth century, that the renewal of cities should be on a large, comprehensive scale rather than through piecemeal interventions. These two processes, although seemingly at odds, were often intertwined. The dominant architectural culture of the period was in many ways a mass of contradictions. A photograph of a typical architect-planner of the period, Leicester's Konrad Smigielski, neatly displays these contradictions (Fig. I.1). He stands in front of images from his plans: above is displayed the city of gleaming towers, *tabula rasa*, internationalism, Corbusianism, and megastructures. Below is the city of *genius loci*, piazzas, Townscape, conservation, and drawings in the style of Gordon Cullen. Architectural and planning culture of the period attempted to embody both these ideals, and it is anachronistic to see them as necessarily opposed. It is therefore generally unhelpful to polarize this period into the binaries historians have used: conservationists versus modernists; New Humanists versus Brutalists; or herbivores versus carnivores.[24] Architects and planners often simultaneously displayed elements of both the brutal and the redemptive.

Architect-planners cared deeply about cities, their potentials and problems, and they brought expertise and an admirable passion to a task that they believed paramount. They saw themselves as countering rather than reinforcing a trend of anti-urbanism that it has been presumed planners are committed to.[25] Their story is nevertheless a tragic one, and this book follows them from a heyday of buoyant confidence through to an intense disillusionment. In doing so, *Boom Cities* provides an unconventional account of the end of modernist approaches to the built environment, showing it from the perspective of planning and policy elites, rather than through the emergence of public opposition to planning.

[24] Michael Frayn, 'Festival', in *The Age of Austerity*, ed. Michael Sissons and Phillip French (London, 1963), first made the distinction between herbivores and carnivores. See Nicholas Bullock, *Building the Postwar World* (London, 2002) for the distinction between New Humanists and Brutalists.

[25] Steven Conn, *Americans against the city* (Oxford, 2014).

Fig. I.1. Konrad Smigielski stands in front of images from his plans, from 'Leicester Plans for her Future', *The Illustrated London News*, 7 November 1964. © Illustrated London News/Mary Evans

Boom Cities consequently offers a messier picture of the move towards greater preservation, which has arguably been the most profound change in the approach to the built environment in Britain of the past half-century. There was a significant shift in this period in which modernist planners developed a philosophy where what was at stake was not just the preservation of several important, mostly pre-Victorian, buildings. Instead, they developed a much more holistic conception of what counted as valuable heritage. As Walter Bor put it in 1967:

> It isn't just a question of preserving a few listed buildings but more often one of preservation and rehabilitation of whole areas with their street network, pedestrian alleyways, scale, colour and texture.[26]

Many in the modernist planning establishment were instrumental in helping to create this new preservationist hegemony of ideas about the way to approach the built environment, although their role remains ambiguous and often contradictory. The role of political elites, and of architects and planners, has been paramount in our understanding of approaches to cities in the 1960s. However, when it comes to dealing

[26] Walter Bor 'A Question of Urban Identity', in *Planning and Architecture,* ed. Dennis Sharp (London, 1967), p. 20.

with the disavowal of modernism, the literature tends to focus on the emergence of public opposition to planning, especially through the conservation movement and various forms of community action.[27] Clearly this represented an enormous and important change in the relationship between the state and society. In the early 1960s even the most radical schemes could be passed through with barely a murmur. In contrast, by the 1970s opposition was widespread, instinctive, and often well organized.[28] Nevertheless, this has led to a rather Manichaean vision of the period, where the plucky St George of the conservation movement slays the implacable and monolithic dragon of the modernist establishment. This 'heroic' narrative has been compounded by the fact that history has often been written by protagonists of the conservation movement themselves.[29] Such perspectives have obscured the way that modernist solutions were, often independently, disavowed by the very planning and political elites who had been at the heart of the massive physical changes imposed on British cities in the 1960s. The presumption that cities would be totally transformed through urban renewal and radical architectural forms appeared increasingly untenable across the political spectrum, and from the perspective of former advocates as much as by long-term dissenters or reactionaries. Whatever its self-perception, the ubiquitous literature of hand-wringing polemic about modernism written during the 1970s ran in tandem with, and not in opposition to, official thinking at the time.[30] The disavowal of urban modernism was pervasive.

In arguing that modernism and preservation were entangled, *Boom Cities* provides a more nuanced portrayal of a subject that has often been treated with a demonizing vehemence—exemplified by the crass cliché

[27] For example, Christopher Klemek, *The Transatlantic Collapse of Urban Renewal, Postwar Urbanism from New York to Berlin* (Chicago, 2011); Alan Powers, *Britain: Modern Architectures in History* (London, 2007).

[28] Adam Sharr and Stephen Thornton, *Demolishing Whitehall: Harold Wilson, Leslie Martin and the Architecture of White Heat* (London, 2014) gives a localized example of this trajectory.

[29] For example: Elain Harwood and Alan Powers, eds, *Twentieth Century Architecture 7: The Heroic Period of Conservation* (London, 2004).

[30] Malcolm MacEwan, *Crisis in Architecture* (London, 1974); Lionel Brett, *Parameters and Images* (London, 1970); Colin Buchanan, *The State of Britain* (London, 1972); Tony Aldous, *Battle for the Environment* (London, 1972); Nicholas Taylor, *The Village in the City* (London, 1973); Colin Ward, *Housing: An Anarchist Approach* (London, 1976); Christopher Booker, *The Neophiliacs: Revolution in English Life in the Fifties and Sixties* (London, 1969). This is a far from exhaustive list, but it is notable that many of these writers had themselves been modernist practitioners or fellow travellers shortly before. Even Jane Jacobs might best be seen as a 'reformer of modernism', as persuasively argued in Peter L. Lawrence, *Becoming Jane Jacobs* (Philadelphia, 2016).

that planners did more damage to cities than the Luftwaffe.[31] Although my approach to the actors involved is a broadly sympathetic one, this is not intended as a contribution to the growing literature that is self-consciously positioned as advocating for post-war British architecture.[32] Rather than focusing on issues of success or failure, the approach taken here is to acknowledge these events as inescapable historical facts, with complex and various repercussions, which need to be historicized to be understood. Instead of making an assessment of the results of plans as implemented, I will interrogate their visions for what they say about the thought-world of those proposing them. The sources used are those conventionally used by planning and architectural historians, but the object of study is people and ideas as much as it is buildings and places. This, then, is a work of *social* planning history, and its methodology allies it with an emerging historiography that uses the built environment and urban policy to explore social and political change.[33]

Reframing the narrative away from issues of implementation allows other questions to be asked: chiefly, how did a set of ideas gather enough momentum to profoundly reshape cities? Moreover, how do we explain the fact that these same ideas became anathema so pervasively within such a short space of time? To answer these questions requires a recognition

[31] This coarse bon mot originated with Sir John Betjeman and had its most famous airing by Prince Charles in 1984.

[32] Especially Elain Harwood, *Space Hope and Brutalism* (London, 2015) and Barnabas Calder, *Raw Concrete: The Beauty of Brutalism* (London, 2016). These books are important for their contribution to the pressing conservation issues surrounding post-war architecture. There is an ongoing and catastrophic demolition of the finest post-war architecture happening now on a scale equal to if not exceeding the assault on Victorian architecture in the post-war period, despite the heroic efforts of the Twentieth Century Society, among others. Nothing in this book should negate the need for a profound reassessment of what ought to be preserved from a remarkable chapter in British architectural history.

[33] For the concept of 'social architectural history' see William Whyte, *Redbrick, A social and architectural history of Britain's civic universities* (Oxford, 2015)—although my focus is on elites rather than users; Erika Hanna, *Modern Dublin, urban change and the Irish past, 1957–1973* (Oxford, 2013); Guy Ortolano, 'Planning the Urban Future in 1960s Britain' and forthcoming book about Milton Keynes; Sam Wetherell, 'Freedom planned: The enterprise zone and urban non-planning in post-war Britain', *Twentieth Century British History*, 27.2 (2016) and forthcoming work on neo-liberalism and cities; Simon Gunn, 'The Rise and Fall of British Urban Modernism' and forthcoming work on traffic; Alistair Kefford, 'Housing the citizen-consumer in post-war Britain: The Parker Morris Report, affluence and the even briefer life of social democracy', *Twentieth Century British History*, 29.2 (2017), pp. 225–58, and forthcoming work on commercial property development; Jesse Meredith, 'Decolonizing the New Town: Roy Gazzard and the Making of Killingworth Township', *Journal of British Studies*, 57 (2018), pp. 333–62; Sarah Mass, 'Commercial heritage as democratic action: Historicizing the 'Save the Market' campaigns in Bradford and Chesterfield, 1969–76', *Twentieth Century British History*, 29.3 (2017), pp. 459–84.

that for architectural ideas to have traction they need to be able to appeal to a shared set of aspirations or ideals. This book therefore uncovers what modernist solutions meant to all of those involved in the decision-making process over the shape of cities, and not just to architects and planners. The reshaping of central areas cannot be understood solely through architectural culture, but needs to be understood through the way that architectural culture became entangled with the political culture and ambitions of the period.

'Modernism' is a notoriously difficult term to define.[34] In the context of the built environment the term suggests both planning concepts—especially automobile-centred transport, top-down and *tabula rasa* planning, decentralization, disregard for much of the existing historic fabric, and slum clearance—and architectural concepts such as radical or high-rise forms, a canon of stylistic functionalist tropes, internationalism over regional variations, and the use of industrialized building systems. Such a broad definition provides only a limited description of the nuances and variety of approaches to the built environment in the post-war period in Britain. The concept of modernism, when elevated to the sole influencing force, has been damagingly Procrustean when discussing British redevelopment in the 1960s, bringing with it a whole range of presumptions. There is a risk that we are made blind to the complexities of motives if we have a frame of reference that does not go beyond the architectural culture of modernism. We also fail to appreciate the full range of actors involved.

Modernism, which has been the key to unlocking this moment in all previous accounts, is here implicitly downgraded as an explanatory tool. Although much of the planning of the 1960s is clearly related to the international, historical, and theoretical cluster of ideas that comes under the title of modernism, it is also shot through with many features that are more commonly understood as postmodern. Although it would be anachronistic to completely eschew the concept of modernism, as it was important to how the period was understood at the time, *Boom Cities* looks towards other explanatory categories, to explain the seemingly contradictory features of complex individuals and the variety of their motives. Planning history is here located within its wider political, cultural, and intellectual milieu, rather than within an internal dialogue.

The first chapter introduces the way architectural and planning ideas were conceived and perceived as responses to concurrent British concerns and ambitions: about growing affluence; about the rise of traffic; and

[34] Ortolano, 'Planning the Urban Future in 1960s Britain', p. 506; Sarah Goldhagen, 'Something to Talk About: Modernism, Discourse, Style', *The Journal of the Society of Architectural Historians*, 64.2 (2005), pp. 144–67.

about Britain's relationship with its past. Chapter 2 shows how these ideas were sustained by a broadly consensual cross-party political culture in central government. Chapter 3 illustrates how these ideas related to local concerns and aspirations, through a representative case study of the Lancashire city of Blackburn. Each of the next two chapters focuses on an individual architect-planner: Chapter 4 on Graeme Shankland; and Chapter 5 on Lionel Brett. These two chapters extend the argument that planning can best be understood through the lens of the political culture that informs and motivates it. Shankland's planning is related to his left-wing milieu, while Brett's is explained through his more patrician and Establishment mentality. Finally, Chapter 6 looks at the way in which the very planning and political elites who had been at the heart of these changes came to disavow the ideas that they had espoused only a few years earlier.

Linking these chapters is a recognition that planning ideals and political ideology did not occur in separate spheres. Not only were the urban visions promulgated by planners informed by a political culture, the flow of ideas went both ways, as the visions of planners were incorporated within the broader social visions of political agendas, often functioning as political propaganda. The book contends that the way British cities were developed in the 1960s was the result of a set of assumptions and ambitions shared across the culture, and not just because a set of architectural ideas were foisted on the country.

1

Optimism, Traffic, and the Historic City in Post-War British Planning

OPTIMISM

Optimism was a recurring theme running like electricity through the discourse of the early 1960s, giving energy to ambition. In the same spirit as Anthony Crosland's *The Future of Socialism* or of Harold Macmillan's affluent society, there was a foundational belief behind the planning documents of the period that continuous economic growth would provide the basis for uninterrupted social progress.[1] Newcastle planner Wilfred Burns, for example, argued as if such progress was a guaranteed fact just because it was part of government policy: 'The national proposals for increasing prosperity give greatly added weight to proposals which aim at improving the standard of environment within the foreseeable future for a large number of people living in outworn or unsatisfactory parts of the City.'[2] A book on redevelopment fervently opined that,

> 'We are planning for the future, and, God willing, there will be a continuing rise in the standard of living, perhaps to a level which it is now difficult to imagine. We must not be afraid therefore of aiming for non-material improvements which today we may fear to be beyond our means. Future generations will not forgive us if we build without vision and do not realize that we have the opportunity to hand on to them decent and civilized cities.'[3]

The promised prospect of an ever expanding economy, resulting in all the cascading benefits of prosperity, encouraged those at the heart of deciding the shape of cities to ask, with Sheffield planner Lewis Womersley: 'What is the good of being a rich country, as we are told we are, if we cannot have

[1] Kevin Jeffreys, *Anthony Crosland: A New Biography* (London, 1999), p. 62, and Glen O'Hara, *From Dreams to Disillusionment: Economic and Social Planning in 1960s Britain* (Basingstoke, 2006), pp. 206–8.

[2] Wilfred Burns, *Newcastle Development Plan Review* (Tyne and Wear Archives, 1963), p. 23.

[3] J. F. Q. Switzer, *Town Centre Redevelopment* (Cambridge, 1963).

these desirable things—if we cannot rebuild our cities in a manner worthy of our day and age, for the convenience and delight of our citizens?'[4] Similarly, Colin Buchanan answered the question, how bold can we afford to be?

> This is really a matter of faith in our own future as a nation. If we believe we have a great future then we must also believe that the standard of living will sweep steadily up, overriding the ephemeral fluctuations of economic life. The long term view must surely be optimistic, a belief that we shall have the resources to remould our environment to our liking.[5]

Britain was in the process of massive changes during these years. These changes were manifest in the rebuilding of cities, and in parallel with these physical changes were titanic social shifts. British society was being transformed by affluence, welfarism, deindustrialization, mass automobile ownership, and new technologies. Planners envisioned the 'breathtaking prospect' of a second Industrial Revolution, driven by universal atomic-energy provision, electronics, and automation.[6] The urban processes of central-area renewal were propelled forward by a concern about contemporaneous social changes. To understand what is distinct about the planning ideology of the latter post-war period, it is necessary to contextualize these plans within the broader concerns of the era. These included: worries about the effects of increasing affluence, and about the relative stagnation of the North of England compared to the London area; the presumption that the post-war period of growth was sustainable; the quest to find Britain a new technocratic role in the wider international scene after the loss of its traditional imperial role; social changes, such as smaller household structures; and 'the development of new shopping customs, of shorter hours of work, and of new means of static communication'.[7] Most fundamental, though, and most intractable, were the challenges thrown up by the growth of car usage.

These rapid social changes were felt to make a new type of approach towards town planning necessary, as opposed to that which had been used in the direct post-war period. Take, for example, the reasons given in 1963 for not following the 1951 Newcastle plan through:

> This review of the City's problems, made more than twelve years after the original proposals were formulated, takes place at a time when conditions in society are very different from those of 1951 or those expected at the time of the first survey... two main changes however have dictated a completely

[4] Lewis Womersley, 'Productivity for What?', *The Listener,* 19 September 1963, p. 407.
[5] Colin Buchanan, *Traffic in Towns* (London, 1963), p. 43.
[6] Anthony Goss, *British industry and town planning* (London, 1962), p. 130.
[7] Buchanan, *Traffic in Towns*, p. 18.

> new type of plan for the City... (a) the growth of traffic; and (b) the prosperity of the nation which, because of changing demands and higher standards reflects itself in the need for and possibilities of redevelopment and environmental improvement which were not contemplated in earlier days.[8]

An expanding economy invalidated the planning of the 1940s, which had been written, as the sociologist Ruth Glass put it, 'in a restrictionist mood—on premises inherited from a period of economic depression . . . it was based on the assumption of a stationary population, economy and culture', and therefore did not provide 'suitable guidance of development in a period of expansion'.[9] Affluence, all the 'abundance of goods and gadgets, of cars and new buildings—in an apparently mounting flow of consumption', was creating novel challenges for planners, calling for new solutions.[10] Architect-planners embraced these forces, but were also nervous about their social and environmental consequences. Beneath an outward veneer of radical futurism, plans often reveal a surprising degree of uneasy conservatism. It was common practice (one might even go so far as to say that it was a tactic) to use a narrative of crisis as a background to plans, in which the strains and stresses on a city from automobile ownership, an ageing building stock, and a growing and increasingly affluent population were presented as near insurmountable, without, that is, the palliative offered by the planner.

TRAFFIC AND URBANITY

The post-war growth of traffic was a major concern of the period, with wide-ranging implications for planning and architectural thought. The 'motor car revolution' was seen to invalidate traditional layouts of cities. The number of licensed motor vehicles in Britain had doubled from 4.5 million to 9 million between 1950 and 1960, and was correctly predicted to carry on rising.[11] It was common to point out that the decentralizing and suburbanizing effects engendered by the automobile had overtaken the cholera and overcrowding engendered by railways as the primary ill of cities.[12] Terence Bendixson pushed the comparison further, seeing Colin Buchanan's seminal

[8] Burns, *Newcastle*, p. 23.

[9] Ruth Glass, *London, Aspects of Change* (London, 1964), p. xix, referring specifically to Abercrombie's *Greater London Plan* of 1944.

[10] Glass, *London, Aspects of Change*, p. xiv.

[11] Simon Gunn, 'The Buchanan Report, Environment and the Problem of Traffic in 1960s Britain', *Twentieth Century British History*, 22.4 (2011), pp. 521–42, p. 523.

[12] See Peter Hall, *London 2000* (London, 1963), p. 160, and Asa Briggs, *Victorian Cities* (London, 1963), pp. 13–14.

Traffic in Towns as providing a role analogous to the reforming reports of the nineteenth century:

> [The Buchanan] Report's real analogues are with the horrific disclosures of the First Factory Inspector's Report of 1839 and with Edwin Chadwick's Report on the Sanitary Conditions of the Labouring Population in 1842. Just as they were the first signs of society attempting to control the effects of industrial change so Buchanan is one of the first realistic examinations of the sort of towns and cities the second machine age is likely to produce. Like them it exposes a social disgrace and by outlining a method of research shows that the problem can be managed.[13]

The argument of *Traffic in Towns* was that if a large proportion of traffic was to be accommodated in large cities without totally destroying their amenity value, there would need to be massive physical reconstruction, and if the community was unable or unwilling to pay for this, then a restriction of traffic would be necessary. Buchanan therefore saw the solution essentially in terms of design. As he put it in an article, urban planning was the 'only way to avoid future chaos': 'We have taken a bull into the china shop and to that old problem there are only two answers—shoot the bull, or, more creatively, build a new china shop specifically designed for bulls.'[14]

The report, following the format of a civil-service paper, presented various shades of the options of traffic restriction or total rebuilding, without definitively advocating either. Certainly the most extreme, and most publicized, of Buchanan's case studies, for a fully automated Fitzrovia on multiple levels with a dizzying armature of multi-lane motorways, was something of a *reductio ad absurdum* (Fig. 1.1). Many commentators on the Buchanan Report, both on its publication and since, have argued that it has been widely misinterpreted as offering, as Buchanan himself wryly put it in 1983, 'a blueprint for the total reconstruction of towns and cities with traffic circulation at different levels, costing a fortune and not very nice to look at into the bargain'.[15] Buchanan's plan for Cardiff from 1966, however, makes clear that he, despite the nuances, certainly was advocating very radical reconstruction indeed.[16] Buchanan was frustrated and protested when the funds for radical reconstruction were not made available.

[13] Terence Bendixson, 'City of Man', *The Spectator*, 6 December 1963, p. 16.

[14] Colin Buchanan, 'Urban planning: "only way to avoid future chaos"', 28 September 1963, p. 5.

[15] Colin Buchanan, 'An Assessment after Twenty Years', *Built Environment*, 9.2 (1983), pp. 93–8.

[16] Colin Buchanan and Partners, *Cardiff Development and Transportation Study: Probe Study Report* (Cardiff, 1966); Gunn, 'The Buchanan Report', pp. 521–42.

Fig. 1.1. The famous and much reproduced three-dimensional scheme for Fitzrovia from *Traffic in Towns.* Drawing by Kenneth Browne. © Open Government Licence

The Minister of Transport, Ernest Marples, certainly read, or misread, the report as a call for radical reconstruction:

> It is fundamental to the whole report that it accepts the motor vehicle as a brilliant and beneficial invention. It is in no sense restricting the motor car. All it says is that we must use our motor cars to the maximum, and yet be sensible and keep some good environmental areas. We have to face the fact, whether we like it or not, that we have built our towns in entirely the wrong way for motor traffic. We want an entirely different type of town.[17]

The rhetoric surrounding the traffic segregation schemes encouraged by post-war plans provides a striking example of the way modernist architect-planners related modernizing schemes to tradition.[18] So widespread was the location of plans in a historical continuum, and so forceful the insistence that they revived elements of traditional urbanism, that one wonders whether this rhetoric was part of an effort of window dressing

[17] Ernest Marples, 'Opening Speech', in *People and Cities* (London, 1963), p. 12.

[18] William Whyte, 'The Englishness of English Architecture: Modernism and the Making of a National International Style, 1927–1957', *Journal of British Studies,* 48.2 (2009), pp. 441–65, argues that English modernists 'stressed their impeccable Englishness, and then went on to argue that modernism reflected a revival of their principles'.

avant-garde principles to make them seem more palatable, or the expression of a genuine ambition. Such rhetoric helps us to begin to tie traffic management together with another phenomenon that profoundly influenced planners: a cross-cultural reinvestment in distinctly 'urban' values, often expressed through the visual tropes of the Townscape movement. Cars were a fundamental assault on the traditional layout of cities, with their pincer movement of imposing suburbanization at the periphery while destroying the amenity at the centre through congestion, hazard, and ugliness. In parallel with the ascendency of radical modernism in this period there was a simultaneous and interlinked reinvestment in the traditional virtues and values of urban life. Architect-planners aimed at creating 'compact, varied, interesting, vital, intensely urban environments', all those qualities that the car and suburbanization were endangering.[19]

The trend towards celebrating the social richness of dense urban development relied on a conception of society as much as it did on aesthetics, and it emerged from the discipline of sociology as much as it did from architecture. As Ruth Glass put it, 'While the visual benefits of high density development are apparent, it is the social benefits that are even more striking.'[20] The Kenilworth Group, set up in the mid-1950s by the social worker Muriel Smith, brought together radical architects and planners with sociologists and social workers to discuss and advocate higher densities. It provided a forum for architects and planners to be influenced by concurrent sociological literature celebrating compact urban life, not least by Kenilworth Group members such as Ruth Glass and Peter Willmott.[21] *Family and Kinship in East London* (1957), written by Michael Young and Peter Willmott, was especially influential. It contrasted the tight-knit community of London's Bethnal Green with the social disintegration of new out-of-town development, and it subsequently 'fired the high density crusade'.[22] Fears about suburban development were particularly acute on the political left because of the conception that less dense development had loosened the bonds of working-class solidarity, replacing it with an acquisitiveness that was seen as ultimately leading to Conservatism. This was an argument made explicitly by Young.[23] The

[19] Buchanan, *Traffic in Towns*, p. 179

[20] Ruth Glass, 'Observations in Lansbury', *Town Planning Institute Journal*, November 1951, pp. 8–14.

[21] See London Metropolitan Archives 'Muriel Smith Papers', LMA/4196.

[22] Atticus, *The Sunday Times*, 14 February 1965, p. 9.

[23] See Michael Young, 'Must We Abandon Our Cities?', *Socialist Commentary*, September 1954, p. 251; J. G. Watson, 'More Money—More Conservative?', *Socialist Commentary*, April 1962; Lawrence Black, *The Political Culture of the Left in Affluent Britain* (London, 2003), pp. 118–23.

influence of these sociological ideas on architectural culture has not been adequately appreciated, in part because Willmott and Young would argue in the 1986 new introduction that *Family and Kinship* attacked 'clever architects', and was intended as a protest and warning against a period of 'collective madness'.[24] This was a bit disingenuous, especially as they had had a rather cosy relationship with architects and planners, and often echoed their concerns.[25] As Willmott wrote in 1963, in a sentence that could be lifted verbatim from any number of plans:

> There are a number of reasons for the crisis and for the growing awareness of it: the fact that so much of our present stock of buildings dates from the Victorian boom of about a century ago and now needs to be renewed; the growth of our population; the rise in living standards . . . and, on top of all these pressures the motor car revolution.[26]

This cross-cultural trend in favour of denser cities was often centred on the slippery term 'urbanity', which melded the word's eighteenth-century import of genteel politesse with a romantic view of the aesthetic and social benefits of compactly laid-out development.[27] It was a word that, significantly, concertinaed the Victorian period, suggesting a direct link between modernism and a pre-Victorian past. The word, one of 'the architectural passwords of the century', entered British architectural discourse through the writings of Arthur Trystan Edwards, and was pushed by planners in the 1940s, especially by Thomas Sharp and in the pages of *The Architectural Review*.[28] In the 1960s 'urbanity' remained a core value, and in the face of the profound onslaught of increasing car usage, radical modernist solutions which segregated pedestrians and automobiles could be presented in the conservative light of being the only way to preserve or recreate this quality. There were two ways to build a town that catered for cars but preserved urbanity: through (in the jargon of the period) vertical or horizontal segregation of vehicles and pedestrians.

[24] Michael Young and Peter Willmott, *Family and Kinship in East London* (London, 1957).

[25] Michael Young, *Chipped White Cups of Dover* (London, 1960), and Willmott's co-authorship of *The Face of Britain: A Policy for Town and Country Planning* (London, 1964). For the influence of the book on architects see Mark Crinson, 'The Uses of Nostalgia: Stirling and Gowan's Preston Housing', *Journal of the Society of Architectural Historians*, 65.2 (June 2006), pp. 216–37.

[26] Peter Willmott, 'Towns of the Future', *The Times Literary Supplement*, 27 February 1963, p. 164.

[27] See H. J. Dyos, *Exploring the urban past, essays in urban history* (Cambridge, 1982), pp. 19–36, for the longer history of the term.

[28] Lionel Brett, letter to *The Architectural Review*, August 1953, pp. 119–20. See also the illuminating critique of the concept of the 'great god of Urbanity, and his cosmetic soul-sister Townscape' in Nicholas Taylor, *Village in the City* (London, 1973), p. 79.

The first way to achieve segregation was through a 'pedestrian precinct', which relegated traffic to the perimeter of a site. Pedestrian precincts were a major feature of the planning vocabulary of the 1950s, most notably in the central shopping areas in the first generation of New Towns. A senior police official, H. Alker Tripp, had set down the idea of segregating traffic through a system of pedestrian precincts in the early 1940s.[29] It was common to relate the pedestrian precinct to earlier forms of development. As Tripp lushly put it himself:

> The streets in the various precincts will then become town streets of the old-fashioned type. They will cease to be maelstroms of noise and confusion, and become companionable places, with an air of leisure and repose; such streets will provide a real promenade for the town dweller and a rest for jaded nerves. We shall get back to Merrie England.[30]

Architect Frederick Gibberd went further in stressing the pedigree, presenting his precinctual shopping centres for Harlow, Nuneaton, and Poplar as being a modern reinterpretation of Renaissance piazzas. Gibberd's 1953 book *Town Design* had elucidated his design method, which was to create abstracted versions of Renaissance Italian precedents, an approach that was an amalgam of Sigfried Giedion's *Space, Time and Architecture* and Camillo Sitte's *The Art of Building Cities*.[31] The book analyses urban spaces, using an abstracted language of plastic compositions in space, enclosure, vistas, optical barriers, and so forth, used whether Gibberd is discussing Florence, Tuscany, or Harlow, Essex. Precincts conjured up a cosmopolitan continentalism. The very word 'precinct', of course, also conjured up the cathedral precinct: pedestrian precincts were therefore 'really not new at all but as old as the medieval market square from which traffic used to be excluded'.[32] *The Architectural Review*'s project 'Westminster Regained', which was exhibited at the Tate, is perhaps the clearest indication that modernist planning was being presented as a revival—the pedestrian precinct and the cathedral precinct were being merged.[33] Planners were keen to stress the analogy, emphasizing the traditional aspect of pedestrianization rather than its modernizing radicalism. The idea of having areas from which through traffic was banned was termed by Buchanan an 'environmental area', an interesting halfway house in the changing meaning of that word towards its now standard ecological usage. Precincts would offer a sanctuary from

[29] Alker Tripp, *Town Planning and Road Traffic* (London, 1942). [30] Ibid., p. 77.

[31] Frederick Gibberd, *Town Design* (London, 1953).

[32] Robert Gardner-Medwin 'Rebuilding Rotterdam and Coventry', *The Listener*, 22 September 1955, p. 456.

[33] Tate Archive, TG92/66; 'Westminster Regained', *The Architectural Review*, November 1947, pp. 159–70.

the pollution and noise of motor-car usage, and indeed modernity itself, in which the traditional sensations of the city would be appreciated.

Pedestrian precincts were a major feature of the planning vocabulary of the 1950s and 1960s. In 1961 the Ministry of Housing and Local Government made a survey of pedestrian shopping precincts in Britain. Jarrow, Poplar, Epsom, Havant, Waterlooville, Cowley, Exeter, Plymouth, Coventry, and Canterbury were the only completed precincts outside the New Towns. In addition, Northampton, Bedford, Cambridge, Croydon, Kirkby, Swindon, and Ellesmere Port had precincts in construction. Seventy-six towns had precinctual schemes in planning phase.[34] Precincting was also a feature in the planning of housing estates such as Chamberlin, Powell, and Bon's Golden Lane and university development like Casson and Condor's Sidgwick site in Cambridge.[35] It was an international phenomenon, from the Lijnbaan in Rotterdam, the Hötorget in Stockholm, to the Kettwiger Strasse in Essen. The high point of belief in precincts in Britain came with the opening of Stevenage Town Centre by the Queen in 1959. It was internationally the most extensive pedestrian precinct yet completed and could therefore be looked upon with pride as an enormous success story, with Stevenage Corporation hardly exaggerating when they wrote:

> The impact of the development of the Town Centre upon the inhabitants of Stevenage, upon the public generally, upon professional opinion and upon the many public and private bodies who have inspected it has been both startling and instructive. The project has received wide publicity from many sources and it attracts an endless procession of visitors from all parts of the country, from Europe and indeed, from all parts of the World.[36]

To many of the more radical of the planning profession, though, the precinctual solution did not go far enough. In 1963 Peter Hall discussed the successes and failures of precincts:

> Until recently, even the most radical central replanning schemes have been conceived in terms of the precinctual solution, standard manuals of planning practice still recommend it. And it has produced the pedestrian shopping malls, which are among the greatest successes of post-war planning... But there are difficulties and defects. All are essentially small-scale solutions, based on a single street or place, or at most a complex of two or three streets.

[34] The National Archives, Kew (hereinafter TNA), 'Central Redevelopment Schemes' (15 November 1961), HLG 136/8.

[35] Alistair Fair, '"Ideal Campus": The Sidgwick Site, Cambridge', *Twentieth Century Architecture 11: Oxford and Cambridge*, ed. Elain Harwood, Alan Powers, and Otto Saumarez Smith (London, 2012), pp. 102–20.

[36] Hertfordshire Record Office, 'Annual report to the Minister of Housing and Local Government', 1960. Hertfordshire archives, CNT/ST/5/1/AP/R28 VOL 2.

> The reason is that vehicle access must be provided at the back of all the premises... These demands mean the virtual sterilization of large areas of land immediately around the shopping precincts and produce aesthetic problems which have not yet been satisfactorily met, the desolation of the back-sides of central Coventry, or central Stevenage, detracts very seriously from the whole concept.[37]

Vertical segregation seemed to offer a remedy to these problems, whereby all the pedestrian functions of the city would be placed on a 'deck' or 'podium', which segregated it from traffic, parking, and servicing underneath. Buchanan called this kind of architecture 'traffic architecture'. Traffic architecture was promoted by both those belonging to a self-proclaimed architectural avant-garde and those closer to the mainstream of planning thought. Important early instances are Alison and Peter Smithson's Berlin Hauptstadt competition; Victor Gruen's plan for Fort Worth; Chamberlin, Powell, and Bon's Barbican scheme; the work of Buchanan's *Traffic in Towns* team; in new universities such as Denys Lasdun's University of East Anglia and the Architects Co-Partnership's University of Essex; around South Bank; in the schemes for the town centres of Hook and Cumbernauld New Towns; and William Holford's Piccadilly Circus scheme.[38] By the early 1960s such three-dimensional solutions were beginning to feature in plans for provincial cities and in developers' schemes. Chapter 3 will examine one of these in depth. One of the important things about such schemes was that, for them to be practicable, they needed to be carried out over a considerable area. As Buchanan put it:

> It is abundantly clear that these traffic architecture techniques cannot be applied over small areas. It is essential to be able to command the development or redevelopment of sizeable areas. The creation, for example, of an elevated pedestrian environment obviously cannot be achieved in penny packet instalments.[39]

Multilevel segregation gave a spur to the need for comprehensive redevelopment over large areas rather than in piecemeal chunks, and therefore for a more brutal approach to the existing fabric of the city. This was something that made the rhetoric so appealing to developers, due to the profitability of 'comprehensive development of whole sites on an enormous scale'.[40] It

[37] Hall, *London 2000*, p. 164.

[38] Alison and Peter Smithson, *The Charged Void: Urbanism* (New York, 2005), pp. 45–63; Chamberlin, Powell, and Bon, *Barbican Redevelopment 1959: Report to the Court of Common Council of the Corporation* (London, 1959); William Holford, *Piccadilly Circus Future Development—Proposals for a Comprehensive Development* (London, 1962).

[39] Buchanan, *Traffic in Towns*, pp. 68–9.

[40] Brian P. Whitehouse, *Partners in Property* (London, 1964), p. 33.

also gave the task of redevelopment, and the need for planning, added urgency. Again, quoting Buchanan:

> Even as this Report is being written the opportunities are slipping past, for in many places the old obsolete street patterns are being 'frozen' by piecemeal rebuildings, and will remain frozen for another half century.[41]

It is worth stressing that a system of decks is opposed to Le Corbusier's urbanism, which saw the whole ground level free for countryside, with motor traffic above. Indeed, Le Corbusier was characteristically vociferous in his attack on placing pedestrians above traffic, arguing that if 'man had the agile feet and the miraculous tail of a monkey it might make sense. But in fact it is madness. Madness, madness, madness. It is the bottom of the pit, a gaping pit of error: the end of everything.'[42] (He goes on for some time in the same vein.)

The ultimate source of the idea for vertical segregation of pedestrians onto an upper walkway (although not a deck) could be Ludwig Hilberseimer's Bauhaus project, *Schema einer Hochhausstadt*, of 1924.[43] The second volume of Thomas Adams's *Regional Plan of New York and its Environs* (1931) had posited the possibility of a system of upper walkways before denying its efficacy, although it inaugurated a common trope in relating the idea to Venice.[44] Hans Bernoulli's *Die Stadt und ihr Boden* (1949) was a source cited by Chamberlin, Powell, and Bon for the multilevel city.[45] Aileen and William Tatton Brown's article 'Three Dimensional Town Planning', published in *The Architectural Review* in 1941 at the high point of the Blitz, is an important British precedent, with its 'creation of a completely new ground level for pedestrians'.[46] This envisaged continuous pedestrian movement on top of flat roofs connected by bridges, rather than buildings rising out of a deck. It is in the experiential description of 'a day in the life of John Citizen' (a very 1940s term) that the Tatton Browns' article most predicts the way that multilevel segregation of the 1960s would be envisioned:

> The new town would present, first of all, the impression of a big exhibition, a vast area of display free from the perils of the motor car. The novelty of the promenades and bridges would excite his curiosity and stimulate his desire to

[41] Buchanan, *Traffic in Towns*. p. 69.

[42] Le Corbusier, *The Radiant City* (London, 1964), p. 123.

[43] Ludwig Hilberseimer, *Großstadtarchitektur* (Stuttgart, 1924), pp. 18–19.

[44] Thomas Adams, *Regional Plan of New York and Its Environs* (New York, 1931), p. 313.

[45] Hans Bernoulli, *Die Stadt und ihr Boden* (Zurich, 1949).

[46] Aileen and William Tatton-Brown, '"Three-dimensional town planning": first of two articles dealing with some principles of town planning relevant to the reconstruction problem', *The Architectural Review*, September 1942, pp. 82–8, p. 83.

> explore: not only the main routes, but small courts off the beaten track, raised terraces, cloisters and colonnades, places where he could sit and rest and watch the world go by. There would be room for him to come into contact with architecture on a more human and intimate scale than has ever been possible before in the centre of any great city.[47]

Despite the seeming futurism of such 'three-dimensional' planning, planners were keen to locate the idea of the multilevel city in a historical continuity. It was common to reach for historical exemplars when describing three-dimensional schemes. See, for example, the extensive list found in the book *Planning for Man and Motor*.[48] The plan for the Barbican also makes extensive use of historical precedents:

> The principle of a podium with terraces above is, of course, not new and can be seen today in Carlton House Terrace. The old Adelphi was a complex example of the application of this principle of separating traffic on different levels . . . The best example of a city where foot and service traffic is completely segregated is Venice, where all supplies are carried to the city on canals while pedestrians walk on pavements which cross the canals by bridges.[49]

The reference to John Nash's Carlton House Terrace (1827–32) and to Robert Adam's Adelphi (1768–72) may strike a reader as odd when considering what a radical proposal Chamberlin, Powell, and Bon were making. The merging of radical forms and historical suggestions was nevertheless a central part of their approach. The plans for the Barbican are replete with references to traditional London typologies. Alongside the modernist housing typologies of point blocks and slabs raised on piloti, the Barbican attempts to reintroduce into this radical scheme many spaces that are evocative of London's *genius loci* London's garden squares, mews housing, crescents, Albany in Piccadilly, and the Inns of Court were all cited. The belief that planning a city on a deck would allow architects to reinvest in traditional forms, but in a way free from the horrors of traffic, was common at the time.

Wilfred Burns described upper-level walkways in Newcastle in such terms: 'The upper level pedestrian ways, freed from vehicular traffic will take on new forms varying from the narrow intimate shopping way to the wide pedestrian square or the enclosed arcade.'[50] What was so appealing about these schemes was that they seemed to balance both tradition and

47 Aileen and William Tatton-Brown, '"Three-dimensional town planning": Part 2, "Application"', *The Architectural Review*, January 1942, pp. 17–20.

48 Paul Ritter, *Planning for Man and Motor* (Oxford, 1963), pp. 44–5.

49 Chamberlin, Powell, and Bon, *Barbican Redevelopment*, p. 5.

50 Burns, Newcastle, p. 73.

Fig. 1.2. Another, perhaps more representative, image from *Traffic in Towns*, showing the deck connecting with the Georgian Fitzroy Square. © Open Government Licence

modernity; indeed, they used radical forms to save something of the traditional functions of cities from modernity (Fig. 1.2). Even the most radical schemes for horizontal pedestrian segregation were not presented as part of some futurist reimagining of the city, but the ambition, as Colin Buchanan related it, was to reinvest in something of traditional urbanism:

> This deck would, in effect, comprise a new ground level, and upon it the buildings would rise in a pattern related to but not dictated by the traffic below. On the deck it would be possible to re-create, in an even better form, the things that have delighted man for generations in towns—the snug, the close, varied atmosphere, the narrow alleys, the contrasting open squares, the effects of light and shade, the fountains and the sculpture.[51]

MODERNISM AND THE HISTORIC CITY

Buchanan's fantastical scheme for Fitzrovia in *Traffic in Towns* involved the demolition of the listed, Georgian Fitzroy Square, much of it designed

[51] Buchanan, *Traffic in Towns*, p. 46.

by the neoclassical architect Robert Adam (1728–92). Buchanan suggested that 'This was not intended to show any disrespect to Fitzroy Square and other buildings worth preserving, but simply to explore factual possibilities.'[52] The 'radically new urban forms' that architect-planners were suggesting often necessitated the total redevelopment of large areas, and 1960s planning is frequently castigated for its despoliation and destruction of historic buildings. Many post-war architect-planners nevertheless displayed a pronounced admiration for buildings that would have been deemed, in the jargon of the day, 'monuments of historical interest', and gave them an elevated position within the 'civic design' aspect of their plans. When it came to historic buildings in the post-war period, what was at stake was giving important buildings an improved setting or environment, often through the creative use of demolition, and therefore at the expense of the more everyday historical fabric of the city.

Two drawings from Frederick Gibberd's 1947 plan for St Pancras help to introduce what had become the orthodox approach to historic buildings by the beginning of the 1960s (Fig. 1.3).[53] They depict the setting of William Inwood's Greek revival Church of All Saints in Camden, as seen from Pratt Street as it then was and as proposed for the future. The plan calls for all of the detritus of slums, mixed uses, noxious industry, and traffic mess to be swept away, so as to bring 'a touch of the country into the heart of the town'. The church, however, was to be 'retained, both as an example of Greek revival architecture' and also because it was deemed 'valuable from a civic design point of view'. In the second image the period of 1837 to 1945 has been collapsed so that the modern world is brought directly into dialogue with that of the Greek revival. The church can now be enjoyed among a pedestrianized landscape of trees and cafes, to be appreciated by coffee-drinking sophisticates.

The church was pathetically hidden in the first image, its spire peeking ruefully over the rooftops; in the second image, demolition of surrounding buildings has opened up new vistas and made it the central feature of a composition, albeit a semi-informal composition. The church stands now within a green space, as if it had been transformed, almost, into a modernist 'object' building. The modern additions are deferential towards the older church in both their scale and siting. They are in a colourlessly modern style Gibberd might well have described as urbane. All Saints had been handed over to the Greek Orthodox Church in 1947, although there is no mention in the plan of this functional use, or of its place in the community. Though giving the church a central, indeed a dominating,

52 Buchanan, *Traffic in Towns*, p. 157.
53 Frederick Gibberd and C. S. Bainbridge, *Plan for St Pancras* (1947).

Fig. 1.3. 'Existing and proposed views of All Saints, seen from Pratt Street'; Frederick Gibberd and C. S. Bainbridge, *Plan for St Pancras* (1947). © Gibberd Garden Trust

Fig. 1.4. Photograph of Pratt Street, 2018; author.

position, it has been deconsecrated, aestheticized, and abstracted by the plan. In this Camden scheme, All Saints takes the position of what Gibberd stodgily called in his theoretical writings a 'dominant vertical feature in space'.[54]

Nothing came of Gibberd's scheme, but what we find on the site today comes as a surprise. What Gibberd rendered as an indiscriminate and messy slum, can never really have been anything of the sort. Instead, walking down Pratt Street we find the quiet elegance of an early Victorian Terrace (Fig. 1.4). This is emblematic of a blindness towards the value of the everyday fabric of the traditional city, sweepingly judging it as an indeterminate slum. This minor example of Gibberd's approach to an existing church can be taken as representative of certain features of the approach of modernist architect-planners to existing historical buildings. One can see many of the features of Gibberd's approach to All Saints Camden in the much more famous examples of the grandee architect-planner William Holford's plan for the St Paul's Precinct, Thomas Sharp's for the area around Exeter Cathedral, or Walter Bor's for the area around the Tower of London.[55] The central feature of all these schemes was the creation of carefully modulated vistas on an historic monument, and a

[54] Gibberd, *Town Design*.

[55] Holden, Charles, and Holford, William, *Reconstruction in the City of London* (London, 1947); Sharp, Thomas, *Exeter Phoenix* (London, 1946).

pedestrianized frame from which to contemplate them. In all cases the aim was for semi-informal views, rather than grand axial vistas. It was common to argue that modernist planning—because it was freer than beaux-arts planning—was more able to accommodate the historical fabric. As will be seen, such an approach continued into many plans of the 1960s.

Creating spaces for old architecture was a central feature of the Townscape approach, which applied picturesque principles to new urban planning. This approach is often written about as if it were only a critique of modernist planning practice, and remained purely in the realms of theory and on paper. But it was widely applied by architect-planners, as can be seen by the example of a plan for Northampton, which was prepared by Wilson and Womersley and had the architectural illustrator Gordon Cullen as 'Townscape advisor'.[56] The planners needed to prepare the city for the increase in population by a further 100,000 people, which would accompany its designation as an expanded town. The Townscape element of the plan was based around uniting five of the city's churches. As the plan put it, 'The primary structure of the new townscape proposals is related to the five churches. Each of the four peripheral churches is connected to All Saints church by a central route, each route having its own individual character.'[57] (Figs 1.5 and 1.6.) Here is a description of one of these visual sequences, which were illustrated by Cullen's beguiling illustrations:

> The sequence north to St Sepulchre's Church from [All Saints' Church] is first contained by the façade of the Ram Hotel and then by the horizon as the crest of Sheep Street is seen. It is finally enclosed by a proposed terrace of housing which continues the curve of the listed buildings in Sheep Street and focuses attention on the Round Church and Spire of St Sepulchre's which suddenly comes into view as Sheep Street is left behind.'[58]

The churches are made part of a sequence of impressions and images, one not to be appreciated from a fixed position, as in a beaux-arts scheme, but by a roving eye.[59] The churches have been co-opted into a 'civic design' conception, which has little relationship to their functional use. Though these buildings from the past are elevated to a central role for the image of the city, this did not entail a wholesale acceptance of the importance of conservation, especially when it came to the fabric of the Victorian city. As the plan put it, 'There are very few old buildings other than some of the churches that escaped the fire in 1675 . . . Most of the town centre is

[56] Wilson and Womersley, *Expansion of Northampton, Planning Proposals* (London, 1968).
[57] Ibid., p. 118. [58] Ibid., p. 118.
[59] For a comparable approach see Nikolaus Pevsner, *Visual Planning and the Picturesque* (Los Angeles, 2010).

Fig. 1.5. Drawing by Gordon Cullen of a pedestrian approach to the Church of the Holy Sepulchre, Northampton, from Wilson and Womersley, *Expansion of Northampton, Planning Proposals* (London, 1968). © Gordon Cullen Estate/ University of Westminster Archive

69. St. Giles Square and the new Arts Centre

Fig. 1.6. Cullen drawing of St Giles Square, looking towards All Saints' Northampton, from Wilson and Womersley, *Expansion of Northampton, Planning Proposals* (London, 1968). © Gordon Cullen Estate/University of Westminster Archive

comprised of 19th Century buildings that are now rapidly coming to the end of their useful life.'[60] For a town plan which advertised its central conception as uniting the various spires, the planners nevertheless sanctioned the demolition of E. F. Law's Gothic revival St Andrews, of 1841–2. As all of this suggests, what was considered historic, and therefore worthy of retention, was limited.

When it came to fitting buildings into historic locations, there was a large and consistent literature advising how to do this in a way that maintained a modernist style. Typical was Thomas Sharp, who argued that the key was the maintenance of character. What was central for him was not disrupting the established rhythms or scale of a place, and in important contexts using 'materials identical or very similar to those used for the present buildings'.[61] It was, however, not necessary to maintain the same style; indeed, 'there need be no suggestion that modern architecture is inevitably disruptive, and that new buildings should be designed in imitation of the old. It would be absurd and stultifying to suggest anything of the kind.'[62]

Translating such ambitions into buildings was not always easy. For one thing, it was very hard to square with industrialized building methods, leading to such questionable assertions as the plan for Chester suggesting that 'Exposed aggregate and shutter-faced concrete suit Chester's face: Coloured glass and plastic panels do not.'[63] Secondly, many of the new typologies of buildings demanded by plans, from car parks to shopping centres, were simply too large for such politesse—indeed, they worked better when approached with a bit of bloody-minded confidence. Thirdly, it is a moot point whether anyone but a connoisseur will pick up on those buildings that do attempt to blend in with an established street scene through such subtle allusions. There are some wonderful examples of historically allusive modernist architecture, notably the Oxbridge buildings of architectural firms such as Powell and Moya or Howell, Killick, Partridge, and Amis, but in lesser hands the results were often spineless and dull.[64]

[60] Wilson and Womersley, *Expansion of Northampton*, p. 17.
[61] Thomas Sharp, *Town and Townscape* (London, 1967), pp. 25–6.
[62] Ibid. p. 23.
[63] Donald Insall, *Chester, a Study in Conservation* (London, 1968), p. 37.
[64] See Kenneth Powell, *Powell and Moya* (London, 2009); Otto Saumarez Smith, '"A Strange Brutalist Primitive Hut", Howell, Killick, Partridge and Amis's Senior Combination Room at Downing College, Cambridge', *Twentieth Century Architecture 11: Oxford and Cambridge*, ed. Elain Harwood, Alan Powers, and Otto Saumarez Smith (London, 2013)

This chapter has shown how architect-planners understood their schemes as responding to widely perceived political and social problems. Although they identified themselves as modernists, they were not merely enacting a blueprint fixed and ossified by the interwar masters of the modern movement, but their ideas were evolving during this period in the face of rapid social and technological change. In all this British architect-planners do not conform with the urbanist Jane Jacobs's influential portrayal of planners and architects of this period:

> It is disturbing to think that men who are young today, men who are being trained now for their careers, should accept *on grounds that they must be 'modern' in their thinking*, conceptions about cities and traffic which are not only unworkable, but also to which nothing new of any significance has been added since their fathers were children.[65]

Architect-planners were swept up in a cross-cultural moment of economic optimism. They celebrated a social and aesthetic quality they defined as 'urbanity'. Even if their conception of what should be included in a definition of the historic city was limited, they nonetheless attempted to balance both tradition and modernity; indeed, modern solutions were presented as the only way to preserve a city's urbanity in the face of expanding automobile usage. The set of ideas propounded by architect-planners chimed with the ambitions of politicians in central government, where they would briefly achieve an almost uncontested ascendancy, as Chapter 2 will show.

[65] Jane Jacobs, *Death and Life of Great American Cities* (New York, 1961), p. 371.

2

Blue, White, and Red Heat

Central Government and City-Centre Redevelopment

BLUE HEAT: TORY MODERNISM

In his 1962 book *The Anatomy of Britain* Anthony Sampson asked the question, 'How potent, one wonders, is the influence of architecture?' He speculated whether Foreign Office policy would 'be more up to date if it were housed in a steel-and-glass block?' rather than its present home in the Victorian edifice designed by Sir George Gilbert Scott. 'Surroundings, I expect, *do* influence attitudes, and it is the social habits and rituals of the Foreign Office that have helped to hold back the realization of change.'[1]

The Wilson government's support of the ambitious Whitehall plan of 1965, by a team headed by the architect Sir Leslie Martin, with Colin Buchanan in charge of traffic planning, is a strong indication of the Labour government's commitment to a modernist planning philosophy. The comprehensive plan involved making Parliament Square into a pedestrian precinct, the demolition of swathes of Whitehall including the Foreign Office, the building of new offices in megastructural ziggurats, and the construction of a road tunnel under the Embankment (Fig. 2.1).[2] The plans were to give a modern, dynamic, and progressive image to government.[3] It is tempting to see the Whitehall scheme as a physical embodiment of the 'white heat' moment generally, or more specifically of

[1] Anthony Sampson, *The Anatomy of Britain* (London, 1962), p. 299.

[2] *Whitehall, a Plan for the National and Government Centre* (London, 1965); Ian Rice, '"Ziggurats for Bureaucrats": Sir Leslie Martin's Whitehall Scheme', *Architectural Research Quarterly*, 8.3–4 (2004), pp. 313–23; Adam Sharr and Stephen Thornton, *Demolishing Whitehall: Harold Wilson, Leslie Martin and the Architecture of White Heat* (London, 2014).

[3] For a comparable example of the symbolic role of architecture in the early 1960s in an institutional setting see William Whyte, 'The modernist moment at the University of Leeds, 1957–1977', *Historical Journal*, 51 (2008), pp. 169–93.

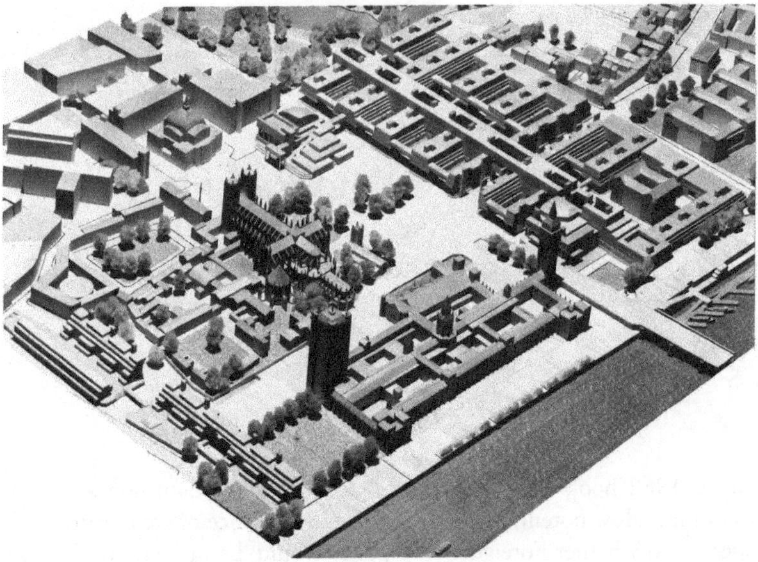

Fig. 2.1. Model of the ambitious plan for Whitehall, 1965; Leslie Martin, *Whitehall, A Plan for the National and Government Centre* (1965). © Open Government Licence

the economist Thomas Balogh's influential Labourite critique of the conservatism of the civil service, which would lead to the Fulton Report in 1968.[4] As Alan Powers argues, 'Images of modern architecture formed a natural backdrop for [Wilson's] vision of Britain's future.'[5] However, Martin and Buchanan were appointed in April 1964 by the Minister of Buildings and Public Works, Geoffrey Rippon, that is to say, before the change of government. As this suggests, the desire to reshape the face of cities in the early 1960s into an image of modernity was tantamount to orthodoxy in these years. Furthermore, the Conservative-controlled government was a fertile ground for radical planning ideas.

The Conservative embrace of modernism has been obscured in most accounts of the period.[6] This is partly due to the general phenomenon that, although modernism has been employed in a wide international array of political and institutional contexts, it has not shaken off its associations with the socialist values of many of its early proponents. The fact that in

[4] See Peter Hennessy, *Whitehall* (London, 1989), pp. 171–98.

[5] Alan Powers, *Britain, Modern Architectures in History* (London, 2007), p. 127.

[6] Housing policy is an exception. Patrick Dunleavy, *The Politics of Mass Housing in Britain, 1945–75* (Oxford, 1981), pp. 104–81.

Britain Thatcherite Conservatism was implicated in the traditionalist reaction against modernism further cements the deeply ingrained association of modernism with the Left. There are also historiographical reasons for overlooking the way the Conservatives were associated with British modernism. Until recently, writing about British modernism has mostly been polemical.[7] Those attacking modernism have tended to do so from a right-wing perspective, and have been only too ready to associate modernism's perceived failures with the failures of a state-led socialism.[8] On the other hand, defenders of modernism have argued, in the words of one historian, that 'we need to be a bit more forgiving of our forebears' passion to alleviate suffering', and have subsequently tended to focus either on the social commitment of individual architects or else on buildings for the welfare state such as schools or public buildings. They have consequently tended to avoid the developer-led modernism of office blocks and shopping centres that occurred in central areas.[9]

During the parliamentary term 1959–64 many radical ideas about the reconstruction of cities were appropriated from an avant-garde town-planning discourse by politicians, forming the basis of what was perceived at the time as a consensus for how to deal with cities. Ideas such as comprehensive redevelopment on a vast scale, the segregation of vehicular and pedestrian traffic, higher densities, virulently anti-suburban attitudes, and an almost unquestioned use of a modernist idiom were held up as ideals. In a parliamentary speech on the subject of urban renewal in 1962, the Conservative MP Bill Deedes noted that a 'whole range of organizations have been turning their minds to a consideration of this central, major problem in recent months'. He went on to cite a number of documents about the subject, produced by both left- and right-wing organizations, from *Socialist Commentary* to the Bow Group.[10] Taken

[7] A striking example is Owen Hatherley, *Militant Modernism* (London, 2009). For an example from the opposite end of the spectrum, see Roger Scruton, 'The Architecture of Stalinism', *Cambridge Review*, 99 (30 January 1976), pp. 36–71.

[8] Most famously in David Watkin, *Morality and Architecture: the Development of a Theme in Architectural History and Theory from the Gothic Revival to the Modern Movement* (London, 1977).

[9] Leif Jerram, *Streetlife, The Untold History of Europe's Twentieth Century* (Oxford, 2011), p. 273; John Allan, *Lubetkin: Architecture and the Tradition of Progress* (London, 1992); Nigel Warburton, *Ernö Goldfinger: the Life of an Architect* (London, 2003); Miles Glendinning, *Modern Architect: the Life and Times of Robert Matthew* (London, 2008); Andrew Saint, *Towards a Social Architecture: The Role of School-Building in Post-War England* (London and New Haven, 1987); Adrian Forty, 'Being or Nothingness: Private Experience and Public Architecture in Post War Britain', *Architectural History*, 38 (1995), pp. 25–35.

[10] The reports mentioned were: Timothy Knight et al., *Let Our Cities Live* (London, 1960); *Signposts for the Sixties: a Statement of Labour Party Home Policy submitted by the National Executive Committee to the 60th annual conference 2–6 October 1961*; Peter Hall,

together, he argued, these 'indicate the astonishing consensus of informed opinion that this matter represents a great social task'.[11] Citing a similar group of texts, a committee set up by the Civic Trust, an organization founded in 1957 by the then Minister of Housing, Duncan Sandys, also noted 'a remarkable measure of agreement on the current problems of economic and physical planning'.[12] Both parties mined the same influential 1950s British planning examples, especially those of Coventry, Sheffield, and the London County Council (LCC), as models for what the city of the future should look like. Although this was rarely acknowledged, many of the concepts and terminology of redevelopment, such as 'urban renewal', came from the United States.[13] Pedestrianization was an obsession of the planners of the period, a theme much taken up by central government. There was a new receptivity within both parties towards the ideas of modernist planners trained after the Second World War, rather than planners associated with the first generation of New Towns and the Town and Country Planning Association, let alone any planner who could be characterized as traditionalist. The difference in the rhetoric of left and right was in how far radical transformations were to be achieved through public or private means.

The thirteen years of Conservative government from 1951to 1964 had seen massive changes to the physical face of the country, although these were primarily directed towards the area of housing.[14] Their 1951 manifesto had committed the Conservatives to building 300,000 new homes a year, a figure exceeded by Harold Macmillan as Minister of Housing. Unlike his predecessor as Minister, Aneurin Bevan (a disciple of American urbanist Lewis Mumford), Macmillan displayed little curiosity about architectural aesthetics, and was criticized for being interested in quantity at the expense of quality.[15] The one qualitative statement on architectural matters to be found in his diaries from this period deals with a trip to Sheffield and the gestating plans for the premier megastructural 'streets in

Malcolm MacEwan, and Peter Willmott, *The Face of Britain: a Policy for Town and Country Planning* (London, 1961); F. J. McCulloch, *Land Use in an Urban Environment* (Liverpool, 1961); *Change and Challenge* (London, 1961); Town and Country Planning Association, *The Paper Metropolis* (London, 1962); the then unpublished *Urban Redevelopment: Report of a Committee Appointed by the Civic Trust* (London, 1962).

[11] W. F. Deedes, House of Commons debate, 13 April 1962, Hansard vol. 657, 1652.

[12] *Urban Redevelopment: Report of a Committee Appointed by the Civic Trust.*

[13] Murray Fraser and Joe Kerr, *Architecture and the Special Relationship, The American Influence on Post-War British Architecture* (London, 2007).

[14] See Peter Weiler, 'The Rise and Fall of the Conservatives' "Grand Design for Housing", 1951–64' *Contemporary British History*, 14.1 (2000), pp. 122–50.

[15] Vincent Brome, *Aneurin Bevan* (London, 1953), p. 114; D. R. Thorpe, *Supermac; the Life of Harold Macmillan* (London, 2011), p. 285.

the sky' estate, Park Hill: 'The architect seemed very good. Some new flats (on the hill) should be very good.'[16]

Housing numbers remained an important electoral issue, with Alec Douglas-Home promising 400,000 new homes a year.[17] In the 1966 election the Tory pledge went up to 500,000 new homes a year.[18] Looking back at his time as Minister in 1987, Keith Joseph wrote, 'I didn't really have a philosophy. I was just a "more" man. I used to go to bed at night counting the number of houses I'd destroyed and the number of planning approvals that had been given... Just *more*.'[19] Despite this, for the Conservative Party housebuilding *did* have an ideological basis as well as an electioneering one, showing the strong influence of Noel Skelton's idea of a 'property owning democracy' on the party leadership.[20] The other way in which the Conservative government had radically affected the built environment in Britain during these years was through the unleashing of a property boom, following the deregulation of building licences in 1954.[21] The controversial effect this had on the skyline of London, and the enormous fortunes made by property developers, would form an important backdrop for debates about city-centre redevelopment.

The renewed interest in positive activity in city centres (rather than a laissez-faire approach which left it to property developers) can be seen as part of a switch in Conservative ideology towards managing, rather than creating, affluence—a physical manifestation, perhaps, of Macmillan's economic 'New Approach' and the 'Modernization of Britain' policy drive.[22] The Buchanan Report and the Parker Morris Committee Report on housing standards, *Homes for Today and Tomorrow* (1961), both by official advisory committees to the government, were signs of a more *dirigiste* attempt to grapple with the qualitative elements of urban life in what was proclaimed as an age of affluence.[23] Buchanan described a problem which had arisen 'directly out of man's own ingenuity and

[16] Peter Catterall, ed., *The Macmillan Diaries* (London, 2003), 12 Dec. 1953.

[17] D. E. Butler and Anthony King, *The British General Election of 1964* (London, 1965), p. 88.

[18] John Ramsden, *The Winds of Change: Macmillan to Heath, 1957–1975* (London, 1996), p. 143.

[19] Quoted in Morrison Halcrow, *Keith Joseph: a Single Mind* (London, 1989), p. 31.

[20] Thorpe, *Supermac*, p. 83; D. R. Thorpe, *Alec Douglas-Home* (London, 1996), pp. 81–2; D. R. Thorpe, *Eden: The Life and Times of Anthony Eden, first Earl of Avon 1897–1977* (London, 2003).

[21] Oliver Marriott, *The Property Boom* (Abingdon, 1989).

[22] See John Tomlinson, 'Conservative Modernization, 1960–64: Too Little too Late?', *Contemporary British History*, 11.3 (1997), pp. 18–38.

[23] Alistair Kefford, 'Housing the citizen-consumer in post-war Britain: The Parker Morris Report, affluence and the even briefer life of social democracy', *Twentieth Century British History*, 29.2 (2017), pp. 225–58.

growing affluence'.[24] Affluence was also the self-congratulatory foundation on which it was suggested housing ought to be built:

> Since the end of the war, the country has undergone a social and economic revolution, and the pattern of living is still changing fast. There is full employment, a national health service, and the various social insurance benefits. In material terms people are better off than ever before. . . . These changes in the way people live, the things which they own and use, and in their general level of prosperity . . . make it timely to re-examine the kind of homes we ought to be building, to ensure that they will be adequate to meet the newly emerging needs of the future.[25]

These reports came out of the same moment as many government reports that subjected particular subjects to intense scrutiny, and they share much in common with the Crowther Report, *15 to 18,* on the future of secondary education; the Newsom Report, *Half Our Future*, on secondary modern schools; the Robbins Report, *Higher Education*; the Trend enquiry into the organization of the civil service; and, most infamously, the first Beeching Report, *The Reshaping of British Railways*.[26] Though by 1963, when the majority of these reports were released, the Profumo affair and the satire boom would highlight all that was antiquated and patrician about the Tories, these reports suggest an intellectually propulsive government, and one not fearful of promising significant state investment in bold projects. They were to form the basis for the Conservative Party's modernizing and centrist 1964 manifesto, *Prosperity with a Purpose*, which promised to 'apply the principles of the Buchanan Report to comprehensive campaigns of town replanning'.[27]

The Bow Group, a think tank for Conservatives under the age of 35 set up in 1951, released a pamphlet, *Let Our Cities Live* (1960), which was an early manifestation of the coming together of Conservative thinking and the ideas of radical planners.[28] Its principal author was a 27-year-old businessman, Timothy Knight. Another author was the Architectural Association trained architect Brian Falk, who was later a director of the commercial architectural firm Covell Matthews & Partners, and co-author, with the planner Jaqueline Tyrwhitt, of a book on city planning.[29]

[24] Buchanan, *Traffic in Towns,* p. 17.

[25] Parker Morris Committee Report, *Homes for Today and Tomorrow* (London, 1961).

[26] Thorpe, *Supermac,* pp. 501–6.

[27] *Prosperity with a Purpose, The Conservative 1964 manifesto.*

[28] For the Bow Group's influence in this period see Tim Bale, *The Conservatives Since 1945: The Drivers of Party Change* (London, 2012), p. 99.

[29] http://www.scottisharchitects.org.uk/architect_full.php?id=400463; Martin Meyerson, Jaqueline Tyrwhitt, Brian Falk and Patricia Sekler, *Face of the Metropolis* (New York, 1963).

A surveyor and a property developer were also involved. Mirroring an argument reminiscent of the influential town planner Thomas Sharp, the pamphlet stated that suburbia was an unintended consequence of Garden City ideals: 'So suburbia spread around and between the cities, giving birth to suburban life, a curious phenomenon of the twentieth century so alien to [Ebenezer] Howard's ideals.'[30] The document is a proclamation of the need to reinvest in a romantic ideal of urban life, in a way that strongly echoes arguments common amongst architect-planners at the time:

> The image of the Big City as a creation of the 'snorting steam engine' belongs to the nineteenth century. It is our proposal that we should shake off this image of the conurbation as a Victorian horror. We must find a way of having conurbations without the conditions we associate with them. This is the challenge of the next decade and we believe that in order to succeed, planners first must accept conurbations as here to stay and . . . to grow; second they must concentrate on overall designs for the Big Cities allowing them to grow without impairing their efficiency.[31]

Traffic was already seen as the 'key to urban planning', with the authors advocating an alternative to either 'obliterating the city by a network of roads, flyovers, cloverleaf junctions, and multi-storey junctions', or to banning traffic outright, which 'would be as disastrous as cutting off the supply of blood to the brain, and just as impracticable'.[32] The motor car was to be made 'the servant and not the master of the city', through segregation, fast inner-city roads, and improved commuter railway links. The pamphlet proposed much higher densities: 'It should be the objective of all rehousing schemes to fit as many dwellings as possible in the available space'; although this would involve 'building tall blocks of flats', they also advised copying experiments by the LCC and in Scandinavian countries in 'new forms of terrace and courtyard houses and flats'.[33] It would be possible to incorporate high-density living into the Macmillanite vision of the affluent society:

> Does this picture of high density city development instead of garden city sprawl entail a different kind of society? Can its social conditions be made acceptable in the light of our aspirations for an ever increasing standard of living? At first glance this may smack too much of Huxley's 'Brave New World', but if the varying needs of population and household structure are analysed it will be found that they are not incompatible with the developments we envisage.'[34]

[30] Knight et al., *Let Our Cities Live*, p. 1. Thomas Sharp, *Town and Countryside* (London, 1932); Thomas Sharp, *Town planning* (London, 1940).

[31] *Let Our Cities Live*, p. 8.

[32] *Let Our Cities Live*, pp. 11–12.

[33] *Let Our Cities Live*, p. 10.

[34] *Let Our Cities Live*, p. 10.

The authors argued that 'the spur to redevelopment will come from the private sector, and the planners would be able to use this growing activity to mould our towns and cities into modern shape'.[35] To make sure rebuilding was on a large enough scale, they suggested a land-pooling system to help with central redevelopment. The end result remained the modernizing one of 'rebuilding our cities so that they can function properly'. Local authorities would achieve the desired aim of an efficient city that would act as the 'foundation for an ever increasing British standard of living' by requiring developers to 'incorporate in their schemes facilities which only indirectly benefit them such as basement car parking, subways, and elevated or segregated pedestrian walks'.[36]

In 1960 the Civic Trust held a conference on the subject of 'Rebuilding Cities'.[37] The conference resulted in the setting up of a committee of politicians and planners, who published a pamphlet in 1962.[38] Politicians from both parties attended the conference, as well as a veritable who's who of modernist planners and architects.[39] Minister of Housing Henry Brooke's opening address argued that 'if only the centre could be made attractive the whole town might begin to move into new prosperity'.[40] As the summary of conclusions of the conference put it, this would involve rebuilding for the motor-car age: 'The street layout in town centres is often completely out of date and unsuited to the motor age. It may be desirable to separate pedestrians from road traffic by the provision of vehicle-free shopping areas, pedestrian bridges and high-level pavements.'[41]

A further Conservative pamphlet, *Change and Challenge,* came from a committee appointed by Home Secretary Rab Butler in March 1960, to 'consider what should be the aims of town and country planning in an age of rising standards of living, increasing leisure and modern industrial development'.[42] It was headed by the M.P. Sir Colin Thornton-Kemsley (who was then a trustee of the Town and Country Planning Association), and involved several Tory MPs (including Enoch Powell until he resigned on becoming Minister of Health), industrialists, local-government figures, and the academic geographer Professor Michael Wise. The pamphlet had a broader canvas than *Let our Cities Live*, looking more generally at national

[35] *Let Our Cities Live,* p. 40. [36] *Let Our Cities Live,* p. 39.

[37] Civic Trust, *Rebuilding Cities, Report of Conference held at Middlesex Guildhall Friday 15th July 1960* (1960).

[38] *Urban Redevelopment.*

[39] They included Lionel Brett, Colin Buchanan, Hugh Cadbury Brown, Peter Chamberlin, A. W. Cleeve Bar, Jane Drew, Maxwell Fry, Frederick Gibberd, George Grenfell Baines, Sir William Holford, Leslie Lane, Graeme Shankland, Richard Sheppard, and Stanley Wardley.

[40] *Urban Redevelopment,* p. 13. [41] *Urban Redevelopment,* p. 5.

[42] *Change and Challenge: Next Steps in Town and Country Planning* (London, 1962), p. 1.

planning mechanisms, but it was still concerned with the new types of cities it was felt were needed to deal with traffic problems. It predicted universal car ownership as inevitable, but this was seen benignly as a 'symbol of spreading prosperity'.[43] Cars, however, made old towns impracticable:

> What has finally shattered the old scene, both in small towns and large ones, during the past generation or two has been the arrival of the universal motor-car – with its threat of delay, distraction and death. The same street pattern still exists but it is now filled with a tangle of buses, taxis, delivery vans, private cars, cycles and pedestrians, both stationary and moving (or at least wishing to), delaying, harassing, injuring and even killing each other.[44]

The conclusion made from this analysis was that redevelopment would have to be carried out comprehensively, so as to achieve segregation of vehicles through both vertical and horizontal means. They held up Coventry city centre as an exemplar.[45] The authors advised that urban motorways would have 'an essential part to play in moving motor traffic in big cities'. They cited the American William H. Whyte's *The Exploding Metropolis* as a warning against allowing American-style suburbanization.[46]

According to Conservative MP Richard Nugent, who had served on the *Change and Challenge* and the Civic Trust committees, giving architects a broad canvas to work on through comprehensive redevelopment would vindicate modern architecture:

> When one criticises architects for putting up hideous offices, and one attacks modern architecture in general, one should remember that, if architects are given a chance in a large enough area to use modern styles, materials and engineering, they can not only achieve excellent modern accommodation but the beauty of exciting lines, freshness and something which puts character into the life of a town. But the first essential is that they be given a large enough area in which to do it.[47]

Nugent had also been chairman of the Committee on London Roads, which had argued that 'We should like to see more schemes for keeping pedestrians and road traffic apart... we hope that similar ideas (the Barbican and the South Bank with upper level walk-ways, etc.) will be considered whenever large scale redevelopment in congested areas takes place.'[48]

As Minister of Transport, Ernest Marples was another important Conservative promoting urban renewal during this period. He had made his name as Macmillan's parliamentary secretary during the housing push

[43] Ibid., p. 7. [44] Ibid., p. 14. [45] Ibid., p. 17. [46] Ibid., p. 34.

[47] Urban Central Redevelopment, House of Commons debate, 13 April 1962, Hansard vol. 657, ccl 645–74.

[48] *Committee on London Roads Report* (London, 1959), p. 11.

of the early 1950s. His background was in the construction industry, which was a cause of embarrassment and charges of conflict of interest, especially after the contract for the Hammersmith Flyover was given to Marples Ridgeway.[49] Many Conservatives had similar connections with the construction industry and other interested parties, and the promotion of large-scale, state-led, infrastructural projects provided business for these sectional interests. The Buchanan Report was commissioned by Marples after a concerted effort to deal with what he described as the 'traffic thrombosis in the heart of London' through a mixture of restrictive methods—such as the first appearance of yellow lines and parking meters in Britain—and engineering projects such as the Hyde Park Underpass.[50]

Keith Joseph was Minister of Housing and Local Government from 1962 till 1964. Though now best known for his role in the formation of Thatcherism, he was recognized at the time as one of the dynamic and modernizing 'professional executives', along with figures such as Marples and Rippon, in the government.[51] He had been a director of the construction firm Bovis, which his father had run. He would later be embarrassed by his time at the Ministry, congratulating a new Minister in the 1980s with the words, 'Well done. You'll find lots of problems in your new job. I caused many of them.'[52] But at the time he boasted, in language reminiscent of architect-planners, that his 'vision' was 'to reconcile the town and its traffic, and create within the years to come, out of the squalor and shapelessness of so much of the past, a new 20th century urbanity worthy of the best in our history'.[53]

People and Cities, the report of a 1963 conference organized by the British Road Federation in association with the Town Planning Institute to discuss the Buchanan Report, presents an opportunity of hearing discussions between planners, Conservative politicians, and developers. The planners who gave talks were among the most radical then practising: Walter Bor (ex-LCC, chief planner at Liverpool), Arthur Ling (Donald Gibson's successor as chief architect and planning officer at Coventry,

[49] Charles Loft, *Government, the Railways and the Modernization of Britain: Beeching's Last Train* (London, 2006), p. 55.

[50] *The Times*, 27 November 1959, p. 8;D. J. Dutton, 'Marples, (Alfred) Ernest, Baron Marples (1907–1978)', *Oxford Dictionary of National Biography* (Oxford, 2004).

[51] 'The Tory Menu: Jam Tomorrow', *The Guardian*, 14 October 1964, p. 10.

[52] Quoted in Brian Harrison, 'Joseph, Keith Sinjohn, Baron Joseph (1918–1994)', *Oxford Dictionary of National Biography* (Oxford, 2004).

[53] Sir Keith Joseph, House of Commons debate, 10 December 1962, vol 669, cc 68. See also Keith Joseph's speech on 'Planning for Growth' to the Royal Institution of Chartered Surveyors reprinted in *The Chartered Surveyor*, 96.1 (July 1963), p. 16.

later planner of Runcorn New Town), Wilfred Burns (ex-deputy at Coventry, chief planner at Newcastle), and Hugh Wilson (chief architect and planning officer of Cumbernauld). These men were undoubtedly in the avant-garde of their profession, but their language and rhetoric were far less colourful than the statements made by other guests.

Marples opened the conference with the extraordinary declaration: 'I believe that the old Roman concept of a road, a pavement and a building—the way we have been building for over a thousand years—is now outdated.'[54] Former editor of *The Economist* Sir Geoffrey Crowther saw the Buchanan Report as offering a separate path of development to Americanization: 'unless we pay particular attention to [the Buchanan Report] it is the American state of affairs that we shall slip into.' He used a narrative of extreme crisis to argue for denser anti-suburban cities: 'After all, we are not planning for Utopia; we are planning for the Black Hole of Calcutta. We must go upwards; we must stand on each other's shoulders; we must try to dis-invent suburbia; we must try to find means of persuading people to abandon the habits of a century and come back to living, if not exactly over the shop, at least in the same part of town as the place where they do their work.'[55]

The property developer Leslie Sydney Marler, who, referencing figures involved in the ongoing Profumo affair, ruefully admitted that the public image of his profession 'came out somewhere half way between Miss Keeler and Mr. Rachman', called for developers to be given the opportunity of comprehensively redeveloping areas on a vast scale.[56] His speech was certainly brash, but it was also notably well informed about the planning philosophy of the period. He thanked architectural critic and teacher Robert Furneaux Jordan, planner Walter Bor, and LCC traffic planner Leslie Lane for informing his ideas. His vision was 'the eighteenth-century idea [he had already mentioned Thomas Cubitt and the Grosvenor Estate] multiplied say, five times vertically but also five times laterally'. He illustrated his lecture with a scheme for three tower blocks in Knights bridge, prepared in conjunction with the LCC, which is one of the more grandiose schemes of the period. It was on a parcel of land that he boasted was equivalent to Trafalgar Square. Each of the three blocks, the tallest of which was forty storeys high, were to rise out of a podium roof, which cars

[54] *People and Cities: Report of the 1963 London Conference, Organised by the British Road Federation in Association with the Town Planning Institute* (London, 1963), p. 12.

[55] Ibid, p. 25–6. Crowther was chairman of the steering committee for *Traffic in Towns.*

[56] Property developers had a significant role in the Profumo affair.Richard Davenport-Hines, *An English Affair* (London, 2013), pp. 149–86.

would access via a ramp. Also included was a 'pedestrian only shopping piazza'. He wished it had been bigger, 'but of course this, amongst other things, would involve the destruction of Harrods, and Harrods is Harrods; frankly, I have not got the nerves to suggest it'. Without working on such a vast scale, individual tall buildings would remain 'twentieth-century buildings on nineteenth-century sites'.[57] This was an argument often used in planning circles. He went on to contrast the ability of private enterprise to repair the war damage of the City of London—'not always wisely . . . but repaired they have been'—with the Corporation of London's failure to do anything to the 'vast acreage . . . of desolation round Barbican'.[58]

The planner Arthur Ling, who was politically on the far Left, summed up the conference in a way that highlights the fact that the Conservatives had taken much from the modernist project, but not its politics: 'One thing [that] has struck me in this conference is the few times that *people* have been mentioned, although the title is "People and Cities". We have heard about planning for traffic, we have heard about planning for profit, but we have not heard enough about planning for people.'[59] Modernist architecture was nevertheless central to the self-presentation of the Conservative Party in this period, acting as a Janus face with the attributes of the country house, the grouse moor, or the golf course more conventionally associated with the Tories. The bold scale of modernist solutions was a central element of what Tories took from modernism, as modernist planning would provide ever greater sites for profitable redevelopment. The engagement with modernism went further than this, though: it was used to give form to the future envisioned by the Conservatives through the mantras of prosperity and affluence. Modernism, despite its early connection with the socialism of the Bauhaus, is clearly as amenable to as broad a range of political symbolic meanings as any other style of architecture. As the architectural writer Colin Rowe put it, 'Disraeli "caught the Whigs bathing and stole their clothes"; and something of the same kind has happened in the recent history of architecture, with the result that the symbolic trophies of an epoch of reform are now paraded by all parties alike.'[60]

[57] *People and Cities*, p. 98.

[58] *People and Cities*, p. 105. Another vivid insight into property developers of the period can be found in John Gale, 'Jack Cotton Explains', *Twentieth Century*, Summer 1962, pp. 77–82.

[59] *People and Cities*, p. 245.

[60] Colin Rowe, 'The Blenheim of the Welfare State' (originally published 1959),in *As I Was Saying: Texas, Pre-Texas, Cambridge* (Boston, 1996), p. 144. Disraeli's original quotation has a different import.

THE LABOUR PARTY AND CENTRAL-AREA REDEVELOPMENT

The Labour Party was divided between modernizing and traditionalist impulses in the 1950s, although, as in the Conservative Party, reforming and modernizing ideas were gaining ground after the 1959 election.[61] Amongst Labour Party politicians the results of the relative return to free-market development unleashed by the Conservatives in the 1950s, most visibly in the office-building boom in the City of London, was widely contrasted with what was seen as the much more successful development by the more powerful and architecturally radical local authorities, especially Sheffield, Coventry, and London. For example, Labour MP Roy Jenkins wrote in *The Labour Case*: 'There have been very few buildings of architectural distinction erected in Britain since the war, but those that exist are mostly in the public sector . . . Compare the L.C.C. housing project at Roehampton, which is a positive addition to the skyline of London, with any private residential scheme, for houses or flats, which has been envisaged.'[62] Similarly, Anthony Crosland complained about a return under Conservative policy to private development:

> Greedy men, abetted by a complacent Government, are prowling over Britain and devastating it. . . . Excited by speculative gain, the property developers furiously rebuild the urban centres with unplanned and aesthetically tawdry office blocks; so our cities become the just objects of world-wide ridicule for their architectural mediocrity, commercial vulgarity, and lack of civic pride. Encouraged by Tory policy, the private builder neglects working-class housing and builds for the middle classes; so millions still live in oppressive and overcrowded conditions, while green-tiled Tudor bungalows spread further into the countryside. The Conservatives have condoned the re-creation of all of the worst speculative horrors of the inter-war years, which in the glow of post-war optimism we thought were never going to be repeated.[63]

He saw the more radical architectural work of the 1950s as giving the blueprint for 'a programme for reform in the 1960s':

> Under the lead of the LCC, Sheffield, and Coventry, there is now perhaps a slight improvement in municipal architecture and town planning . . . The

[61] Lawrence Black, *The Political Culture of the Left in Affluent Britain* (London, 2003).
[62] Roy Jenkins, *The Labour Case* (London, 1959), p. 145.
[63] Anthony Crosland, *The Conservative Enemy, A Programme of Radical Reform for the 1960s* (London, 1962), p. 183. Whether such a suburban pastiche as a 'green-tiled Tudor bungalow' had been built in the interwar period, let alone since the Second World War, is surely a moot point.

> New Barbican will be the most ambitious and distinguished piece of comprehensive redevelopment since Nash. The universities and the War Office, Liverpool and the City of London, are all recent converts to mid-twentieth-century ideas.[64]

Crosland advocated large-scale comprehensive redevelopment to achieve cities ready for the motor car:

> Piecemeal redevelopment, block by block, may allow minor road-widening and some increase in off-street parking. But it freezes the existing road pattern, which in Britain is usually quite unsuited to the needs of the motor age. A comprehensive redevelopment would always include a major change in the road pattern and a complete separation of pedestrians and motor traffic in selected areas.[65]

He was passionately anti-suburban, lamenting, in language appropriated from Ian Nairn's articles in *The Architectural Review*, 'the relentless invasion of the countryside by "Subtopia" and the gradual obliteration of the distinction between town and country.'[66] He advised building high to counter this: 'Personally I should be prepared . . . to pay any subsidy to encourage more high buildings in cities in the interests of preserving the countryside—whatever the *Sunday Express* said about government waste, or the *Economist* about the "distortion" of resources.'[67] He criticized the fact that vast super-high-density, high-rise schemes such as the Barbican and High Paddington had not been built.[68]

The Labour Party policy statement *Leisure for Living* had similarly argued that 'Public indifference, private avarice, and, in some places, municipal ignorance are largely responsible for the growth of what has been nicknamed "Subtopia".'[69] The pamphlet is remarkable for the level of its approval of modernist architecture, even praising 'Anti-Ugly Action', a group of students from the Royal College of Art who demonstrated in front of new traditionalist buildings.[70] Also held up were the 'courageous and forward-looking' buildings by local authorities, such as the LCC's Lansbury and Roehampton estates, Harlow, Peterlee, and Stevenage New

[64] Crosland, *The Conservative Enemy*, p. 195.

[65] Crosland, *The Conservative Enemy*, p. 191.

[66] Anthony Crosland, *The Future of Socialism* (London, 1956), p. 526; Ian Nairn, *Outrage* (London, 1956).

[67] Crosland, *The Future of Socialism*, p. 526.

[68] Crosland, *The Future of Socialism*, p. 526. Chamberlin, Powell, and Bon's Barbican would, of course, be built; construction started in 1965. Kadleigh's scheme for 8,000 people housed in towers rising out of a podium spanning Paddington goods yard remained on the drawing board. See Sergei Kadleigh, *High Paddington, a town for 8000 people* (London, 1952).

[69] Labour Party, *Leisure for Living* (London, 1959), p. 16.

[70] Gavin Stamp, 'Anti-Ugly Action', *AA Files* 70 (2015), pp. 76–88.

Towns, Churchill College, Cambridge ('a satisfactorily contemporary building'), Basil Spence's Coventry Cathedral, and the schools built by 'progressive local education authorities'.[71] Also cited was TUC headquarters, Congress House, which was, it boasted, 'uncompromisingly of the present age'.[72]

Referencing the American economist John Galbraith's *The Affluent Society,* Labour Party leader Hugh Gaitskell argued in 1962 that 'a country gets the architecture it deserves', and the last decade had been one characterized by 'private wealth and public squalor'.[73] Rebuilding in the City of London had been 'a national monument to mediocrity, the tomb of good taste, the greatest missed opportunity of the century.' He warned that 'subtopia swallows more and more of the countryside', and suburbia involved 'the squandering of social life, a rubble of people and talent and leisure'. Exceptions included the 'really fine examples of good development such as Coventry' and the 'imaginative, exciting comprehensive plans of Birmingham and Newcastle'. He promised comprehensive 'positive planning, in which decisions are taken by those responsible about the shape that the whole life of a town should take'. He advocated a policy of 'building high' as well as further New Towns to counter 'the red brick rash and the suburban sprawl with all the congestion that follows'. Preservation was also important, to achieve for future generations 'fine buildings, both ancient and modern, and green fields'. This would be expensive, but the community must be prepared 'to pay for a civilised way of life'.

The 1964 Labour manifesto famously promised 'A New Britain—mobilising the resources of technology under a national plan; harnessing our national wealth in brains, our genius for scientific invention and medical discovery; reversing the decline of the thirteen wasted years'.[74] Recreating cities for the motor age in line with the Buchanan Report would be a central part of this:

> Nowhere is planning more urgently needed than in our transport system. The tragedy of lives lost and maimed; growing discomfort and delays in the journey to work... the chaos and loss of amenity in our towns and cities—these are only some of the unsolved problems of the new motor age... Urgent attention will be given to the proposals in the Buchanan Report and to the development of new roads capable of diverting through traffic from town centres.[75]

[71] *Leisure for Living,* pp. 16–18. [72] *Leisure for Living,* p. 19.

[73] Hugh Gaitskell, 'Paying for the Future', *Twentieth Century: Up! Rebuilding Britain,* summer 1962, pp. 33–8.

[74] *'A New Britain' Labour Party Manifesto 1964.*

[75] *'A New Britain'.* See also Peter Jenkins, 'Mr Wilson's Points for a New Britain', *The Guardian,* 10 February 1964.

Following the unpopularity of the first Beeching Report, which closed down many rural railway lines in favour of an expanded motorway system, there was some attempt by the Labour Party to present themselves as the party of public transport.[76] Nevertheless, universal car ownership was regularly presented as an egalitarian and democratic aim: 'Higher living standards almost automatically have a socially equalizing effect. There is far less keenly felt difference between a rich man in a Cadillac and an ordinary man in a Chevrolet than between a rich man in any sort of a car and a poor man whom he sweeps into the ditch as he drives along the dirt roads of a subsistence level country.'[77] For MP Tony Benn, 'When we talk about the scientific revolution at political meetings, the vision conjured up in the minds of most of those who come to listen is of a car, or a new car, or a faster car, of their very own.'[78] Furthermore, restricting car usage or ownership was politically difficult in the early 1960s due to the risk of losing the votes of the 750,000 people working in the car industry.[79]

The Labour Party produced two pamphlets on the subject of urban renewal in 1961.[80] *Signposts for the Sixties* argued that rebuilding 'our cities so that they will be a source of pride' could only be achieved through planning which was 'bold, comprehensive and co-ordinated at the centre'.[81] The Fabian Society also produced a number of policy documents throughout the period dealing with questions of town planning.[82] Also worthy of note was Socialist Commentary's *The Face of Britain*, written by the sociologist Peter Willmott, the geographer Peter Hall, then engaged in writing a book imagining a fully motorized London, and Malcolm MacEwan (the formerly communist editor of the *Architects' Journal* and *RIBA Journal*).[83]

During the period 1959–64 both political parties appropriated a cluster of ideas from radical planners. A style of modernizing rhetoric was rife, practically unquestioned, and repetitively stated ad nauseam. In this the period conforms to what Christopher Booker characterized as a pervasive culture of 'neophilia', and to what Raphael Samuel argues was a ruling

[76] *'A New Britain'.* [77] Jenkins, *The Labour Case*, p. 55.

[78] Anthony Wedgwood Benn, 'The Motor God' (originally published in *The Guardian*, 15 May 1964), *The Regeneration of Britain* (London, 1965), p. 133.

[79] Loft, *Government, the Railways and the Modernization of Britain*, p. 58.

[80] *Signposts for the Sixties: Towns for our Times: A Labour Party looking ahead Pamphlet, 4* (London, 1961).

[81] Ibid., p. 20.

[82] J. B. Cullingworth, *Restraining Urban Growth: the Problem of Overspill* (London, 1960); John Greve, *The Housing Problem* (London, 1961); J. B. Cullingworth, *New Towns for Old: the Problem of Urban Renewal* (London, 1962); Harry Brack, *Building for a New Society* (London, 1964).

[83] Hall, MacEwan, and Willmott, *The Face of Britain*.

ideology that was 'forward-looking and progressive'.[84] On the surface, regardless of who won the 1964 election, the outcome would be Butskellite city centres, remoulded in the aspect of something like Coventry—a nation of shopping precincts. Consensus only went so far as these ideas were used to clothe different political agendas. The main difference in rhetoric was in how these transformations were going to be financed. The Conservatives promised a new prosperity through large-scale infrastructural projects and planning that would help to unleash private development, while the Labour Party argued that the work of more interventionist public authorities provided a blueprint for the future development of cities.

THE JOINT URBAN PLANNING GROUP

It was not just in the realm of rhetoric that radical ideas were gaining ground, but, more seminally, in the machinery of central government itself. Although the Ministry of Housing and Local Government [MHLG] was only one of the departments to have a role in city-centre redevelopment, this section focuses on a single aspect of MHLG's advocacy of modernist planning through the Urban Planning Group. In 1961 MHLG had set this group up to 'guide and advise local authorities'.[85] An early report on the Group wrote that it was partly set up in response to the rapid increase of central-area redevelopment schemes in preparation, as well as to 'a spate of outside activity and publications on urban renewal', listing the Civic Trust conference, *Let Our Cities Live*, *Change and Challenge*, and the *Socialist Commentary* report.[86] The Group comprised four architect-planners (including the head of the Group, F. H. Littler), an engineer-planner, a highway engineer, a research officer, and a traffic planner. On the administration side were an Assistant Secretary and a Principal.[87] Unlike the Planning Advisory Group, another group set up by MHLG, the Urban Planning Group was not composed of well-known planners.[88] One of the Group's first actions had

[84] Christopher Booker, *The Neophiliacs: Revolution in English Life in the Fifties and Sixties* (London, 1969), esp. p. 149; Raphael Samuel, *Theatres of Memory* (London, 1994), p. 51.

[85] *The Times*, 28 November 1963, p. 12.

[86] 'The Urban Planning Group of the Ministry of Housing and Local Government', *Official Architecture and Planning*, June 1963, pp. 541–2.

[87] TNA, '"What is the Urban Planning Group?", 5 December 1962, Extension of Joint urban planning group and Inclusion of Ministry of Transport', HLG 136/167.

[88] See John Delafons, 'Reforming the British planning system 1964–5: the Planning Advisory Group and the genesis of the Planning act of 1967', *Planning Perspectives*, 13.4 (1998), pp. 373–87, and H. W. E. Davies, 'The planning system and the development plan', in *British Planning: 50 Years of Urban and Regional Policy*, ed. Barry Cullingworth (London, 1999), pp. 45–61.

been to send a letter to all the heads of local-authority planning branches, so as to accumulate 'information about town centre schemes in various stages of preparation up and down the country'.[89] They created an exhibition, which was not open to the public but was intended for 'the benefit of local authority members and officers visiting Whitehall'.[90]

One of the Group's roles was to provide 'specific advice on particular schemes'.[91] They were interested in 'schemes which tackle renewal in a progressive and unconventional manner'.[92] In meetings with planning departments, planners who were 'very conscious of the traffic problems in the centre' such as Norwich's H. C. Rowley, were asked by Littler to collaborate on the department's study of central-area redevelopment.[93] Others, such as Berkshire's county planning officer, were given the suggestion 'that it was undesirable to proceed... until soundly based replanning proposals were worked out over the central area at large'.[94] To guide Berkshire in the right direction, 'The Newcastle approach of Burns was mentioned', and they were sent off promising that they intended 'to do some more thinking about this important aspect of planning'.[95] Occasionally a planner would have to be reined back, such as happened with the 'starry-eyed approach' of Graeme Shankland (Liverpool's planning consultant, and the protagonist of Chapter 4), who advised an inner-city motorway for which the government would have to contribute a 75 per cent share of funding. There was a recognition that although they had advocated Liverpool's grand thinking, financial constraints would be necessary:

> We should maintain contact with Liverpool and not leave them too long to their own devices to produce a gold-plated scheme which might prove to be a considerable embarrassment to Departments. I can see that this might well happen since we have been constantly pressing on Liverpool the need to do something adequate and really saying that in the past they have not measured up to their opportunities. With a new and enthusiastic consultant... I think there is some possibility that if we do not keep track of the situation the Departments may find themselves presented with very expensive proposals.[96]

89 TNA, A. Sylvester-Evans, 4 April 1961, HLG 136/8.
90 'The Urban Planning Group of the MHLG', *Official Architecture and Planning*, June 1963, pp. 541–2. There is a picture of the exhibition on p. 541.
91 TNA, 'What is the Urban Planning Group?', HLG 136/167.
92 TNA, J Delafons, 11 December 1961, 'Central Area Redevelopment Schemes', HLG 136/9.
93 TNA, Minutes of Meeting, 27 November 1961. HLG 136/8.
94 TNA, Minutes of Meeting, 7 March 1962, Central Redevelopment Schemes, HLG 136/8.
95 TNA, Minutes of Meeting, 7 March 1962, Central Redevelopment Schemes, HLG 136/8.
96 TNA, Letter signed F. H. Littler, 21 March 1962, 'Inner Ring Road Redevelopment Proposals', HLG79/1288.

The Group's main function was authoring reports giving advice to local authorities on town-planning issues. They were to be 'the main medium for giving guidance to planning authorities on various urban planning matters'.[97] Their bulletins included *Town Centres: Approach to Renewal* (1962), *Residential Areas: Higher Densities* (1962), *Town Centres: Cost and Control of Redevelopment* (1963), *Town Centres: Current Practice* (1963), *Development Plan Maps* (1964), and *Parking in Town Centres* (1965). Cumulatively, these set out a number of objectives for the replanning of towns and cities, under the banner 'Urban Renewal'—'a new phrase for an age old process'—which propounded the recognizable set of ideas, whereby 'under the rapid social and technological changes more conscious action is needed to guide renewal processes'.[98] They were influenced by similar bulletins issued by the US federal government, and by the publications of the Ministry of Education's building branch.[99] The bulletins foreshadow the interests of the Buchanan Report, where the 'primary objective must be to sort out conflicting types of traffic and provide adequately for each—in particular to separate pedestrians and vehicles so that both can move freely and safely'.[100] They lamented that:

> Some town centres are in little better physical shape than the slums which surround them . . . Old shops become unsuitable for modern retailing methods or too small for the number of customers. Old office buildings cannot be adapted to modern business methods. Old town halls cannot hold the staff needed to deal with the wide range of local government services. The components of the old town centre become outgrown and out of date.[101]

Central to the vision was that private and public cooperation would be needed to achieve all this: 'Town centre redevelopment is essentially a matter for co-operation between local government and private enterprise, and the bulletin has advice on how to secure this.'[102]

A proposed notional exemplar of a 'town map' shows all of the familiar tropes of the period (Fig. 2.2). Slums, noxious industry, and unsightly buildings were to be swept away and, even in this imagined town, the town hall is deemed obsolete and inadequate for modern needs. Replacing

[97] TNA, 'Urban Planning Bulletins' (undated, but 1961), HLG 136/24.

[98] [Ministry of Housing and Local Government,] *Planning Bulletin no. 1, Town Centres: Approach to Renewal* (London, 1962), p. 2.

[99] TNA, N. Litchfield to A. Sylvester Evans, 20 March 1961, HLG 136/24; TNA, A. Sylvester Evans to Mr. Street, 17 March 1961, HLG 136/24.

[100] *Bulletin no. 1.*, p. 3.

[101] *Bulletin no. 1.*, p. 2.

[102] *Bulletin no. 1*, p. 1. See Stephen V. Ward 'Public–Private Partnerships', in *British Planning, 50 Years of Urban and Regional Policy*, pp. 237–8.

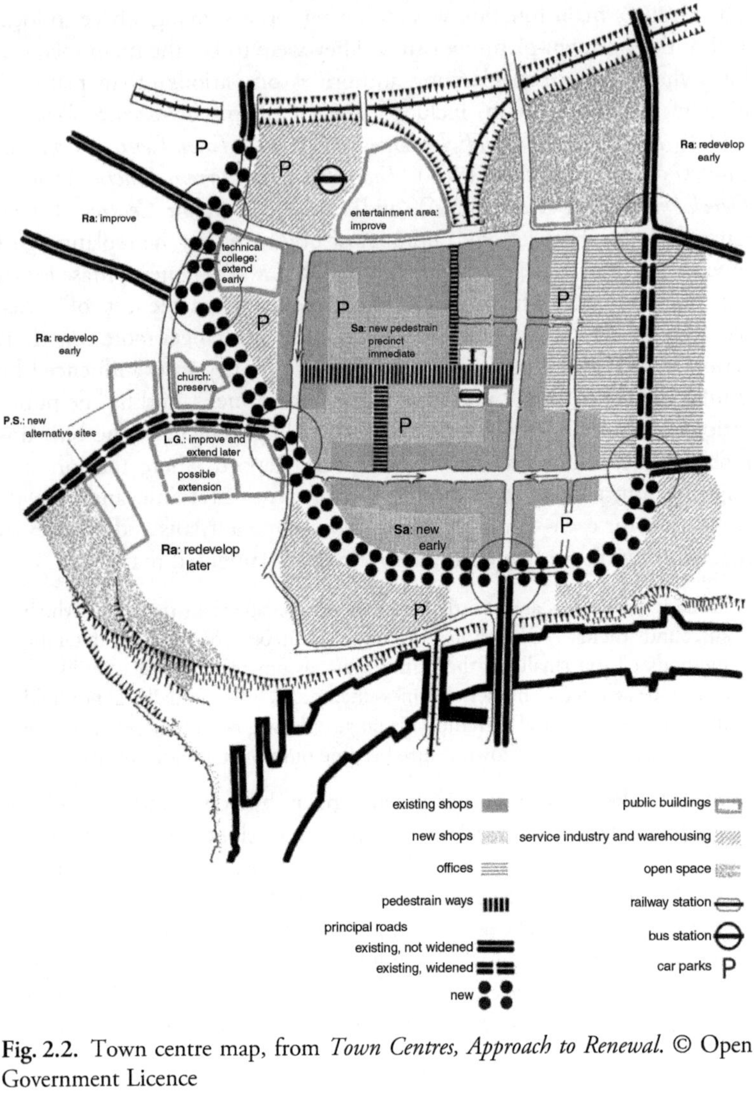

Fig. 2.2. Town centre map, from *Town Centres, Approach to Renewal.* © Open Government Licence

this generic Victorian city was to be an archetypal modern one, with its central pedestrian precinct and shopping area, encircled by a bus and service road. Adjoining this central core is a ring of development for parking, offices, high-density housing (at the anti-suburban density of 100 persons per acre), and civic and entertainment zones. Encircling the whole inner area is an urban motorway in a loop.[103] Here was a replicable vision for a Macmillanite urban utopia. In line with Conservative Party rhetoric at the time, the reports argued that renewal 'cannot be carried through without private enterprise'.[104] Local-authority involvement would be limited to unifying land ownership through the creation of comprehensive development areas, and to providing planning expertise that would 'open up new opportunities for profitable redevelopment'.[105]

The reports were anti-suburban, not just in their upholding of higher densities and the way they advertised such projects as Cumbernauld, the LCC Alton Estate, or Sheffield's Gleadless Valley, but also in the belief that 'Redevelopment gives an opportunity to attract people back into the centre to live, and there are signs that people would like to live there, given good conditions. This adds vitality to the centre.'[106] In Planning Bulletin no. 4, *Town Centres: Current Practice*, we find all the usual suspects of 1950s urbanism: Harlow, Stevenage, Sheffield, Cumbernauld, and Coventry town centres. Even the then unbuilt megastructural project St John's Precinct in Liverpool, is included and commended for showing the possibility of redevelopment 'planned as essentially one great building in which all the different uses are inter-related and form part of the same architectural concept'.[107] This was a project at the forefront of planning thought, and was praised in 1963 by Peter Hall as displaying a 'sophistication of the principle' of vertical segregation.[108] It was also, perhaps better explaining its inclusion, the result of a public–private partnership between Liverpool's Conservative-controlled city council and Ravenseft Properties Ltd.

The reports effectively gave the ministerial green light to such specialist, even avant-garde, town-planning concepts as comprehensive redevelopment, urban renewal, higher densities, and pedestrian segregation. They sent a clear message to local authorities that this kind of language, both visual and conceptual, was the key to ministerial approval—which might help to explain the homogeneity in the plans of the following period. The bulletins are visually presented in the style commonly used for modernist plans of the 1960s, using bold colours, modern typography, and illustrations in the style of the influential architectural illustrator Gordon Cullen. They are written with a succinct clarity, so that the effect must have been, as *The Spectator* put it, such that even 'the dimmest town councillors must feel, as they read the Ministries' illustrated bulletin, that they ought to

[103] *Bulletin no. 1.*, map. [104] *Bulletin no. 1.*, p. 6. [105] *Bulletin no. 1.*, p. 6.

[106] [Ministry of Housing and Local Government, and Ministry of Transport,] *Planning Bulletin no.4, Town Centres: Current Practices* (London, 1963).

[107] *Planning Bulletin no.4.* [108] Peter Hall, *London 2000* (London, 1963), p. 167.

have thought of this before'.[109] T. H. Carline's plan for the town centre of Folkestone directly proclaims the influence: 'We were at one with the recommendations which the Ministry of Housing and Local Government were making to local authorities. We therefore tried to follow the general pattern which was being suggested in those Planning Bulletins which had been published at that time.'[110] Liverpool's city-centre plan was also able to 'embody much of the most recent professional and administrative thought' as outlined in the bulletins.[111]

In 1963, to deal with the Buchanan Report, the group was expanded to become the Joint Urban Planning Group [JUPG], now serving both MHLG and the Ministry of Transport, as well as the Scottish Development Department.[112] It had been agreed at 'our first talk about the Buchanan Report . . . that our two Departments would need to set up a joint unit to grapple with the impact of the report on the problems of urban planning'.[113] The Group was to be 'responsible for developing the techniques required for implementing the concepts embodied in the Buchanan Report and for other aspects of urban planning'.[114] However, the JUPG would become increasingly involved in putting a brake on radical planning rather than stimulating it. This was certainly how the MHLG Permanent Secretary Evelyn Sharp advocated they should proceed with reference to Buchanan: 'I got the impression from Mr Buchanan that he thinks that so long as he and his group continue with the sort of study he has been making it doesn't much matter what we do. His notion seemed to be that L.as. [local authorities] could take his report(s) and carry on from there. I would have thought he could not be more mistaken: that on the question: So, what do we do? The two Departments have got to bring the report(s) down to earth, to cost, practicability, priorities; and that on this there is all the way to go.'[115] As will be seen, this would be the focus of the JUPG's activities in the coming years.

109 Kenneth J. Robinson, 'Sick Transit . . . ', *The Spectator*, 10 Aug. 1962, p. 12.

110 T. H. Carline, 'Folkestone: Planning Proposals for the Town Centre of a Seaside Resort', *Town Planning Review* (1966), p. 259.

111 Francis J. C. Amos, 'Liverpool' in John Holliday, ed., *City Centre Redevelopment* (London, 1973), p. 203. See also John Poulson, *Southport, Town Centre Map* (1964).

112 Confusingly, this cooperation was welcomed prematurely in 'Editorial Notes' in *The Town Planning Review*, October 1962, p. 165, and 'Save Town Centres: Adapting to the Car Age' in *The Guardian*, 25 July 1962, p. 4. The first Bulletin did have a foreword by Hill and Marples, but was the work of MHLG alone. The cooperation prefigures the merging of the two departments as the Department for the Environment, and reflects current thinking on the need for integrating land use and traffic planning.

113 TNA, Dame Evelyn Sharp to Sir Thomas Padmore, 26 July 1963, MT45/655.

114 TNA, Evelyn Sharp and Thomas Padmore, circular no. 1/64, MHLG and MOT, 17 January 1964, HLG 136/99.

115 TNA, Evelyn Sharp to Mr James, 20 May 1963, HLG 136/167.

The JUPG was only one of the elements impacting the way that city-centre areas were redeveloped, and the group's advice was enacted in various ways in local contexts, under the pressures of different local authorities, planners, and financial considerations. British cities approached the redevelopment of their central areas with a multitude of locally orientated ambitions—as Chapter 3 will demonstrate. Other departments such as the Ministry of Transport and the Board of Trade, as well as non-governmental agencies such as the road lobby, also exerted influence on development. The forcefulness with which a radical modernist agenda was pressed by MHLG in the early 1960s is nonetheless striking. Looking at the advice given by the Joint Urban Planning Group can help to give a context for the homogeneity in the presentation of local-authority plans in the early 1960s. The JUPG was not particularly innovative in the planning ideas it propounded. Their 'town map' was nonetheless used as a blueprint, and tropes such as the pedestrian precinct and the motorway ring road would often be recycled as clichés in the plans written over the decade. As Alan Bennett parodied it in 1967,

> How many times in the last ten years has one seen the same drawing: that spacious sun-baked piazza, the motor-cars tucked vaguely away somewhere, those fine flourishing trees, those outdoor restaurants, the whole thronged with Precinct People, a race of tall, long-headed men. Municipal Masai, who lounge about every architect's drawing in a languor presumably induced by the commodiousness of their surroundings. I wonder how many local councils have been gulled into demolishing their town centres by such drawing-board dreams.[116]

AFTER THE 1964 ELECTION

When Richard Crossman, Member of Parliament for Coventry East, succeeded Keith Joseph as Minister of Housing and Local Government, his first policy statement argued that 'I want to emphasise that the rebuilding of old towns will become an increasingly important preoccupation of this Ministry.'[117] He was greeted by the planning profession enthusiastically; as Percy Johnson Marshall put it after hearing Crossman's inaugural lecture to the Town Planning Institute, 'At last, it seemed to me, we had a politician in Parliament who understood our problems; and this made me feel really extraordinarily exhilarated.'[118] The obvious difference

[116] Alan Bennett, 'Views', *The Listener*, 30 November 1967, p. 692.
[117] 'Mr. Crossman on his Housing Policy', *The Times*, 29 October 1964, p. 16.
[118] TNA, 'Planning Advisory Group, Papers Circulated', HLG136/142.

between the rhetoric of the two parties during the parliamentary term 1959–64 had been in how redevelopment would be financed, with the Conservatives unsurprisingly giving more focus to the role of private development. Despite this maintained contradistinction between the two parties, within nine days of being appointed Labour's Minister of Housing and Local Government, Richard Crossman, 'went to dinner... to meet [Harry] Hyams, the millionaire director of Wimpy and a property magnate who Arnold [Goodman] thought was a possible adviser on housing or director of the housing drive... It was clear after we had discussed things for a long time that he was prepared with his million pounds in the bank, his house full of Rembrandts and Picassos, to try Labour politics as an extra.'[119] The property developer, one of the millionaires who had become rich from the abolition of building licences in 1954, and who was behind the infamous development of the commercial architect Richard Seiffert's Centre Point office development, would become Crossman's advisor.[120] Crossman would come to feel that, at least in terms of preservation, 'local authorities are far worse than private developers. They will often destroy buildings and leave a huge open space for years afterwards because they have planned things so badly.'[121] The work of the JUPG was easily co-opted by Wilson's 'modernization' agenda. *Planning Bulletin no. 1* was republished verbatim in 1965, down to the Tory ministerial introductions and advice on securing private enterprise, suggesting the continuity of approach between the two administrations.[122]

One important link between the two parties in the period 1959–64 had been the foundational ideological belief behind the planning philosophy of the period that continuous economic growth would provide the basis for uninterrupted social progress. As the decade progressed, such confidence began to appear increasingly naive, with Crossman distancing himself from the more radical proposals of the Buchanan Report: 'We have to find ways and means of making life in towns tolerable in traffic terms. I venture to say—speaking as a practical politician—that brilliant as the Buchanan Report was, it was a demonstration that the wholly desirable

[119] Richard Crossman, *The Diaries of a Cabinet Minister: Volume 1 Minister of Housing 1964–66* (London, 1974), p. 30.

[120] David Cadman, 'Property Finance in the UK in the Post-War Period', *Land Development Studies,* 1.2 (1984), pp. 68–9.

[121] Crossman, *Diaries of a Cabinet Minister,* p. 177.

[122] As John Delafons, a principal civil servant at the time, argues in a discussion of the changeover from Joseph to Crossman, 'It is a feature of the British political process that a new administration does not automatically jettison all its predecessor's policies and initiatives.' Delafons, 'Reforming the British planning system 1964–5', p. 379.

is financially impossible. Any politician who studies its implications has to face the fact that if this is the minimum we are not going to get it.'[123] Buchanan would use his plan for Cardiff to warn of the 'great difficulties' that would result from the government's pronouncements, such as the *National Plan* and Ministry of Transport circular 8/65.[124] These did not present 'a very optimistic outlook', warning as they did of the government's reluctance to provide significant investment for redevelopment.[125] When Minister of Transport Barbara Castle met Colin Buchanan ('a dedicated, rather shy person', as she described him) for lunch in 1966, she found that he couldn't grasp the blunt fact that 'one just can't find the money for his schemes'.[126] With government also financing a massive increase in the building of council houses, as well as a new round of New Towns, public money for city-centre redevelopment was in short supply.

Given this context, it is unsurprising that MHLG's focus on town planning became less likely to deal with sweeping changes, and more likely to look towards conservation or rehabilitation. Even before the election there was a realization within the JUPG that 'it was unlikely that any major Buchanan-type road programmes could be put into effect [in the next 10–15 years] and yet the Government had to show that the problems involved are being tackled urgently'.[127] Two JUPG studies, both of which were initiated before the election, are determinedly unvisionary. A study of Deeplish, an area of Rochdale, suggested rehabilitation rather than renewal, with 'a modest level of investment' at least in the intervening period before renewal could be enacted.[128] This was despite what Crossman described as the 'primitive, dismal life in Deeplish'.[129] The Denington Committee Report would go further, and was 'a major reverse for the favoured approach to renewal in the early 1960s'.[130] The Reading traffic study, which started out with the objective of developing 'the application of Buchanan concepts of primary road networks and environmental areas to towns as a whole', ended up, through the financial 'need to avoid major

123 TNA, Crossman speech to Town Planning Institute, HLG136/142.

124 *The National Plan* (London, 1965); TNA, 'Circular 8/65', MT 47/553.

125 Colin Buchanan and Partners, *Cardiff Development and Transportation Study: Probe Study Report* (April 1966).

126 Barbara Castle, *Diaries, 1964–70* (London, 1990), p. 108.

127 TNA, Sixth meeting, JUPG Environment Study Group, 28 September 1964, HLG 136/168.

128 MHLG, *The Deeplish Study: Improvement Possibilities in a District of Rochdale* (London, 1966).

129 Crossman, *Diaries of a Cabinet Minister*, p. 340.

130 Central Housing Advisory Committee, *Our Older Homes: a Call for Action* (London, 1966); Jim Yelling, 'The Development of Residential Urban Renewal Policies in England' Planning for Modernization in the 1960s', *Planning Perspectives,* 14 (1999), p. 9.

Fig. 2.3. Transport interchange from *Leicester Traffic Plan* (1964), p. 70. © Leicester County Council

works', suggesting little more visionary than a one-way system and a number of traffic-light interchanges.[131]

The first plan to be released which included an integrated land use and traffic plan was for the city of Leicester (Fig. 2.3).[132] Headed by Konrad Smigielski, the plan was an overblown version of the kind of tropes found in the *Planning Bulletin no. 1* map: it suggested pedestrianizing the entire centre, apart from electric rickshaw taxis, and encircling it with an inner city motorway with several 'traffic architecture'-style transport interchanges, composed of underground train line, a monorail, eight floors of car parking, and a helipad on top. The JUPG, which made a report on the plan, was sceptical: 'It is extremely doubtful if the concept as propounded is tenable, particularly as regards the interchange car parks.'[133] The Group saw it as having been 'prepared more for publicity purposes than as a technical document', and was especially damning about its financial viability: 'In the present financial climate it seems hardly realistic to plan for an expenditure of

131 TNA, 'Outline Programme July–October 1964', HLG 136/211; TNA, HLG 136/210. See also Joe Moran 'Crossing the road in Britain, 1931–1976', *Historical Journal*, 49.02 (2006), pp. 477–96, for the history of the less radical approaches to traffic management post-Buchanan.

132 Konrad Smigielski, *Leicester Traffic Plan* (Leicester, 1964).

133 TNA, 'Leicester Traffic Survey', HLG 136/200.

£3.2 million per annum over the next ten years in a town with a population of 273,000; the present rateable income of Leicester is £5.7 million.'[134]

A benefit of the Leicester plan was to make the JUPG think more seriously about public transport: 'The Leicester planners let their fancy roam and suggested a monorail, different types of taxi and a re-arranged bus service. But the essential point is that even on this plan—which must be regarded as grossly over-estimating the amount of capital Leicester can expect over the foreseeable future—public transport was still needed on a substantial scale.'[135] For Leicester, the JUPG advocated a public transport solution, and a type of rhetoric that had been largely absent from discussions about traffic in the early 1960s finally reached the agenda: 'A public transport solution would, incidentally, give a better service to the young, the old and many of the disabled. It must seriously be doubted whether a town which provides badly for these substantial groups can be called really civilised.'[136]

Leicester may be an extreme case, but the experience of having to rein back the more radical aspects of plans, due to government inability to finance schemes, was typical. Take, for example, Haringey's three-dimensional scheme for Wood Green, presented to the MHLG in 1966. It received short shrift:

> Because of the present economic situation the Government is restricting capital expenditure on central area redevelopment schemes of this kind. The Ministry officers have criticised the scheme as being too 'elaborate' and are not prepared at this stage to indicate that a pedestrian deck system would be approved. They have pointed out there may be difficulties in financing the deck structure where government grants are concerned.[137]

With central government backing out, it was left to local authorities to find the money through the kind of public–private partnership that had been advocated by the Conservative government before the election, as indeed Haringey did, carrying out the scheme in partnership with Electricity Supply Nominees from 1969.[138]

The kind of language used from 1959 to 1964 advocating the radical renewal of cities did not totally disappear from political discourse as the decade progressed, but what did evaporate was the confidence about what could be achieved. A striking example of the loss of confidence can be

[134] Ibid.

[135] TNA, 'Land Use and Transportation Planning, The Role of Public Transport, The Case for an Examination.', HLG 136/200.

[136] Ibid.

[137] D. W. Frith, *Wood Green Central Area* (April 1967), p. 3.

[138] 'History of the Scheme', *Haringey Central Area* (London, 1979). See also Robert K. Home, *Wood Green Shopping City* (London, 1984).

found in the 1966 Labour Party manifesto, in which Harold Wilson continued the themes of 1964:

> The Britain we want has yet to be built. Many of our cities and towns are bursting at the seams with growing populations. Those spawned by the industrial revolution grew without vision or plan. They are utterly inadequate to the needs of today. But whether planned or unplanned, all our towns are choked with traffic, and their population overspill threatens the unspoiled countryside around.[139]

However, there was less economic confidence that this could be achieved, and the spirit of 1959–64 was beginning to appear wildly over-optimistic:

> In their pre-election boom the Conservatives gave the impression that money, resources and skilled labour were available to meet any and all of these demands simultaneously. It is now plain that the grandiose plans they announced were uncosted and mutually inconsistent. The industries concerned – building and civil engineering – cannot expand without limit when other demands of the economy are taken into account. Although their efficiency is being improved and their output increased, demands will outstrip resources for years ahead and there will be a constant shortage of skilled labour. Moreover, the resources available are strictly limited. That is why, in this crucial field of physical reconstruction, priorities must be clearly defined and strongly enforced.[140]

The high-water mark of confidence in a modernized environment had already been passed by the mid-1960s, and a more pragmatic and conservationist ethic was beginning to find favour. From the perspective of central government, this switch was initially the result of the need for financial stringency rather than because of a significant ideological turn against the radical tenets that had been propounded only a few years before. The Labour Party was forced to back-pedal from the ambitions of the early 1960s, and, ironically considering their rhetoric in the early 1960s, presided over many city-centre schemes completed by the kind of public–private partnerships that had been advocated and developed under the Conservative Party. Looking at the period through the lens of central government, the loss of confidence in large-scale renewal and a movement towards a more conservationist ethic were already under way by the mid-1960s. This was not initially due to a reaction against modernist principles—although, as will be seen, it would develop in tandem with such a reaction—but came about in large part because of a realization that government could not afford to provide funds for such projects in the darkening economic climate.

[139] 'Time for Decision', 1966 Labour Party Manifesto. [140] Ibid.

The way that central government approached town-centre redevelopment in the early 1960s displays the political culture in microcosm, with visions of large-scale modernization based on an ill-founded economic optimism. In this the rebuilding of British inner cities ought to be seen not just as something that played out in isolated local contexts, or as the result of a purely architectural discourse, but also as part of a larger history. The physical planning of British cities shares much with the 1960s planning moment generally, relying as it did on the presumed continuation of an economic golden age which in the end was unsustainable.[141]

Chapter 3 will show how ideas being pushed by central government related to local concerns and ambitions in Blackburn, an early and very ambitious exemplar of city-centre redevelopment. Blackburn is typical of a story that was played out in cities across the country, but the chapter will also explore its unique local circumstances.

[141] See Glen O'Hara, *From Dreams to Disillusionment: Economic and Social Planning in 1960s Britain* (Basingstoke, 2006), pp. 206–8.

3

Blackburn Goes Pop

City-Centre Redevelopment in a Provincial City

PLANS AND MODERNISM

In 1960 Blackburn was a city with a declining population of around 106,000, and, as was frequently pointed out, was 'a fairly typical example of the Lancashire towns which had their beginnings at the time of the Industrial Revolution.'[1] It was described with a certain topographical lyricism in 1955:

> Blackburn is said to be the greatest cotton-weaving centre in the world. Its great mills and many chimneys fill the Blakewater valley, while on either side, rows of small streets clamber up the curved hill-side in steep 'ridge and furrow', in sharp contrast with the beautiful open country that lies immediately to the north and east.[2]

The city was yet to experience the Asian immigration that would change the demographic of the city, meaning that today the 'eye is drawn mainly to the gold and green domes and minarets', rather than to the mill chimneys.[3]

Over the course of the 1960s this essentially Victorian scene was largely to be swept away, replaced by a megastructural melange, a consumerist paradise, a beacon for an affluent and modern age. Blackburn Shopping Centre was built by the Blackburn Corporation in partnership with the Laing Development Company, and was planned and designed by the Preston-based architectural firm Building Design Partnership (BDP).[4] Within a faience-tiled structure, with white tiles picking out the non-structural

[1] TNA, J. L. M. Metcalf, 'County Borough of Blackburn, Report of Public Inquiry into Objections to 1. Proposals for alterations and additions to the Development Plan for the County Borough of Blackburn. Market Place; Comprehensive Development Area.' HLG 144/72.

[2] Peter Fleetwood-Hesketh, *Murray's Lancashire Architectural Guide* (London, 1955), p. 132.

[3] Derek Beattie, *A History of Blackburn* (Lancaster, 2007), p. 326; Clare Hartwell and Nikolaus Pevsner, *Lancashire: North* (London and New Haven, 2009), p. 110.

[4] See the firm's official history, Hugh Pearman, *61/11, BDP Continuous Collective* (2011).

Fig. 3.1. Blackburn Shopping Centre: 'EXISTING'; *Blackburn Central Development* (1961). © Building Design Partnership

elements and bronze cladding for the structural,[5] the shopping centre was to contain 138 small shops, 4 larger stores, and 4 supermarkets, as well as hotels, restaurants, a cinema, a clock tower, and a 15-storey office tower block. It was a town centre built for the new automotive age, using its sloping site to achieve total segregation of pedestrians and traffic. With service vehicles demoted to basement level, a pedestrian deck stretched back across the site from Lord Square at ground level. The roofscape was to be devoted to parking space for 1,517 cars (Figs 3.1 and 3.2).[6] As Blackburn Labour councillor George Eddie boasted in a 1961 brochure:

> It is a plan that has vision and courage. This is not a case of knocking down a street and rebuilding. Blackburn is going to have the sense and courage to knock down its whole town centre, replan it, and build in accordance with modern needs and ideas. We propose to do that with 150 acres of our town centre.[7]

[5] Maurice Bowra complained that modern buildings were made 'entirely of some ghastly stuff called cladding'. Plausibly the tiles were chosen because they would be easily cleaned in an industrial atmosphere.

[6] *Blackburn Central Area Redevelopment: Phase 1* (n.d., 1970?), RIBA Library 711.523–163 (42.72B)//BLA.

[7] Laing Development Company Ltd, *Blackburn Central Development* (1961). A copy, the only I have been able to locate, was consulted in the Frances Loeb Library, Harvard

Fig. 3.2. Blackburn Shopping Centre: 'PROPOSED'; *Blackburn Central Development* (1961). © Building Design Partnership

The Laing scheme was submitted to Blackburn's Civic Development Committee on 2 May 1961, and was considered 'so comprehensive in nature, so attractive from a planning point of view and had so many advantages that on the 4th of May 1961 the Corporation approved it'.[8] The Corporation were to remain the ground landlords, but granted Laing a 99-year lease.

BDP's George Grenfell Baines was the consultant architect for the planning phase, and Keith Scott took over for the detailed scheme. An exhibition was held in the city's library for five weeks from 4 May, showing the plans and model.[9] It was arranged that 'members of the Corporation's technical staff were constantly available to explain the scheme to any enquirer'. A total of 20,927 people visited the exhibition.[10]

University. It is a beautifully produced document, neatly fitting into what Shapely sees as the model of plans produced for 'civic boosterism'.

[8] TNA, 'The Main Proposals', HLG 144/72.

[9] Ironically, the original plan included the demolition of this Victorian library of 1872–4 by Woodgate and Collcutt, described by Pevsner as 'Gothic with touches in the direction of Arts and Crafts. Sculptural panels by Seale.' Thankfully, it survives and now houses Blackburn Museum.

[10] TNA, 'The Main Proposals', HLG 144/72.

Despite such publicity, the shopping centre was presented as a fait accompli, leading to the feeling amongst many that, 'The Plan has been "bulldozed" through without any general consultation with members of the public.'[11]

The shopping centre was to be on a 15-acre (6-hectare) site, while other plans were also being formulated for the rest of the 146 acres (59 hectares) of the centre, with only a small area around the cathedral where the 'special character will be preserved'.[12] An inner-city ring road was another priority, and it was argued that the 'traffic problem is so urgent that the main road framework will have to be carried out in the very early stages and quite independent of any other redevelopment proposals', as 'the Town Centre roads were designed principally for use by horse-drawn traffic'.[13] Roads were another area where much of the cost of development would not fall entirely on the rates, as, if approved, the Ministry of Transport would fund a significant percentage of the construction costs. Vehicle registration in Blackburn was below the national average, but had risen from 75 to 149 per 1,000 population between 1950 and 1961. High-density residential redevelopment in tower blocks grouped around green areas was also proposed, and it was hoped they would 'feed the centre'.

The shopping centres of the 1960s are part of a banal, everyday modernism that is invisible and unloved. Whether through snobbery or puritanism, architectural historians have tended to ignore shopping centres. They don't fit into the narrative in which British modernism is seen as allied to the progressive and reforming social programmes of the welfare state, such as housing and schools, that architectural historians have focused on.[14] Most shopping centres of the period follow Colin Buchanan's caustic judgement: 'I do not know one of these projects which is not a disappointment when visited, and which does not fill one with regrets at the lack of quality in design and finishes, at the brashness and the stickers, at the loss of the sense of intimacy and services which the older shops provided, and even at the goods that are sold.'[15] But BDP, as is evidenced by their two recently listed projects, Preston Bus Station and

[11] Ibid. [12] Ibid.

[13] F. V. Powell, *Development Plan Amendment no. 19 Comprehensive Development Area (Market Place)* ([Blackburn,] 1962). The ring road would be built, and was christened Barbara Castle Way, a dubious honour for Baroness Castle of Blackburn—the only Minister of Transport without a driving licence.

[14] Kathryn Morrison, *English Shops and Shopping: an Architectural History* (London and New Haven, 2004), is a notable exception. Other types of historian tend to see shopping centres as the invisible adjunct of larger processes such as mass consumerism, the growth of multiples, or Americanization. There is, however, a strong American literature on shopping centres, e.g. Richard Longstreth, *City Centre to Regional Mall, Architecture, the Automobile and Retailing in Los Angeles, 1920–1950* (Cambridge, MA, 1997).

[15] Colin Buchanan, *The State of Britain* (London, 1972), p. 54.

the Halifax Headquarters Building, was one of the few architectural practices of the period really able to exploit the aesthetic possibilities of a project of this scale. Although it is impossible to appreciate now, due to a 1990s recladding and substantial demolitions from 2007, Blackburn was a step above the American-style, inward-looking box mall. Behind the admittedly limited glamour of another Debenhams and another BHS, there was a considerable élan in both its conception and realization (Figs 3.3, 3.4, and 3.5).

The shopping centre had an almost constructivist, multidimensional quality, breaking up its massive scale with a picturesque massing. The detailing was tough and urbane, without resorting to the mannered and elephantine belligerence of Geoffrey Copcutt's Cumbernauld town centre or Owen Luder Partnership's Tricorn in Portsmouth. It is probably the first built English iteration of the avant-garde idea of a megastructure—the concept of building all the multiple functions of a city in a single building.

Blackburn Shopping Centre was a representative of new ideas about how to achieve the segregation of pedestrians and traffic. Had the centre been designed a few years earlier, it would almost certainly have been in the form of a pedestrian precinct. Blackburn combines elements of vertical and horizontal segregation of pedestrians and traffic, with a classic pedestrian precinct, down to the clock tower and fountain, at Lord Square (Fig. 3.6). From here there was an overall slope across the site, making up a cross fall of over 20 feet (6 metres), so that services could be introduced at grade at the lower end, whilst a deck stretched back across the site from the square.

Then as now, shopping centres received very little critical attention from the architectural press and establishment, but Blackburn was something of an exception. It was one of only five new town centres to have been awarded a Civic Trust Award, and one of only two town-centre schemes to have been covered by *The Architectural Review*.[16] Much of the collaged imagery for Hubert de Cronin Hasting's *Civilia: The End of Sub Urban Man* is taken from Blackburn (Fig. 3.7).[17] Ian Nairn praised the scheme in a 1972 BBC documentary as having 'a very great style, a canal style, an industrial north style'.[18]

[16] Keith Scott, *Shopping Centre Design*, (London, 1989) p. 12; 'Central area redevelopment, Blackburn, Lancashire', *The Architectural Review*, February 1970, pp. 119–24.

[17] Ivor de Wolfe, *Civilia: The End of Sub Urban Man, a Challenge to Semidetsia* (London, 1971).

[18] Ian Nairn, 'Nairn Across Britain, Trans-Pennine Canal' first broadcast in 1972, available at http://www.bbc.co.uk/programmes/p01rwfkm. Keith Scott had produced his MA thesis in 1952 on 'The Mills of Preston', a copy of which is held at the Harris Museum, Preston.

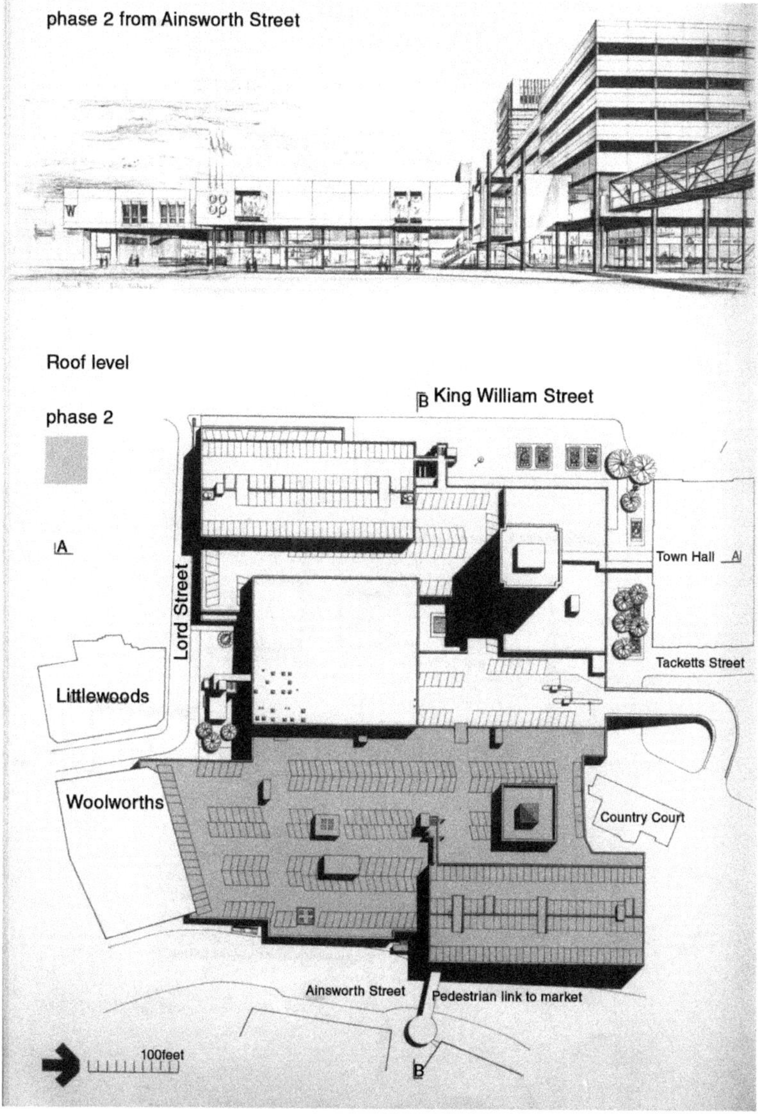

Fig. 3.3. Phase-2 perspective from Ainsworth Street and Roof Level Plan; *Blackburn Central Area Redevelopment* (no date). © Building Design Partnership

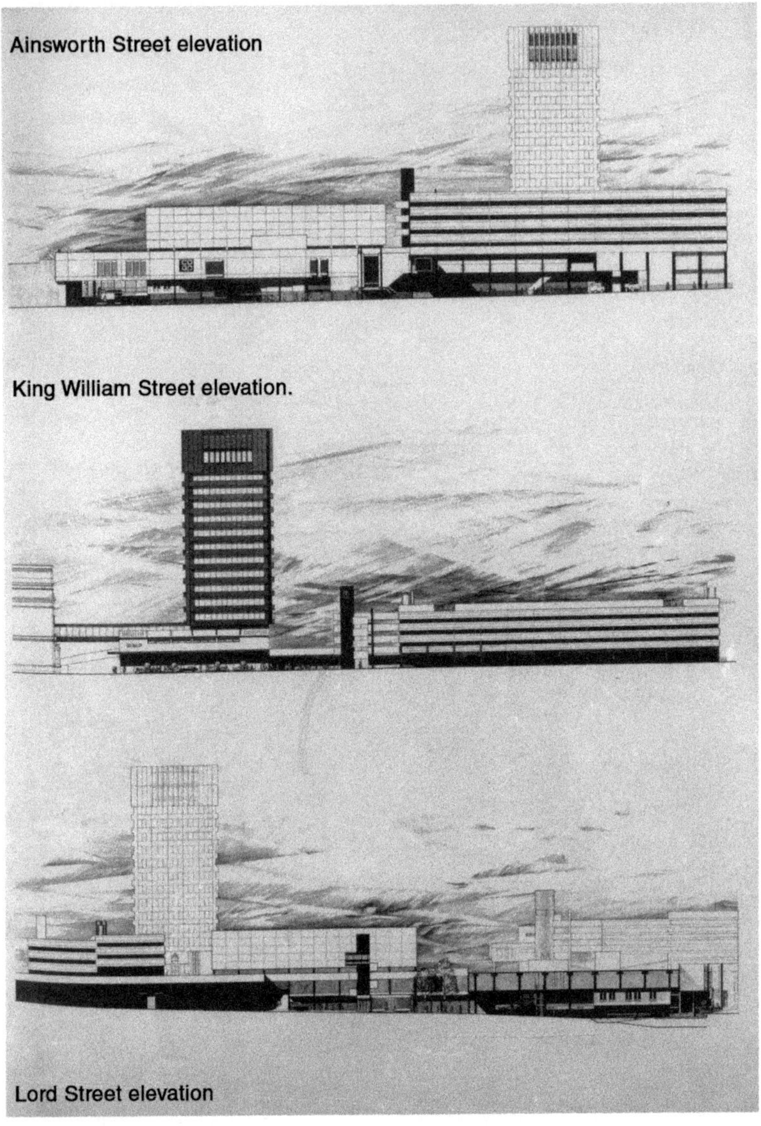

Fig. 3.4. Blackburn Shopping Centre elevations. © Building Design Partnership

It is worth stressing that Blackburn Shopping Centre is worthy of respect for its visual panache and the considerable care taken in its design. Judgement of the scheme should certainly go beyond the fact of it having a flat roof and lacking traditionalist trappings. BDP went on to produce

Fig. 3.5. The clock tower seen from the shopping precinct, 1969. © RIBApix

one of the first postmodern town centres at Ealing, in 'full blooded vernacular... reflecting the spirit of Edwardian Ealing', which in its way is rather splendid. Learning lessons from Robert Matthew Johnson Marshall and Partners' Hillingdon Civic Centre, Ealing mixes stripped-back features from local landmarks such as S. S. Teulon's St Mary's with a lot of

Fig. 3.6. Car park access stair tower on Lord Square, 1969. Photograph Peter Bairstow. © RIBApix

plate mirror glass, creating a style that might be described as suburban-disco-gothic.[19] Both shopping centres, whether of the 1960s or the 1980s, share the same evils, which have little to do with style and much to do with their gargantuan scale and the way they privatize a town centre.

Whatever the aesthetic nuances or otherwise of the scheme, by any measure knocking down the entire central area of a city and replacing it with a shopping centre and car park was a simply astonishing thing to do. Many cities in Britain were doing something similar at this period, with the cities of Lancashire at the forefront of the process. In 1963 there were as many as forty-five town centres in Lancashire alone (which then incorporated Merseyside) where 'town centre schemes have either been

[19] Scott, *Shopping Centre Design*, p. 33. On Hillingdon see Gavin Stamp, 'Suburban Affinities', in, *Twentieth Century Architecture 10: The Seventies* (London, 2012), pp. 137–51.

Fig. 3.7. Blackburn Shopping Centre in *Civilia: The End of Sub Urban Man.* © RIBApix

approved or are with the Minister of Housing or are in the course of preparation'.[20]

The question as to why Blackburn demolished its town centre and replaced it with a shopping centre is a challenging one. As the scheme's own chief architect, Keith Scott, later admitted, in the decades following the 1960s such a plan 'would be deemed megalomania'.[21] There can be few examples of a historical process of this scale that has become so incomprehensible to everyone, even those intimately involved, in such a short space of time. Is it the best we can do to understand the process through Christopher Booker's concept of 'neophilia'—a collective madness which swept through society in the 1960s?[22]

The scheme cannot be understood solely through the lens of the architectural culture of modernism. BDP's aesthetic clearly allies the practice with the generation who, as Peter Mandler puts it, defined 'themselves *against* what they saw as "picturesque English-Festival-style compromise" and for

[20] TNA, 'Notes on Urban Renewal, from HLG', PREM 11/4313.

[21] Scott, *Shopping Centre Design*, p. 11. John Eddleston's evocative photographs of Blackburn just before these changes took place are reproduced with informative commentary at http://www.blackburnpast.com.

[22] Christopher Booker, *The Neophiliacs: Revolution in English Life in the Fifties and Sixties* (London, 1969).

something starker, harder, more ruthless'.[23] But even if we categorize BDP as brutalists, this does not necessarily mean they were brutal—although much of their approach at Blackburn certainly was.[24] Although there is admittedly little of the redemptive aspect of 1960s architectural culture in evidence at Blackburn, in a different urban context a contemporaneous plan for Chester, Grenfell Baines's rhetoric, while still part of an undeniably modernist plan, took on quite a different register. The Chester Plan, written directly for the council and not for a developer as at Blackburn, warned that,

> It must be remembered that the motives of the commercial developer are usually quite different from those which motivate the Planning Team. The Team (which includes the City Council) has a responsibility to all established traders in the City. The commercial developer has no such allegiances or responsibilities.[25]

Grenfell Baines went on to argue for the need for Chester to come to terms with 'the disappointing trends of our time . . . the disappearance of regional distinctions and specialty . . . family businesses fail or are bought out by multiples'. He therefore advised that the council should sponsor 'a shop to sell handmade wares—a school of bakery making homemade bread and cakes, pottery, weaving, Welsh crafts'.[26] In Chester, redevelopment was merely a matter of 'filling a few decayed teeth rather than taking out the whole mouthful, good and bad'.[27] Grenfell Baines was keen to praise 'an interesting Victorian building and we do not like to think of any building of merit and character disappearing'.[28] Modernist architecture and planning ran on a starkly different course in Blackburn with its shopping centre than at Chester with its craft shops because of the political and cultural environment in which it occurred. The architect-planners of the scheme, to appropriate a metaphor from Ayn Rand, were at the confluence of a range of forces advocating radical reconstruction, rather than at the fountainhead.

DEINDUSTRIALIZATION AND THE VICTORIAN PAST

The assumptions about the future behind a projected shopping centre involved a belief in the inexorable progress of a meliorist programme,

[23] Peter Mandler, 'John Summerson (1904-1992): the Architectural Critic and the Quest for the Modern.', in *After the Victorians: Private Conscience and Public Duty in Modern Britain* (London, 1994), p. 240.

[24] It is a paradox that *brutalism* is one of the few style labels to have initially been used in self-identification, only to subsequently become a term of abuse, in the opposite etymological journey to such terms as *gothic* or *baroque*.

[25] George Grenfell Baines, *Chester, A Plan for the Central Area 1964*, p. 14.

[26] Ibid., p. 15. [27] Ibid., p. 27. [28] Ibid., p. 31.

creating the cascading benefits of affluence—that 'there will be an improvement in economic conditions accompanied by a rise in disposable income, an increase in the number of cars, better houses requiring more spent on durable goods, and more spent on food, particularly the luxury foods'.[29] An almost wishful repetition of the mantras of prosperity and affluence was especially, and paradoxically, prevalent in the north-west mill towns that were already experiencing the tremors of the process of deindustrialization. George Eddie's pronouncements about the Blackburn plan are representative: 'We have great faith in the industrial future of this town and we believe it will become the shopping centre for a very wide area. We are certainly prepared to invest in its future prosperity.'

Such rhetoric strikes an unexpected note in a city whose post-war history has been characterized as one of 'decline and stagnation.'[30] In a 1961 perspective of the shopping centre, one can see the industrial townscape of belching mill chimneys, smudgily depicted in contrast to the clean lines of the shopping centre, rising behind (Fig. 3.8.). Blackburn's industrial past, and its uncertain industrial future, similarly looms over the planning of the scheme—even if it does so mostly invisibly. In a city experiencing the precipitous collapse of its primary industry, cotton, it was impossible to be unaware of the lurking question—'is it too good to last?'—that has been characterized as the flip side of Macmillan's affluent age.[31] Of the fifty working mills in 1955, only thirty survived into the 1960s. Blackburn had a focus on weaving rather than spinning, making it the most open to competition from Asia, and subsequently it was hit hardest by deindustrialization even in the context of the region.

Despite some early success in switching the base of Blackburn's economy from textiles to engineering and other forms of manufacturing, between 1960 and 1967 unemployment would rise from 4.9 per cent to 10.4 per cent.[32] With this in mind, it is unsurprising that Blackburn's urban renewal was deeply linked with these events, both as a response to deindustrialization and as part of a campaign to reinvent Blackburn for a changing Britain. The economic optimism which was such a feature of the rhetoric behind Blackburn's planning was skating on very thin ice, and the one mention of the processes affecting Blackburn in the council's brochure was unconvincingly upbeat: 'Blackburn became famous for its weaving industry, but its thriving and vigorous community now enjoys a prosperity based on a wide diversity of industries. The change came

[29] Josephine P. Reynolds, 'Shopping in the North West', *Town Planning Review*, 34.3 (October 1963), p. 213.

[30] Beattie, *A History of Blackburn*, p. 293.

[31] Dominic Sandbrook, *Never Had it so Good* (London, 2010).

[32] David M. Smith, *Industrial Britain, The North West* (London, 1969), p. 145.

Fig. 3.8. Clean lines of the shopping centre with industry in the background; *Blackburn Central Development* (1961), p. 13. © Building Design Partnership

about in the past decade. The centre of the town is unable to express its new vitality.'[33]

Evidence that the Lancashire redevelopment schemes were seen as part of a response to the massive contraction of the textile industry can be seen in a delegation of the Lancashire and Merseyside Industrial Development Association to Harold Macmillan on 2 July 1963. It was led by the Earl of Derby, and included many local-authority figures. They were asking for help in a period when, as they put it, 'Lancashire is passing through a difficult period of transition—its basic industries and associated traditional skills are declining and its nineteenth century environment is becoming obsolete.'[34] The delegation made it clear that this was a problem that would only go on increasing, and that government 'should pay regard not merely to actual percentage rates of unemployment based on Insured Population figures, but should take into account likely future trends'. Although the ostensible primary purpose of the delegation was to ask for an extension of the Industrial Development Certificate system, so as to stop the 'drift to the South' of jobs and industry, it is curious how much of

[33] *Blackburn Central Development* (1961), p. 2.

[34] TNA, PREM 11 4313.

the actual discussion was not specifically about industry but about questions of the built environment.

It is a striking counter to our periodization of post-war Britain that the cityscape of deindustrialization was already such a feature of the debate about northern cities in the early 1960s:

> The nineteenth-century legacy of obsolescence and congestion is, in itself, particularly grave in Lancashire; nonetheless it has been seriously aggravated in more recent times by the continuing contraction in the basic industries which has resulted in the addition of a large number of vacant and uncared for premises, many of them unsightly, near-derelict and of no potential value.[35]

The delegation painted an image of the urban environment calculated to tug at Macmillan's one-nation heartstrings:

> Behind any description of figures of obsolescence there are the human considerations – in this 'grim environment' people live and work, and children are brought up. No statistics and no description can illustrate the pervading squalor, the absence of amenity, and lack of ordinary facilities, in these areas.[36]

Solving these environmental issues would be part of the response to solving the area's economic issues: 'If Lancashire is not to fall into a chronic state of decline; if it is, rather—as it would wish—to play a full role in the future, positive measures must, as a matter of urgency, be taken now, to accelerate the renewal or redevelopment of much of the urban fabric of the country.' If Lancashire remained an area of 'old and decaying towns and of general dereliction, young people (including the vitally needed skilled workers and University graduates) would be attracted to other parts of the country, and industrialists would be unwilling to consider moving into Lancashire'. The shopping centre, it was envisioned, would provide the amenities desired for these two vital groups. In a meeting with the Ministry of Transport, Blackburn councillors had stressed that 'There had been cases of industrialists going elsewhere after a look at the town.'[37] The Board of Trade reinforced this focus on environment, by insisting that there was only so much steerable industry, and that 'migration results from many factors of which lack of jobs is only one'.[38] It is perplexing that the response towards solving, or even just to addressing, labour-market failure focused so much on programmes for the provision of consumer goods and an improved aesthetic environment. Perhaps the central reason that these ill-suited weapons were grasped to

35 TNA, PREM 11 4313. 36 TNA, PREM 11 4313.
37 Meeting at 82 Victoria Street on 10 February 1964, MT 107/184.
38 TNA, PREM 11 4313.

combat deindustrialization was that, in a mixed economy, redevelopment was one of the few areas in which local authorities could rely on private investment. With Macmillan, or for that matter his successors, unable to countenance the level of *dirigisme* that would have been welcomed by the many councillors on the delegation, most vocally represented by Liverpool's Jack Braddock, redevelopment was the only area where the councillors could make a suitably dramatic show of tackling the issue.[39]

Entangled with these fears about a post-cotton future was a historical narrative about Lancashire's Victorian past. This was another important driving motive behind redevelopment and modernization. Echoing G. M. Trevelyan's or Lewis Mumford's writings on Victorian cities, the delegation argued that the nineteenth-century environment of these towns symbolized 'both the rank growth and harsh social conditions of that period and the vast contribution made by Lancashire to the overall strength and prosperity of Great Britain'. Labour councils had a historically conditioned perspective on their cities as being the result of the Industrial Revolution and Victorian laissez-faire capitalism, the continuing repercussions of which they saw it as their mission to address.[40] Returning to George Eddie's pronouncements about Blackburn, we can see that they clearly echo these concerns:

> Like most industrial towns in Lancashire, Blackburn is a product of the industrial revolution. It grew up without any apparent sense of planning, with few buildings that can lay claim to real architectural beauty... Drastic change in the way of re-planning and re-building is inevitable.

The renewed appreciation of the picturesque qualities of Victorian townscapes that gained wide currency by the end of the decade was barely nascent in the early 1960s.[41] Perhaps such appreciation was only possible once the effects of the Clean Air Act of 1956 and the creation of smoke-control areas were properly felt and Victorian architecture ceased to be indelibly linked with industrial dirt and smoke.[42] As the Stockton-on-Tees-born architect Peter Smithson reminisced, 'When you live in the North of England everything is dirty, and you think, modern architecture

[39] It is perhaps relevant that Braddock was opposed as regards the modernizing plans for Liverpool by Walter Bor and Graeme Shankland. See Eric Heffer, *Never a Yes Man* (London, 1991), p. 105.

[40] Simon Gunn, 'The Rise and Fall of British Urban Modernism: Planning Bradford 1945-1970', *Journal of British Studies,* 48:3 (2010), p. 860.

[41] A potent example is Angela Carter, 'Industry as Art', *New Society*, 22 January 1970, pp. 143–4.

[42] See Margaret Drabble, *Arnold Bennett, a Biography* (London, 1974), p. 5, for the novelist's reappraisal of industrial townscapes following effective smoke abatement.

is wonderful.'[43] Appreciation of the Victorian townscape was certainly nowhere to be seen in a report on the buildings of Blackburn's central area, which argued that:

> the buildings in the town centre are predominantly of the older type and erected before 1878. Close examination of the buildings makes it apparent that many are now nearing the end of their useful life and that redevelopment is a matter of urgency. The survey revealed serious decay, overcrowding of rear spaces, inadequate access provision and in some cases structural defects. The general appearance of the shop fronts have changed over the years and this gives a false façade to old and decaying buildings.[44]

The first stage of Blackburn's redevelopment came primarily at the expense not of the everyday decaying fabric of the Victorian city, but of Terence Flanagan's Market Hall. This building was described by a local solicitor as 'a work of art, it is a structure admirably suited to its purpose, well-proportioned, chaste in design and with all ornaments restrained to the point of austerity, its only embellishment is its graceful campanile with its elaborate cornice, characteristic of the style it represents'.[45] BDP's Grenfell Baines, on the payroll of the developer, argued that it 'might have been good architecture when it was erected but it is no longer such'. The one act of preservation, of the Italianate Town Hall (1852–6 by J. Patterson) was justified by Grenfell Baines 'not on the grounds of artistic merit', referring to its 'robustness of appearance', but on the grounds of the 'convenience of its situation and its historic interest'.

Eddie's pronouncements give an impression almost of embarrassment about Blackburn. It was a 'dull, shabby, sooty, uninteresting place. It must put on some glamorous war paint if it is going to succeed in selling itself'. It wasn't just the old that was embarrassing, there was an almost frenzied rhetorical belief in the necessary good of the new:

> There is an old saying to the effect that 'where there is muck there is brass.' That concept is as dead as Queen Anne. Where there is muck, soot and grime there is ill-health, inefficiency, depression and stagnation. Away with such evils. Away with moaners and groaners and all those who fear progress and want to keep things as they are. This is a challenge I issue to this Council and all the citizens of this town – a challenge to the young, the young in years, the young in mind, the young in heart. The future belongs to you. Plan it, build it with vision, courage and faith and, like Browning's hero, march breast forward, never doubting.[46]

[43] Quoted in Mark Crinson, *Alison and Peter Smithson* (London, 2019), p. xv.
[44] Powell, *Development Plan Amendment no. 19.*
[45] TNA, HLG 144/72.
[46] *Bolton Journal and Guardian*, 28 May 1968, p.1.

Redevelopment was further spurred on by a feeling of competitiveness between cities, with one councillor from the North-west stating that: 'We are determined not to lag behind in the race for central redevelopment.'[47] Cities hoped, as a contemporary put it, to 'maintain, consolidate and perhaps achieve better status in the local government framework'.[48] Such competition between cities was made more intense by the growth of automobile ownership, which meant a larger catchment area for shopping: 'With mobility offered by the car, town centres have to compete for shoppers.'[49] In the dense proximity of cities in Lancashire, councillors were constantly looking over their shoulder, so that Manchester, for example, could be castigated by local businessmen for failing to produce any agreed comprehensive plan for the redevelopment of its centre, 'which just made one shudder'—especially when compared with the 'excellent city-centre redevelopment scheme' at the other end of the Manchester Ship Canal in Liverpool.[50] That Blackburn was one of the first out of the blocks in the redevelopment stakes was a point of pride.

All these local concerns were reinforced by the national dialogue about the rapid changes that were sweeping through Britain. In mill cities like Blackburn, such concerns were even more acute. As a journalist put it, there was an 'impatience and near-despair [at] the formidable task of re-creating these cities so that they become truly fit places'.[51] Worries about the social ills caused by suburban development were another important factor. There was a worry that, without rebuilding on a vast scale, town centres would die, creating a lifeless Americanized and suburban Britain. Newcastle's planner Wilfred Burns's fear of American-style out-of-town shopping centres is indicative of a widespread suspicion that such development could 'never be a satisfactory replacement for the town centre or "downtown" shopping district. It can never be part of the wider city culture. From this point of view, therefore, the out-of-town shopping centre must be regarded as inhuman.'[52] The reaction against 1930s-style sprawl that had been codified in the post-war period by the Barlow report was still very much the consensus.[53] Where a large shopping centre was planned for a suburban site, as for example in Cowley on the outskirts of Oxford (planned from 1954, building started in 1960), this was an

[47] Quoted in Reynolds, 'Shopping in the North-West', pp. 213–36, p. 213.

[48] Reynolds, 'Shopping in the North-West', p. 213.

[49] Graeme Shankland Associates, *Bolton Draft Town Centre Map* (1964).

[50] '"Manmade hell" in South Lancashire', *The Guardian,* 9 January 1964, p. 4.

[51] Joseph Minogue, 'Rebuilding the Inner Cities', *The Guardian,* 26 March 1962, p. 9.

[52] Wilfred Burns, *British Shopping Centres* (London, 1959), p. 103.

[53] Nicholas Low, 'Centrism and the Provision of Services in Residential Areas', *Urban Studies,* 12.2 (1975), pp. 177–91.

exception, pushed by specific local needs.[54] When in 1965 a developer proposed a suburban shopping centre at Haydock Park, 'the towns of South Lancashire, with big central area redevelopments in hand, rose with one voice against the project' and the plan was rejected by the Ministry.[55] Such rhetoric celebrating centralization over dispersal easily melded with the longer tradition of local-authority civic pride, and the need to retain both rates and voters.[56]

CIVIC PRIDE—COUNCILLORS AND SHOPKEEPERS

Keith Scott, the lead architect at Blackburn, gave a candid, possibly hyperbolic, description of Labour councillors of the period:

> They are frequently blue-collar workers, almost always in the PAYE tax bracket and they are often given great articulacy by support from academics from the local polytechnic. Together they know little about the arcane world of business – indeed tend to deride it – but this leaves them free to be visionaries and they are quick to grasp overall strategy. Implementation and practical matters make them short-tempered and they are prone to retreat into rhetoric. That cuts little ice with a developer who is seeking to get on with the job.[57]

Labour councils were, therefore, as Oliver Marriott put it, 'much more occupied with the glory of their towns, keen to embark on grandiose projects, and impervious to the squeals of small shopkeepers'.[58] These were all important attributes at Blackburn.

As Chapter 2 showed, the type of public–private partnership between developer and local authority used at Blackburn was developed as part of Conservative Party policy, through the official pronouncements of the Ministry of Housing and Local Government's planning bulletins. Blackburn actually predated the first of these bulletins. This was seen as a point of pride: 'It might be said that Blackburn's present proposals could have

[54] [National Economic Development Office,] *Cowley Shopping Centre* (London, 1968), p. 1.

[55] 'The Shopping Line', *New Society*, 5 August 1965, p. 4. See also Liverpool and Bolton planner Graeme Shankland's argument against Haydock Park, in '£19.5m plan assumptions "reasonable"', *The Guardian*, 25 November 1965, p. 13.

[56] See, for example, Charlotte Wildman, 'Urban Transformation in Liverpool and Manchester, 1918-1939', *Historical Journal*, 55.1 (2012), pp. 119–43.

[57] Scott, *Shopping Centre Design*, p. 14.

[58] Oliver Marriott, *The Property Boom* (Abingdon, 1989), p. 126.

been put forward as a blueprint for the Minister's bulletin.'[59] Paradoxically, though, in local cases Conservative-controlled authorities tended to be far less gung-ho about central-area redevelopment, and the majority of ambitious town-centre schemes happened in Labour-dominated councils. This was due to an ideological fissure between the local and central Conservative parties—a fissure that was also causing acrimonious friction over the scrapping of resale price maintenance in 1964, which also saw the government siding with multiples over private traders.[60] In the case of Blackburn there was near unanimity on the council for the redevelopment, and the leader of the Tories, Bob Mottershead, was vice-chairman of the Civic Development Committee. He and Eddie were frequently described by the local press as 'the Two Dictators'.[61] Nevertheless, to understand what happened at Blackburn it is important to recognize not just the forces pushing for redevelopment, but also those pushing against redevelopment, and why they were ignored. Keith Scott gives a portrait of Tory councillors in the period:

> Tories tend to cling to the belief that theirs is the party of private enterprise, pragmatism and business acumen, all very necessary attributes of a developer. One might assume therefore that a meeting of minds can be anticipated. In fact this does not happen. Tory councils are usually made up of self-made businessmen and they own drapers shops, small jewellers and confectionery stalls. They are generally freeholders and have a very acute sense of what is good for their own business, but it would not occur to them to spend time working out what is good for their competitors. In short, they are strong on detail, light on strategy and getting them to take the broad view on a project involving every trader in town can be very hard work indeed.

The type of local businessmen described by Scott were a central ingredient in the way schemes panned out all over the country—although in the case of Blackburn their only allies on the local council were Liberals, not Conservatives.[62] Before the advent of significant organized local activism and the rise of preservation movements, local businessmen were the most substantial counterforce to redevelopment. Their voices were overridden at Blackburn. But that is not to suggest they did not exist. They most certainly did. A total of 226 objections were lodged, and a

[59] TNA, 'Reply to certain criticisms made by Objectors', HLG 144/72.

[60] Ian Gilmour, *Whatever Happened to the Tories: the Conservatives since 1945* (London, 1998), pp. 207–8. It is significant that the scrapping of rpm increased the profitability of shopping centres.

[61] 'The Big Face-Lift Begins', *The Blackburn Times,* 13 January 1961, p. 1.

[62] 'Build New Blackburn with Vision and Courage', *The Blackburn Times,* 23 March 1962, p. 11.

spirited campaign was led by the local solicitor and president of the local Liberal Association, E. C. Marsden:

> Over and over again [Marsden] has been asked in one form or another 'is there no way in which this scheme can be stopped' and he appears at the inquiry as a Blackburnian having a pride in the past of his town and, despite the local authority, a belief in its future.[63]

Out of 388 existing shops in the town centre, the scheme would involve the demolition of 251. The proposal eliminated not only the primary shopping street, King Street, but also many other secondary shopping streets. With rents of around £150 per annum usual in these secondary streets, and the minimum price charged by Laing for a spot in Phase 1 of the new scheme £950, it was clear, as the objectors stated, 'This must mean that the multiples will come in and private traders will be driven out of this central area.' Quoting from several of the local shopkeepers who lodged objections gives insight into the trauma experienced. A builder and a plumber were among those 'satisfied after careful consideration of the finances that if the proposed scheme should be implemented the effect on their business and their 125 employees would be disastrous', while a hardware and ironmongery store pleaded that they 'have been freeholders for 130 years and wish to remain freeholders'. But this was not just seen in personal terms, with the Market Place 'replaced by remote islands of concrete and chromium and the small trader and multifarious organisations which for so many years have efficiently formed the hub of the town would have to depart and give place to the large multiple firms with their unfortunate standardisation and impersonal service'. This was an ideological conflict, with two conceptions of civic pride at odds. The small businessmen, with their locally oriented spirit of civic pride and understandable attachment to their property, were being ignored by their natural allies in the Conservative government, who were intent on projecting an agenda of modernization. These local shopkeepers were left powerless when coming into conflict with a Labour council, which in trying desperately to find a new role for the city, formed an unlikely alliance with big business to make a grand gesture. As the owner of a wholesale fruit and veg store saw it, it was 'a marriage of opposites with financial gain the object and human and social considerations of little or no concern to either of the parties'. There was also a stream of anti-Semitic xenophobia running alongside this championing of Blackburnian tradition, with one councillor suggesting that the town was 'going to belong to a lot of Jew boys'.[64]

[63] TNA, 'Objections', HLG 144/72.

[64] 'New Tow Centre Critics Slated', *The Blackburn Times,* 7 April 1961, p. 1.

The shopkeepers defined themselves as standing for a local, traditional, and individualist pragmatism:

> Blackburn Market Hall is the only establishment in the town, conducted by local private enterprise, which performs the function of a multiple store and as such it offers healthy competition to the encroachment of international finance and helps the town preserve something of its old traditions of thrift and independence.[65]

In Blackburn, the concerns of these small businessmen were met by the inspector for the council, J. L. M. Metcalf, with haughty dismissal: 'It is suggested that the best people to represent public opinion are the democratically elected representatives and not individual bodies in the town.'[66] Metcalf's sharpest disdain, from the lofty heights of the expert, was reserved for a Liberal councillor who suggested the scheme should be put to a referendum: 'This objection has been an irresponsible waste of several hours of public time and money. It would be a waste of time dealing with the planning points put forward, they are put forward without any special qualifications and must be treated as such.' George Eddie called these criticisms from the Chamber of Trade 'stupid', and argued that 'The whole of their criticisms arise from the fact that they are concerned how redevelopment might hit their pockets. It is not the town they are concerned about but their personal, selfish, vested interest.'[67]

This was a local iteration of a national issue, with the National Chamber of Trade leading a campaign highlighting the nationwide plight of shopkeepers displaced by central-area redevelopment.[68] David Robertson (MP for Streatham) was one of a number of MPs who attempted to lobby Keith Joseph on the issue, pointing out that in common with many Tory MPs he owed a debt to shopkeepers: 'Almost every shopkeeper was canvassing support for the Conservative cause. The giant multiples were of no use to me politically because their boss had not a vote in my constituency.'[69] Joseph responded blandly, but the Ministry's private reaction to these entreaties was that 'it was not for the Department to try to perpetuate obsolete forms of trading [and that] the independent trader has a

65 TNA, 'Objections', HLG 144/72.

66 TNA, 'Reply to certain criticisms made by Objectors', HLG 144/72.

67 'New Town Centre Critics Slated', *The Blackburn Times*, 7 April 1961, p. 1.

68 See National Chamber of Trade memorandum, *The Plight of Displaced Independent Traders* (London, 1963).

69 TNA, Letter from David Robertson, M.P., to Keith Joseph, 6 November 1962, HLG 136/61.

place on merits in the town centre but that the Department's interest is to secure redevelopment and not to protect existing traders as such'.[70]

It is worthwhile to briefly compare what happened in Blackburn with two other plans for market areas, but in cities with a different political and regional context: Leicester and Salisbury. In Leicester, there were several schemes from developers 'proposing radical replanning of the area in the form of a modern shopping centre'.[71] In Leicester there was also vociferous opposition: 'The Market Area, . . . owing to its position, history and character of uses, could be described as the very heart of Leicester.' It is not surprising that the matter of its redevelopment provoked a considerable and often violent controversy. The idea of a radical replanning was particularly strongly opposed by the Market Traders' Association and the market stallholders, who argued that any scheme needed to 'ensure the preservation of the individual character of the market area as an area of private businesses operated by persons whose lives are centred in the City'.[72] In Leicester, though, these dissenting voices were victorious, and the scheme was scaled back and replaced with a '"face-lift" scheme for the Market Area for use as the basis of a more detailed scheme to be prepared and implemented by the various traders through a co-ordinating Committee to be established by themselves'.[73] This was to be prepared in consultation with the Civic Trust. Ian Nairn and Kenneth Browne from *The Architectural Review* were even hired as 'experts in urban landscape'. The tone of the eventual report for the area, like that for Chester outlined above, is wildly different from Blackburn's:

> The open market, although the oldest form of shopping, cannot be considered an anachronism. New forms of shopping, [do] not necessarily replace old ones and the open market has a definite role in a modern city amongst the retail shop, department store and the supermarket . . . Leicester's open market should remain where it is without a substantial reduction of stalls.[74]

Perhaps the character of Leicester's intriguing planner, Konrad Smigielski, who would eventually resign over a conservation issue, had something to do with these differences.[75] But it is notable that Leicester did not abandon its shopping centre; it just moved it to a less sensitive site, mostly

[70] TNA, Meeting on displaced traders, 22 January 1963, HLG 136/61.

[71] Konrad Smigielski, *Market Area Leicester, Report of the City Planning Officer* (Leicester, 1963).

[72] Leicestershire Record Office (hereinafter LRO), 'General Meeting of Leicester Central Area Traders' Association, 3 July 1963', Town Planning Minutes 1964, DE3277/213.

[73] LRO, Town Planning Minutes, 14 May 1963, DE3277/213.

[74] Smigielski, *Market Area Leicester*.

[75] See Harry Martin, 'A love affair with Leicester: Konrad Smigielski, ex-chief planning officer of Leicester', *Building Design*, 29 November 1974, pp. 14–15; Simon

occupied by the Corporation's omnibus depot. Smigielski's draft plan for this shopping centre follows exactly the planning precepts of the Blackburn shopping centre: 'a multi-deck scheme with shops on the ground and first floors, an entertainment centre on the upper floors, multi-level car parking provision, and an underground service road system.'[76] The Haymarket Shopping Centre opened in 1973; the developers were Littlewoods, and the architects were Building Design Partnership.

In Salisbury the appointment of a modernist architect-planner actually stemmed the tide of radical redevelopment. Here the developers were Hammerson, who from 1961 were proposing a precinctual shopping centre—with rooftop car deck for 200 cars—on the site of the New Street Chequer. The site was mainly comprised of a cattle market, but also included a number of historic buildings—most notably the thirteenth-century George Hotel on the High Street. Hammerson argued that without the shopping centre Salisbury would 'forfeit what could be a thriving and prosperous future', especially in light of plans under way for expanding Basingstoke and Andover. At a public enquiry the council's anxiety about the process of public–private development was made clear by their counsel:

> I think everybody dealing with these plans for central re-development, are still only feeling their way; Planning Authorities, Developers, indeed, to some extent, the Minister, because his Bulletins which have been extremely helpful are only very recent publications. It is a new field of Planning, and a vital one.[77]

Max Lock was brought in as planner in 1961. He saw it as his job to 'to reconcile the increasingly chaotic state of warfare that exists between (i) TRAFFIC, (ii) TRADE and (iii) TRADITION'.[78] His plan was very much on the side of the shopkeepers; it was 'not merely a preservationist plan but in fact, is one step ahead of those who would exploit the City by excessive concentration of shopping anywhere because it seeks to conserve the trade of the whole city'.[79] His plan makes a distinction between young and old towns: 'A young town without much history or architectural maturity can be planned and reshaped to respond flexibly to modern

Gunn, 'Konrad Smigielski and the planning of post-war Leicester', in *Leicester: A Modern History* (Lancaster, 2016), pp. 267–91.

[76] LRO, 'Haymarket Comprehensive Redevelopment Area', DE3277/214.

[77] Wiltshire and Swindon Archive Centre (WSAC), Graham Eyre (Counsel for Salisbury City Council), at the summing up of the public enquiry, 30 October 1963, G23/141/6.

[78] WSAC, Max Lock at the public enquiry, 30 October 1963, G23/141/6.

[79] Ibid.

engineering demands in a way that an old and historic town cannot.'[80] Taking his cue from Patrick Geddes's idea of conservative surgery, Lock argued that, 'The problem in Salisbury is therefore, primarily one of 'civic surgery' which, because Salisbury is an old town and not a young one, must be gentle, reasonable—neither drastic nor excessive.'

The perceived pressures of commercial development and traffic were felt equally in all of these cities. But modernist approaches to solving these problems were not homogeneous but modulated according to how various actors perceived the cities they were working in. There was not a city in Britain that escaped the process completely, but it was in cities like Blackburn that the more nuanced concerns of British architect-planners were conceived as least applicable.

One is left with the impression that Blackburn Corporation was so desperate to get private development involved in the formidable task of reinventing the city for a post-cotton age, that it was overawed by the slick operation of Laing and BDP.[81] The Corporation ended up allowing redevelopment to happen in the areas where it was not actually needed, at the expense of Blackburn's historic fabric and established shopkeepers, rather than in the areas of industrial dereliction where such an intervention might have been more welcomed by posterity. Blackburn's shopping centre is definitely not a building from a vanished era. It was wrestling with problems which remain intractable and pertinent: how to mould private investment towards giving a new role to a city whose meaning had been so tied up with a now defunct industry.

The tragedy of Blackburn is as much about the destruction of civil society the buildings contained as of the buildings themselves. Although nothing came of it, a 1972 report, also by BDP, for a new cultural centre for Blackburn belatedly acknowledged that more than retail and wholesale demolition was required to create a vibrant town centre, and it also marked a rejection of the policy of complete renewal:

> The redevelopment of Blackburn's city centre has proceeded so far on the basis of complete renewal. The commercial precinct now covering over ten acres was achieved by the demolition of all existing buildings and a further phase has still to be completed. It can therefore be argued that from now on the main task of renewal will be to preserve what is good and merge new work into the existing fabric of the old.... The new Cultural Centre presents a fine opportunity to develop this policy and to demonstrate in three

[80] Max Lock and Partners, *Salisbury, The Redevelopment of the City Centre* (June 1963).
[81] Ronald Hough, Blackburn's Chief Planning Assistant, is notably absent from the narrative.

dimensions how Blackburn's notable past can be welded to a vital and prosperous future.[82]

BDP's shopping centre is itself currently being redeveloped, but the developer behind the plans for the new centre assured me that the replacement would also be graced with a clock tower. This means that Blackburn, in little over half a century, will have had three clock towers symbolically representing the city's civic identity.

Blackburn's redevelopment was highly controversial. This meant that central government took note. Subsequently I found a much richer archival trail for what happened in Blackburn than in other local-authority archives, where the decision to rebuild is often only evidenced by a plan, a brief note in the council minutes, and the glass and concrete buildings around the city. Blackburn helps us to see city-centre redevelopment as a local response to a national dialogue about cities, and to the global historical process of deindustrialization. To understand city-centre redevelopment, a historian needs to be able to shift through these different scales.

Chapter 4 will focus on an architect-planner, Graeme Shankland, who worked on plans for two other Lancashire cities which were facing similar challenges to those experienced by Blackburn. Through these plans Shankland developed a much more subtle and appreciative approach to industrial cities than that taken at Blackburn. The chapter will continue to develop the thesis that planning in this period was an intensely political activity, and was responding to concurrent social and technological shifts. From this point on another key argument of this book will become increasingly paramount: that the tenets of radical modernism unravelled, not just because of outside pressures but also because of a shift in the thinking of architect-planners themselves, towards new priorities and new commitments.

[82] Building Design Partnership, *A New Cultural Centre for Blackburn, A Feasibility Study* (1972).

4

Planning for Affluence

Graeme Shankland and the Political Culture of the British Left

THE BUTCHER OF LIVERPOOL?

Graeme Shankland (1917–84) conforms in many ways to the popular image of a 1960s planner, with his lyrical advocacy of inner-city motorways and his suggestion of enormous programmes of renewal in 'outworn' Victorian city centres. He was an advocate of the belief that 'our problem in Britain is that it is our generation which must completely renew most of the older parts of our larger towns and cities'.[1] Shankland's plan for Liverpool is notorious. Gavin Stamp described it as a 'nightmare' which was mercifully only partly completed.[2] Raphael Samuel labelled him 'the butcher of Liverpool'.[3] Journalist Simon Jenkins's antipathy towards planners developed after viewing Shankland's Liverpool plan: 'I was looking at Bomber Harris. This was the end of the beautiful city and that reaction has infused everything I have thought since about planning and architecture.'[4] At best, Paul Barker sees him as misguided: 'I think, for example, of the destruction of the centre of Liverpool by well-meaning planners like Graeme Shankland.'[5]

Shankland complicates this received image of the 1960s planner as bogeyman because he also displays many of the virtues that we tend to associate with the reaction against 1960s comprehensive redevelopment. He was a pioneer in championing the preservation of Victorian structures (even industrial ones) and was a member of the Society of Architectural

[1] Graeme Shankland, 'British Towns and Cities: the New Chance', *The Listener*, 17 June 1965, p. 892.

[2] Gavin Stamp, *Britain's Lost Cities* (London, 2007), p. 111.

[3] Raphael Samuel, *Theatres of Memory* (London, 1994), p. 67.

[4] Quoted in Huw Morris, 'Siding with Communities', *Planning*, 15 (2008), p. 15.

[5] Paul Barker, 'Non-Plan Revisited: Or the Real Way Cities Grow', *Journal of Design History*, 12:2 (1999), pp. 95–110, p. 108.

Historians of Great Britain from 1960. Furthermore, he displayed sensitivity towards the existing individual characters of northern cities: 'Crumbling and chaotic they may be, but they also have a unity and character which enable them to be comprehended.'[6] Contra Jane Jacobs's influential view of planners as having no sympathy towards the beneficial qualities of urban life, he was emphatically pro-city, attempting, for example, to bring housing back into central areas. In addition, in contrast to a narrative of British post-war urbanism which stresses 'the Corbusians coming to Britain', Shankland was vocally critical of Le Corbusier.[7] As the architectural theorist and teacher Colin Rowe reported, Shankland 'felt that Le Corbusier's tendency to make man in his own image, to project this image on society and often impose a formal pattern regardless of circumstances, in some degree vitiated his contribution'.[8] He was actively influenced by the Townscape movement, which advocated the application of a picturesque sensibility to modern development, especially through his close involvement with the architectural draughtsman Gordon Cullen.

These are all ideas we might more readily associate with the type of philosophy advocated by *The Architectural Review* during the post-war period rather than avant-garde, modernist urban renewal. In contrast to accounts that stress a polarized architectural culture, Shankland's plans are an amalgamation of radical renewal and experimental forms with more nuanced concerns.[9] It was a dichotomy that the critic and historian Reyner Banham was able to observe at the time: 'Graeme Shankland is currently giving Liverpool a traffic plan that starts with the proposition that the function of cars is to move, and fast... But Shankland is being very tender with the urban texture wherever he can, and he has Gordon Cullen (of Townscape fame) to advise him and his team on how to preserve and enhance it.'[10]

If we are to understand Shankland through the familiar categories and conventions of architectural history then his *oeuvre* in the late 1950s and early 1960s appears schizophrenic, veering as it does between the very forefront of both modernist and postmodernist ideas of the city. This interpretive problem arises only if we try to categorize him either as a

[6] Graeme Shankland, 'Picture of Britain 1959', *Architectural Design*, January 1960, p. 49.

[7] Peter Hall, *Cities of Tomorrow* (London, 2002), p. 234.

[8] Colin Rowe, 'Le Corbusier: Utopian Architect', *The Listener*, 12 February 1959, p. 289.

[9] See Reyner Banham, 'Revenge of the Picturesque: English Architectural Polemics, 1945-1965', in *Concerning Architecture: Essays on Architectural Writers and Writing presented to Nikolaus Pevsner*, ed. John Summerson (London, 1968), pp. 265–73; Nicholas Bullock, *Building the Post-War World, Modern Architecture and Reconstruction in Britain* (London and New York, 2002), pp. 95–130; Christopher Klemek, *The Transatlantic Collapse of Urban Renewal, Postwar Urbanism from New York to Berlin* (Chicago, 2011).

[10] Reyner Banham, 'The Embalmed City', *New Statesman*, 12 April 1963, pp. 528–30, p. 530.

dehumanizing modernist or as a humble conservationist. Such categories are clearly insufficient for understanding Shankland—or, indeed, his period. Relating Shankland to the context of the political culture of the time provides a way to understand how seemingly conflicting ideas were able to coexist within a single philosophy.

By seeing Shankland's approach as allied to the meliorist aims of the British Left, the ostensible contradiction that finds his ideas on both sides of some historical divide dissolves. Although it is common to view the architecture of the 1960s as the expression of Wilsonite 'white heat',[11] this chapter builds on a more nuanced account of left-wing political culture, which understands it as being conflicted—like Shankland's work—between modernizing and more traditional concerns.[12] Shankland's biography and statements show him to be very much engaged with a post-1956 left-wing milieu, and his plans embody many of the ambiguous and conflicted feelings about affluence and the possible consequences of an untrammelled project of modernization which were prevalent among the British Left at the time. In particular, there was a widespread sense on the Left that affluence and the post-war growth in automobile usage were destroying traditional conceptions of community and creating a suburban, Americanized Britain. The preconceptions that shaped Shankland's plans grew out of the whole political culture of the Left in Britain as much as any hermetic architectural discourse. While Shankland was not necessarily voicing a specific party-political line, his approach nonetheless responded to, and paralleled, wider debates. His solutions were perceivable at the time as part of a panacea to problems widely appreciated by politicians. Furthermore, Shankland's approach was co-opted by sections of the Conservative Party, which in this period was pursuing *dirigiste* and one-nation policies. His plans were realized, if at all, as much through the Conservative-backed policy of public–private partnership as they were through state intervention.

The main sources for this chapter will be three plans in which Shankland had an important role.[13] Shankland was also a prolific writer of

[11] Alan Powers, *Britain, Modern Architectures in History* (London, 2007), p. 127; Elain Harwood, 'White Light/White Heat: Rebuilding England's Provincial Towns and Cities in the Sixties', *Twentieth Century Architecture*, 6 (2002), pp. 56–70.

[12] Lawrence Black, *The Political Culture of the Left in Affluent Britain, 1951–64* (London, 2003).

[13] The result is not an attempt at a detailed history of physical change in the cities discussed; it is as much a history of things that were not built as things that were. The history of Liverpool's planning alone deserves a book-length treatment, which would necessarily deal with issues outside of Shankland's purview. Here, therefore, the plans will be analysed in a limited way, interrogating them for their ambitions and the rhetoric they use, and relating these ambitions to a wider cultural moment, while generally ignoring the

proselytizing journalism, and was described by the Garden City advocate Frederick Osborn as 'typical of the architectural group that almost monopolises the press and BBC in this country'.[14] Shankland saw himself in the artistic terms of an 'urban designer', creating three-dimensional designs over large areas with the aim of creating 'the city as art'.[15] He proclaimed that if our surroundings 'are beautiful and stimulating they raise our aesthetic standards and deepen our sensitivity'.[16] William Morris is the frequently stated life-long influence behind such a statement.[17] Shankland's aesthetics and approach to urbanism are nevertheless a long way from the rustic medievalism of Morris's *News from Nowhere.*

BIOGRAPHICAL OVERVIEW

Graeme Shankland was born on Merseyside on 31 January 1917 to Violet Cooper (née Lindsay) and Ernest Claude Shankland, who was then the Assistant Marine Surveyor of the Mersey Docks and Harbour Board and by 1926 became Chief Harbour Master at the Port of London. Graeme Shankland left Liverpool at the age of 6, and when he returned as planner his only memories of the city were from being billeted there during the Second World War, 'walking over streets covered in broken glass'.[18] He attended Stowe during J. F. Roxburgh's headmastership and in 1940 graduated from Queens' College, Cambridge, in Architecture and Draughtsmanship. He was already interested in William Morris, writing a letter to *The Listener* about quality in industrial design, in which he mentions lectures by Nikolaus Pevsner.[19] He was also in correspondence with Garden City advocate Frederick Osborn while an undergraduate, and had started to plan a career in town planning.[20]

mechanics of their implementation. For a defence of the validity of using plans as a source for understanding 'ambitions and assumptions', rather than for how they directly affect the built environment, see Guy Ortolano, 'Planning the Urban Future in 1960s Britain', *Historical Journal,* 54 (2011), pp. 477–507.

[14] *The Letters of Lewis Mumford and Frederic J. Osborn: a Transatlantic Dialogue 1938–1970,* ed. M. Hughes (Bath, 1971), p. 312.

[15] Graeme Shankland, 'New Role of Urban Design', *RIBA Journal,* February 1965, pp. 69–74.

[16] Graeme Shankland, *Liverpool City Centre Plan* (Liverpool, 1965), p. 68.

[17] See, for example, Graeme Shankland, 'The Next Ten Years', *Town Planning Review,* 43.3 (July 1977), p. 279; Graeme Shankland, 'William Morris as Designer', in *William Morris: selected writings and designs,* ed. Asa Briggs (London, 1962).

[18] 'Planning Overlord', *The Guardian,* 22 February 1962, p. 19.

[19] Graeme Shankland, 'Artistic Standards of the C.W.S.', *The Listener,* 11 August 1937, p. 310.

[20] Hertford County Archives, DE/FJO/B159/61, Letter from Shankland to Osborn, (9 [March 1939]).

Early in the Second World War he worked as a member of William Holford's team designing hostels for factory workers. Then, having joined the Royal Engineers in 1942, he was commissioned and saw active service in Africa, the Middle East, and what was then Malaya, before being demobilized in October 1946 with the rank of temporary captain. Shankland joined the Communist Party in 1942, and had his letters opened by MI5 until 1958. Those relating to his communism (as well as prurient snooping of his homosexuality) are still held in The National Archives.[21] It was far from unusual for British planners to be Party members.[22] Shankland was also a member of the Communist Party Historians Group, corresponding with Eric Hobsbawm, and was the anonymous *Daily Worker*'s architectural correspondent until 1956.[23] As with many of his generation, he left the Party after sending a letter to Communist Party headquarters protesting against their 'shameful resolution' on Hungary in 1956.

Shankland joined the Architectural Association after demobilization, before undertaking a postgraduate course at the London School of Planning. While at the Architectural Association he visited Sweden and Italy with two other architectural students, Michael Ventris, famous for deciphering the Mycenaean script Linear B, and Oliver Cox, his future architectural partner.[24] He later praised Swedish architecture's 'dry beauty', and saw it as analogous to Britain's attempt to

> turn away from the abstract diagrammatic forms of Le Corbusier and Mies van der Rohe, and a turning towards more national and traditional forms in the light of experience and popular criticism... For national character, manifest in architecture as it must be, is something inevitably developed between the people, the architects and the craftsmen, and transmitted from father to son and professor to student.'[25]

Shankland was more than plausibly a key target of architect James Stirling's gibe, 'William Morris was a Swede'.[26] The Swedish suburban New Town of Vällingby, 'a suburb with a real heart', was an important influence on the unbuilt Hook New Town (to which Shankland

[21] TNA, 'Graeme Shankland', KV 2/3108-3110.

[22] Stephen V. Ward, 'Soviet Communism and the British Planning Movement: Rational Learning or Utopian Imagining?', *Planning Perspectives,* 2.4 (2012), pp. 499–524.

[23] See, for example, 'Green and Pleasant land—For How Long', *Daily Worker*, 13 July 1955, p. 2.

[24] Andrew Robinson, *The Man Who Deciphered Linear B: The Story of Michael Ventris* (London, 2002), pp. 48–59. London, RIBA Drawings and Archives Collection, Oliver Cox, 'Italian Journal, Summer 1948', VOS/90.

[25] Graeme Shankland, 'Architecture in a Welfare State', *The Listener*, 27 March 1952, p. 506.

[26] Bullock, *Building the Post-War World*, p. 71.

contributed) and Boston Manor, an imaginary scheme for the reconstruction of this West London suburb proposed along with Chamberlin, Powell, and Bon.[27]

From the early 1950s Shankland lived in a flat at 36 South Hill Park in Hampstead, 'overlooking last of the Hampstead chain of ponds which form headwaters of the Fleet'.[28] His home was decorated with William Morris's Bower-design wallpaper, and also, according to an informant, with posters 'of a communist nature'. He joined the London County Council (LCC) in 1950, becoming one of three senior planners in the Planning Division along with Walter Bor and Gordon Logie, working first under fellow communist Arthur Ling and then, from 1956, under Leslie Lane. He was in charge of detailed schemes for the Elephant and Castle and the South Bank permanent development scheme, as well as less high-profile jobs in Lewisham and Woolwich.[29] He was reprimanded for his unauthorized involvement with Chamberlin, Powell, and Bon's proposals for Boston Manor, but nevertheless became a key figure in the planning of Hook New Town at the suggestion of Cox, by now also working for the LCC and leading this project.[30] The Hook plan was never realized, but Shankland wrote up the findings; they were reprinted twice, were translated into Japanese and German, and were influential, notably on the design of new universities.[31] In 1962 Shankland became the planning consultant for Liverpool city centre, as part of Walter Bor's larger plan. He formed the private practice Graeme Shankland Associates, which rapidly became Shankland Cox after he was joined by Oliver Cox. The firm's important town-planning projects in Britain during the 1960s include a realized plan for Bolton, and expansionary plans for Ipswich, Winsford, and Reading.[32] He wrote a conservation study for UNESCO on Isfahan,

[27] Graeme Shankland, 'Dead Centre: the Crisis of Planning and the Future of Cities–2', *Architectural Association Journal*, March 1957, p. 194; For Swedish influence, see Peter Carolin, 'Sense, sensibility and tower blocks: the Swedish influence on post-war housing in Britain', in *Twentieth Century Architecture*, 9, *Housing the Twentieth Century Nation* (2008), pp. 98–112.

[28] 'Men of the Year', *Architects' Journal*, 17 January 1962, p. 127.

[29] See Percy Johnson Marshall, *Rebuilding Cities* (Chicago, 1966).

[30] See John R. Gold, *The Practice of Modernism* (Abingdon and New York, 2007), pp. 98–100, and 'Realisation of the Living Suburb: The Boston Manor project...', *Architecture and Building* [London,] Sept., Oct., and Nov. 1958). Cox subsequently joined the Ministry of Housing Development Group.

[31] London Metropolitan Archives [hereinafter LMA], Planning of a New Town Hook, GLC/DG/PRB/22/097; Stefan Muthesius, *The Postwar University, Utopianist Campus and College* (New Haven and London, 2000), pp. 92 and 171.

[32] Shankland Cox and Associates, *Expansion of Ipswich* (London, 1966); Shankland Cox Partnership, *Winsford Plan, Proposals for Town Expansion* (Chester, 1967); Shankland Cox and Associates, *Woodley and Earley Master Plan* (London, 1971).

and gave advice on the French New Town of Cergy-Pontoise, which led to more international projects in the 1970s, especially in Jamaica, where the firm set up an office.[33]

HOOK NEW TOWN

Hook was a project for a New Town for 100,000 people in Hampshire, abandoned during 1960 because of local opposition as well as the political calculation from Tory high command that 'the withdrawal of the Hook proposal would be preferable from the political point of view'.[34] The plan was an attempt by the LCC to achieve their policy of decentralization without suburban expansion.[35] The LCC began looking for a site for such a project from 1955, and alighted on Hook by 1957.[36] Along with the realized new town of Cumbernauld in central Scotland, developed from 1956 and with which it shares many characteristics, Hook represents an intermediate stage between the low-density 'Mark I' post-war New Towns such as Stevenage (designated 1946) and Harlow (1947), and the 'Mark II' New Towns such as Skelmersdale (1961) and Runcorn (1964). Shankland was primarily responsible for writing up the plan, although the contribution of other participants, especially Cox, should not be overlooked.

In common with many of his generation, Shankland historicized his position as being in reaction to the Garden City movement and its bastardization in suburbia: 'I think the time has come to lay the ghost of Ebenezer [Howard, founder of the Garden City Movement].'[37] The Barlow Report of 1940 had set the tone for continuing dispersal away from large cities in the early post-war period, arguing that the 'concentration of population in the great towns, especially since the Industrial Revolution has been marked by a disastrous harvest of slums, sickness,

[33] Shankland Cox and Associates, *The Planning of Isfahan* (London, 1968); Lionel Engrand and Oliver Millot, *Cergy-Pontoise forms et fictions d'une Ville Nouvelle* (Paris, 2015); Shankland Cox and Associates, *La vie dans un grand ensemble: Étude de l'habitat au Puits-la-Marlière en banlieue nord de Paris* (Pontoise, 1971).

[34] TNA, Letter from Rab Butler to Macmillan, 5 April 1960, PREM 11/3128.

[35] Ken Young and Patricia Garside, *Metropolitan London: Politics and Urban Change, 1837–1981* (London, 1981), pp. 289–91; and Gold, *Practice of Modernism,* p. 151.

[36] LMA, 'New town site search—history of investigations leading to selection of the Hook, Hants site', LCC/AR/CB/01/155.

[37] Shankland, 'Dead Centre–2', p. 196. See also Ivor de Wolf, 'Italian Townscape', *Architectural Review*, June 1962, p. 383; Hugh Wilson, 'New towns: what next?' *Twentieth Century*, autumn 1962, pp. 98–106; Timothy Knight et al., *Let Our Cities Live* (London, 1960).

stunted population and misery'.[38] Shankland was one of many planners who, faced with new and increasingly suburban forms of urbanization, were attempting to reinvest in more urban forms of development. He was a founding member of the Society for the Promotion of Urban Renewal (SPUR).[39]

This agenda was made explicit at Hook. The plan was 'an attempt to retain some of the assets of urban life lost in the garden cities—which, from Ebenezer Howard onwards, in trying to break with the unhealthy effects of the dense 19th century industrial city, have lost some valuable characteristics of town life'.[40] Hook was responding to the wide feeling that the first generation of New Towns, as one commentator put it, had 'failed because they are not towns, they are ghettos for young families, they are not urban, they are suburbs with no town, and because they deny by their very shape and environment the cultural richness for which their people are grasping.'[41] The preconceptions of the planning team at Hook were summed up by one of its members, Hugh Morris: 'the original common bond of the team was profound dismay on visiting the new towns... [we] believed that there was an *a priori* case for higher densities'.[42]

Hook was designed to celebrate 'urbanity': it 'should be compact without sacrificing standards of open space.... Urban character in terms of buildings, landscape and relationships between them should be achieved, although the town would be predominantly horizontal in design and developed at a gross overall density probably comparable to other English new towns.'[43] The plan's bibliography shows that the architects were influenced by planners from an earlier generation, such as Frederick Gibberd, Thomas Sharp, William Holford, Geoffrey Jellicoe, and even Arthur Trystan Edwards—each of whom had stressed the importance of urbanity.[44]

The second factor influencing the development was the growth of motor traffic. The town was designed to meet a predicted enormous rise in private car ownership through strict segregation of vehicular and pedestrian circulation. As Colin Buchanan noted, 'The road plan [at

[38] *Royal Commission on the Distribution of the Industrial Population, Report* (London, 1940), p. 8.

[39] See London, RIBA Drawings and Archives Collection, Letter from Shankland to Lionel Brett, 18 November 1956, Brl/4/1.3. For SPUR, see John Gold, 'A SPUR to action: the Society for the Promotion of Urban Renewal, "anti-scatter" and the crisis of reconstruction', *Planning Perspectives*, 27.2 (2012), pp. 199–223.

[40] [London County Council,] *The Planning of a New Town* (London, 1961), p. 41.

[41] John Harlow, 'One New Town', *Universities and Left Review*, autumn 1958, p. 19.

[42] *Architectural Association Journal*, April, 1962, p. 259. See also Graeme Shankland, 'Lessons of the New Towns', *The Times*, 3 July 1961, p. 4.

[43] LCC, *The Planning of a New Town*, p. 16.

[44] LCC, *The Planning of a New Town*, p. 178.

Fig. 4.1. The Market at Hook, with its traditional covered awnings and profusion of advertising, including for *The Scotsman*; *The Planning of a New Town*, p. 59. © London Metropolitan Archives

Hook] was calculated on the basis of 1.5 cars per family, which is... somewhat higher than the present Californian figure.'[45] The town centre was to be on a raised deck above a sunken spinal road, its linear shape meaning that a significant number of dwellings would be within walking distance (Figs 4.1 and 4.2). The central area, which tightly abuts the housing areas, was contrasted in the plan with an image of an American shopping centre surrounded by a car park.

It was hoped that the positive social function of street life could be preserved through a system of elevated pedestrian walkways:

> In the 19th century town the street was still the focus of social life, where people met to talk whilst children played on the doorsteps... All public buildings and spaces, while not deprived of vehicle service, are inter-connected by the pedestrian way, which becomes a new kind of street, with life and movement, but free from the noise and danger of traffic.[46]

[45] Colin Buchanan, *Traffic in Towns, A Study of the Long Term Problems of Traffic in Urban Areas* (London, 1963), p. 167.

[46] LCC, *The Planning of a New Town*, p. 38.

Fig. 4.2. Services banished below the deck. A sense of how this space might have been experienced can be got from the decks at Bath and Essex Universities; *The Planning of a New Town,* p. 59. © London Metropolitan Archives

Such rhetoric was widespread at the time and clearly echoes the concurrent architectural experiments being carried out at Sheffield's Park Hill estate, and in Denys Lasdun's Bethnal Green cluster blocks.[47] It arguably grew out of contemporary sociological conceptions of community. The preconceptions of the planning team at Hook were summed up by one of its members, Hugh Morris, who admitted that perhaps the team had been 'unduly influenced by some rather bogus sociological chatter about new town blues and loneliness current at the time'.[48] Peter Willmott replied that since writing *Family and Kinship* he had found that New Town residents 'liked the openness and garden city character of their town', although it was reported that he himself had admitted 'with unblushing candour that he found it rather depressing'(Fig. 4.3).[49] The Hook study also cited a debt to the sociologist Ruth Glass of the Centre for Urban Studies, whose complaint in 1955 that town planning had 'paradoxically

[47] See Joe Moran, 'Imagining the Street in Post-war Britain', *Urban History*, 39 (2012), pp. 166–86; Mark Crinson, 'The Uses of Nostalgia: Stirling and Gowan's Preston Housing', *Journal of the Society of Architectural Historians*, 65.2 (2006), pp. 216–37; Jack Lynn, 'Sheffield', in *The Architect's Year Book*, IX, *The Pedestrian and the City*, ed. David Lewis (London, 1965), p. 59.

[48] 'Seminar on the planning of the project for Hook New Town', *Architectural Association Journal*, April 1962, pp. 254–60, p. 259.

[49] 'Hook Plan, Did the Team Think?' *Architects' Journal*, 7 February 1962, p. 291. For the research itself see Peter Willmott, 'Housing Density and Town Design in a New Town', *Town Planning Review*, July 1962.

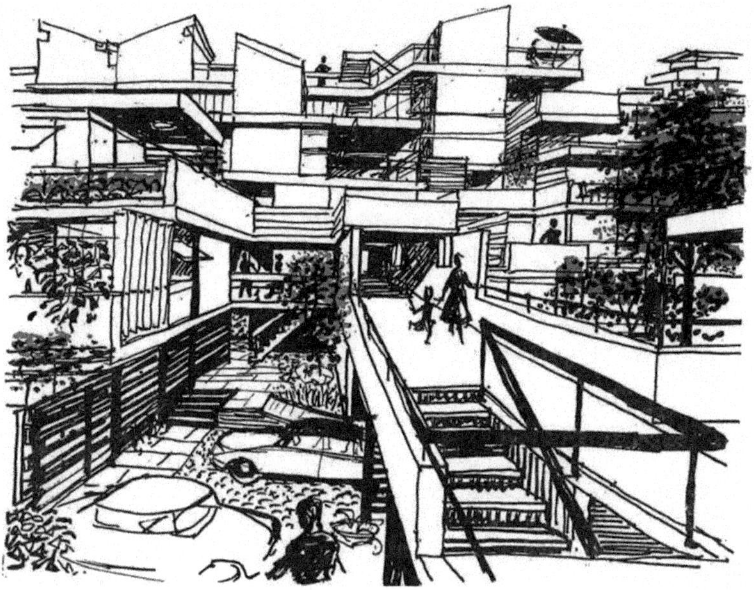

Fig. 4.3. High-density, low-rise housing at Hook, making a virtue of its warren-like, multilevel complexity; *The Planning of a New Town,* p. 46. © London Metropolitan Archives

been the field of the anti-urbanists, who try to shape the town in terms of idealized rustic images', foreshadows the concerns of Hook.[50] Shankland and Cox would have known Willmott and Glass through the Kenilworth Group.[51] Shankland would later work directly with Willmott on a plan for Lambeth.[52]

The third factor important at Hook was the need for a distinct separation between 'town and countryside': 'The town should stand out distinctly from the surrounding countryside and yet be complementary to it... [Hook] achieves a contrast between the hard built-up urban landscape of lakes, playing fields and woods which surround it. It is not so much a garden city as a city in a garden.'[53] This type of language is reminiscent of the anti-Garden City tracts of Thomas Sharp such as *Town and Countryside* (1932). The very images in the Hook plan, drawn in

[50] Ruth Glass, 'Urban Sociology in Great Britain' (1955), reprinted in *Clichés of Urban Doom and Other Essays* (Oxford, 1989), p. 39.

[51] See LMA, 'Muriel Smith Papers', LMA/4196.

[52] Graeme Shankland, Peter Willmott, and David Jordan, *Inner London: Policies for Dispersal and Balance* (London, 1977).

[53] LCC, *The Planning of a New Town*, p. 17.

Fig. 4.4. The benefit of counter-attacking subtopia; not a Garden City but a city in a garden; *The Planning of a New Town,* p. 74. © London Metropolitan Archives

green and black crayon, proclaim this ideal. The uncompromisingly harsh brutalist aesthetic of Hook's housing and town centre was seen as a concomitant of the need to produce this 'essential contrast, between the highly organized building complex of the centre and the free disposition of trees and lakes to the west of the central area'. There is a wonderful image of a couple sitting on a country hill overlooking the town, playing on a common visual motif stretching back at least as far as Ford Madox Brown's 'An English Autumn Afternoon' (1854) (Fig. 4.4). For the centre of the town, the 'danger is that small trees . . . might be used, producing a fussy and "pretty" character. This should be avoided. The pattern should essentially be one of hard surfaces.' The use of a hard aesthetic at Hook is clearly related to a brutalist reaction against the soft Festival of Britain style, but the language used to justify it is reminiscent of Ian Nairn's ideas outlined in *Outrage* (1955) and *Counter-Attack Against Subtopia* (1956), that city centres should be robust rather than polite, where the danger was of the 'reduction of vitality by false genteelism, of which Municipal Rustic is the prime agent'.[54] The images of 'compact housing' at Hook suggest the Townscape mantras of enclosure, sequences of spaces, multiple levels, and views of landscape framed by buildings.

The fourth focus was on questions of social balance, community, and 'the extension of choice through higher densities and the complexity of social patterns'.[55] The plan was prefaced by a description of the 'startling and rapid' social changes of the last ten years, from a society where there 'was a shortage of consumer goods and many items, including petrol, were rationed', to one where 'with the lure of television making itself felt observers are deploring the retreat to the home and the lack of active

[54] Ian Nairn, *Outrage* (London, 1955), p. 363.
[55] LCC, *The Planning of a New Town*, p. 41.

forms of recreation'.[56] As with the preceding New Towns, it was felt that every effort should be 'made to achieve a balance of population'.[57] In common with Cumbernauld, rather than relying on the neighbourhood unit concept of the earlier generation of New Towns, it was believed by the planners at Hook that the physical pattern of the city, especially through its density, would stimulate community:

> Patterns of social relationships are not simply determined by the planned relationships of buildings or the spaces between them. They can, however, be deeply influenced by them for better or for worse as studies by William Whyte [American urbanist, author of *The Organization Man* (1956)] and others have shown. The pattern of social relationships, neither simple, static nor closely predictable, may indeed be influenced by density . . . It is also an idea that does not imply the imposition of over-simplified abstract planning concepts, such as the neighbourhood units, onto the complex, rich and concrete patterns of social life. In beginning to evolve forms related to this idea, the Hook plan represents an attempt to retain some of the assets of urban life lost in the garden cities.[58]

Hook is the manifestation of a social and political vision. Although we might point to the influence of Vällingby, the pronouncements of the Hook team show them to have engaged far more with ideas about the changing face of society than with modernist architectural culture. Reyner Banham later saw Hook as a pioneering example of the international avant-garde concept of a megastructure, the idea of building the multiple functions of a city into one vast structure, writing that there 'is a real megastructural boldness and, indeed, bloody-mindedness about the Hook scheme'.[59] However, the plan is presented in a way devoid of the kind of futurism one would expect of an avant-garde document. Rather, it is grounded in traditional social and political questions.[60] Banham could not understand how Britain, 'a nation of earnest grey functionaries designing socially responsible architecture for the people', as he disparagingly described it, could have conceived such 'visionary architecture' as Hook. It is more explicable if we see Hook's ostensible avant-gardism as the product of its social responsibility rather than as a self-conscious attempt at trendy futurism.

[56] LCC, *The Planning of a New Town*, p. 16.

[57] LCC, *The Planning of a New Town*, p. 17.

[58] LCC, *The Planning of a New Town*, p. 41. On Whyte's advocacy for cities over suburbs see Becky Nicolaides, 'How hell moved from the city to the suburbs', in *New Suburban History*, ed. Kevin M. Kruse and Thomas J. Sugrue (Chicago, 2006).

[59] Reyner Banham, *Megastructure, Urban Futures of the Recent Past* (London, 1976), p. 73.

[60] In this it resembles Fred Pooley's North Bucks New Town, another unbuilt New Town of the period. See Ortolano, 'Planning the Urban Future in 1960s Britain'.

LIVERPOOL

Shankland would bring many of the concepts and approaches that had been developed at Hook to bear on two Lancashire city-centre projects, first in Liverpool and later in Bolton. These two plans would further engage with an idealized vision of a richly social and distinctly urban life, and would use radical planning in a way that attempted to address the social dynamics of a changing Britain.

Shankland was launched into the vortex of city-centre redevelopment when in 1962 he was hired as Planning Consultant for Liverpool's central area, within the context of the Planning Officer Walter Bor's larger scheme (Fig. 4.5). Shankland and Bor were commissioned on the advice of a panel including Sir William Holford (then teaching in London, but formerly of Liverpool), Myles Wright, and Robert Gardner-Medwin (both at Liverpool University). This panel had been set up when the council was Conservative-run in a bid to encourage private-sector investment, but was retained when Labour took hold of the authority in 1963.[61] Between 1962 and 1964 Shankland's team produced eleven planning documents (the last three in association with Bor), dealing with individual features of the plan.[62]

In 1963 Peter Hall was already praising Shankland's plan of September 1962 for the St John's Precinct, suggesting that it showed a 'sophistication of the principle' of vertical segregation.[63] It was boasted of the plan that if 'realised this would be one of the largest pedestrian precincts outside of Venice'.[64] In 1965 the work coalesced in two published plans, one dealing with the inner area by Shankland's team, and another outlining general principles for the whole city by Bor. Even the often-sceptical Ian Nairn was swept up in the feeling of excitement generated by these plans:

> Modern architecture has a fighting chance, with Graeme Shankland as planning consultant and Walter Bor as city planning officer. The results could still be terrible, but at least the opportunity is there. And the city itself seems to have wakened out of a drugged sleep. Everyone knows about the

[61] The Labour council under John Braddock was in fact far less amenable to Shankland than its Tory predecessor, although this changed when Labour councillor Bill Sefton took charge. See Francis J. C. Amos, 'Liverpool', in *City Centre Redevelopment*, ed. John Holliday (London, 1973), pp.175–206, p. 182 , and Eric Heffer, *Never a Yes Man* (London, 1991), p. 105.

[62] Planner John Collins, architect David Gregory-Jones, surveyor Desmond Searle, and traffic engineer Alan Proudlove.

[63] Peter Hall, *London 2000* (London, 1963), p. 167.

[64] Quentin Hughes, *Seaport, Architecture and Townscape in Liverpool* (London, 1964), p. 86.

Fig. 4.5. The Liverpool model's megastructural scale relates to the Three Graces; *Liverpool, City Centre Plan*, cover. © Liverpool County Council

> Mersey Beat, but this could not have been so successful if it had not been a symptom, drawing its vitality from some common resurgence.[65]

Shankland's rhetoric at Liverpool echoes the foundational belief behind the political planning philosophy of the early 1960s that continuous economic growth would provide the basis for uninterrupted social progress. The optimism was self-consciously purposive at Liverpool, and was part of a campaign to achieve what Shankland saw as his 'first job': 'banishing this "smell of defeat"' caused by forty years of economic decline.[66] The plans for central Liverpool were presented by Bill Sefton, when Labour leader of Liverpool Council, as political propaganda for a programme of increasing prosperity:

> All this process of renewal and rehabilitation must take into consideration new factors such as mobility, increased leisure and greater prosperity. New standards of amenity must be accepted for all, and a new environment must be created, in which it will be easy to live a full, healthy and happy life.[67]

The mood of Shankland's plan for the inner area approached euphoria, citing how, though,

> Liverpool has long been familiar to the world as a great seaport . . . since the appearance of the Beatles record *Love Me Do* in the autumn of 1962, the Mersey Sound has flooded the hit parade . . . It is qualities such as these and the football achievements of Liverpool and Everton that regularly hit the headlines in recent years and they form an important part of the mystique that attracts people to the city.

The plan was based upon eulogistically optimistic predictions of a steadily improving future of growing affluence: 'a 20% growth in population by 1981 that looks forward to increasing prosperity . . . People will have more free time. The population of the city region is expected to increase by 400,000 people by 1981. Rising incomes will give most people greater spending power and the growth of education could well lead to increases in intellectual and artistic pursuits.'[68] The city would have to adapt to these changes. In its economic optimism, Liverpool's reconstruction can be seen as part of a 1960s planning moment which relied on the presumed continuation of an economic golden age.[69] Such rhetoric was commonly

[65] Ian Nairn, 'Liverpool: World City', *The Listener*, 11 June 1964, p. 949.
[66] Graeme Shankland, 'Renaissance of a City', *Journal of the Town Planning Institute*, January 1965, pp. 20–32, p. 20.
[67] W. H. Sefton, *Liverpool Interim Planning Policy, Statement* (March 1965), p. 9.
[68] Shankland, *Liverpool City Centre Plan*, p. 30.
[69] See Glen O'Hara, *From Dreams to Disillusionment: Economic and Social Planning in 1960s Britain* (London, 2006), pp. 206–8.

deployed by planners and by politicians on the Left, keen to shape this increased leisure time.[70]

Throughout the 1950s, the Ministry of Housing and Local Government had 'been constantly pressing on Liverpool the need to do something adequate and really saying that in the past they have not measured up to their opportunities'.[71] Liverpool had not seen any significant development since the war. 'For 20 years', *The Times* commented, 'the centre of Liverpool has been like the belly of some mangy stuffed animal in a Victorian museum. Great bald patches caused by bombing serve as temporary car parks; beyond the centre the slums stretch away....'[72] Rapid social changes were felt to make a new type of approach towards town planning necessary. Liverpool's last Development Plan had only been approved in 1958, but it was felt that it 'no longer reflects the accelerating rate of change, the growing complexity of modern life or the mounting impact of the motor car. The Buchanan Report has proved conclusively the obsolescence of these Plans.'[73] Shankland believed that *Traffic in Towns* represented a pivotal moment in post-war town planning:

> Looking back over twenty years there is no doubt in my mind that the Buchanan report *Traffic in Towns*, must be seen as a watershed, and one of the key events which distinguish the planning of the nineteen-sixties from both the forties and the fifties. It was a historic event because it embodied not merely the ideas of one team but so much of the new thinking on urban problems, in a way which threw a flood of light on the real nature of the battle for the environment. In fact it is just this idea of putting the environment first—of forcing us to make up our minds about the kind of place we want—that is the key idea.[74]

According to Shankland, 'The essence of Liverpool's problems today stem from the fact that the essential fabric of the City dates from a hundred

[70] Wilfred Burns, *Newcastle-Upon-Tyne Development Plan Review* (1963), p. 23; Buchanan, *Traffic in Towns*, p. 43.

[71] TNA, Letter signed F. H. Littler, 21 March 1962, 'Inner Ring Road Redevelopment Proposals', HLG79/1288.

[72] 'Liverpool Tries to Catch Up 20 Years', *The Times*, 6 April 1963, p. 9. See also Joseph Minogue, 'Grappling with Liverpool's Slums', *The Guardian*, 2 April 1962, p. 8.

[73] *Liverpool Interim Planning Policy, Statement*, p. 10. This copy was consulted in the collection of the Martin Centre for Architectural and Urban Studies at the University of Cambridge.

[74] Shankland, 'British Towns and Cities', p. 891. Though the Buchanan Report, which suggested ways to mitigate the damage done to urban environments by growing motor-car usage, was released under the aegis of the Conservative Party, transport issues, especially inner-city congestion, had exploded into the political consciousness of both Left and Right during the early 1960s. See 'Socialists and Transport', special edition of *Socialist Commentary*, April 1963; and *'A New Britain' Labour Party Manifesto 1964*.

years ago.'[75] His plan would be based on extensive urban renewal and the implementation of radical forms to create pedestrian oases while allowing for increased traffic flow:

> Liverpool's vast urban renewal programme, coupled with the city's extensive land ownership, provides the unique opportunity to incorporate most of the Buchanan principles into the redevelopment: the comprehensive reshaping of the city can now be based upon the most recent techniques of integrated traffic/ land use planning and the most advanced design ideas in traffic architecture and urban redevelopment.

The report posed the question of redevelopment in terms of reinvesting in urban life in the face of suburbanization. It asked the question: 'Will not the continued spread of cities, the growing use of cars and the crisis in public transport make central areas too inaccessible in the future to be worth renewing?' Shankland denied the suburban answer emphatically:

> Renewal at the centre is vital, and has a special claim above the claims of all other parts of the city. The city centre is the public home of the community, a place worth coming to, a daily meeting place, and a place to receive guests; a place, too, where a wide range of people are encouraged to live; one designed for great civic occasions, for personal recreation, fun and adventure.[76]

It was hoped that the plan would repopulate the centre: 'Bringing people back to live in the central area is another cause to which much energy must be applied. Many people would enjoy true urban living, which a central area could provide.'[77] The separation of pedestrian and vehicular circulation was also a priority through vertical and horizontal segregation. This would mean that 'comprehensive development should be regarded as the rule rather than the exception'.

The plan included an inner city motorway loop, six lanes wide and often elevated, circling a 500-acre (202-hectare) area (Fig. 4.6). It was conceived in a lyrical spirit:

> The gentle curves and generous radii needed to secure regular traffic flow impose a sinuous pattern of a highly new order on the traditional small scale texture of streets and buildings... The motorway becomes an architectural object of great significance in its own right, particularly if it is elevated.[78]

[75] Shankland, *Liverpool City Centre Plan*, p. 55.

[76] Graeme Shankland 'The Central Area of Liverpool: Extracts from the Report on the Draft City Centre Map', *Town Planning Review*, 35.2 (July 1964), p. 117.

[77] Shankland 'The Central Area of Liverpool', p. 122.

[78] *Planning Consultant's Report No. 7, Inner Motorway System* (December 1962). A copy was consulted in the collection of the Martin Centre for Architectural and Urban Studies at the University of Cambridge.

Fig. 4.6. The 'gentle curves' of the Liverpool motorway in the model. © Liverpool County Council

It was felt that, if produced carefully, a 'modern urban motorway can be an object of beauty and magnificence in itself. The views from it can reveal the city in quite a new way.'[79] The motorway superseded an earlier scheme for a much tighter inner ring road, which had been prepared by W. S. Atkins and Partners as consulting engineers. The Royal Fine Art Commission had been instrumental in warning of the 'disastrous' effect that this earlier ring road would have on the inner city.[80] It was common not to appreciate the visual and environmental damage caused by inner-city motorways, but rather to see raised motorways cutting around the inner area of a city as a visual asset, under which urban life could continue.[81] Cullen's drawing of people happily promenading under the road, as if it was some kind of arcade, shows an astonishing lack of imaginative foresight as to how these spaces would be experienced (Fig. 4.7).

Each of the schemes for four redeveloped areas (the St John's Precinct, two comprehensive development areas around Moorfields and Paradise Street, and a vast Civic Centre) was infected by a grandiosity of intention, containing multiple functions set over many acres within a densely planned single megastructure (a term not used by Shankland) (Fig. 4.8). The planning ideas pioneered in Geoffrey Copcutt's multifunctional Cumbernauld Town Centre were in essence applied to an existing city context.[82] The Liverpool plan's gigantism is remarkable. Take, for example, the new central residential community in the Paradise Street area, a Merseyside Barbican on 19.7 acres (8 hectares) (of which 6.5 acres [2.6 hectares] were reserved for a new park), which would contain within a single megastructural superblock a bus station, a shopping centre (with sixty shops, two large stores, and one supermarket), pubs and restaurants, an entertainment centre with a cinema, and car parking for 2,500 cars. It was envisaged that the roof level would be regained with a pedestrian precinct, 'an environment completely free, dedicated to the pedestrian and eminently suited to housing'. Out of this superblock, therefore, would rise five twenty-storey point-blocks, containing housing for 600–800 dwellings, accommodating between 1,300 and 1,750 people—making a

[79] *Planning Consultant's Report No. 7*.

[80] TNA, Inner Ring Road Redevelopment Proposals, HLG79/1288.

[81] See Paul Ritter, *Planning for Man and Motor* (Oxford, 1963), p. 161; Konrad Smigielski, *Leicester Traffic Plan* (1964); Wilfred Burns, *Newcastle, a Study in Replanning at Newcastle Upon Tyne* (London, 1967), p. 25; Scott, Wilson, Fitzpatrick, and Partners, *Report on a Highway Plan for Glasgow* (Glasgow, 1965), p. 65.

[82] See John R. Gold, 'The Making of a Megastructure: Architectural Modernism, Town Planning and Cumbernauld's Central Area, 1955-75', *Planning Perspectives*, 21.2 (April 2006), pp. 109–31.

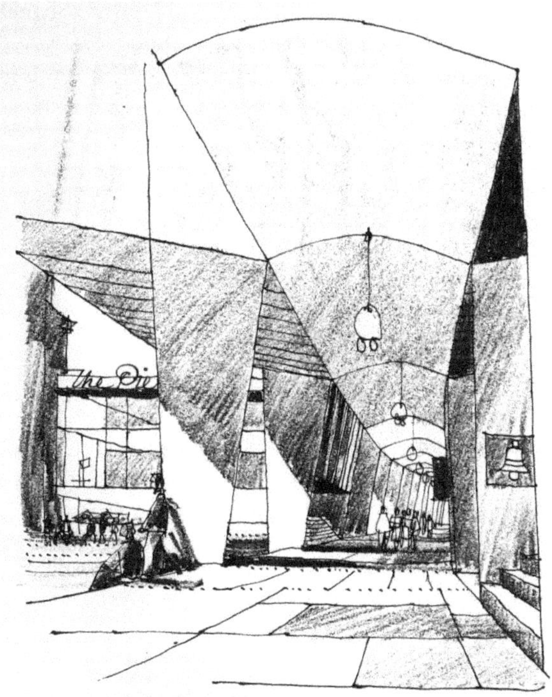

Fig. 4.7. Gordon Cullen's drawing of the underside of the motorway; Walter Bor, 'A Question of Urban Identity', in *Planning and Architecture*, ed. Dennis Sharp (London, 1967). © Gordon Cullen Estate/University of Westminster Archive

Fig. 4.8. Drawing of the Liverpool plan. © RIBA

density of 75–100 persons per acre over the whole site.[83] Shankland cited both the Barbican and Sheffield's Park Hill as influences.[84]

The plan for a new Civic Centre is similarly gigantic. It was hoped that it would be 'a major step towards the integration of the various functions of the central area into a single idea . . . a place in which to live, work, shop, and play'.[85]

> To achieve this objective the Civic Centre area should not be the exclusive reserve of municipal functions but be so designed to incorporate where suitable the livelier uses of the central area including, among others, cultural and entertainment facilities, shopping, an hotel, flats, a swimming pool, licensed premises, restaurants and cafes.[86]

Colin St John Wilson was hired to design the Civic Centre, proposing a £16.6 million scheme with a pinwheel plan (1965–9). A further, simplified project was prepared in 1970, but it was eventually abandoned altogether in 1973.[87] The experience of hiring an architect with artistic ambitions for an important scheme, but failing to bring it to fruition, was a common experience in provincial cities in this period: for example, little came of Leicester's hiring of Chamberlin, Powell, and Bon, or Newcastle's appointment of Arne Jacobsen. Architects of this calibre rarely had the opportunity to build in British city centres. The one megastructure in Shankland's plan for Liverpool that was built was realized by the commercial architect James A. Roberts for the ubiquitous Ravenseft Properties. This was the St John's Precinct: an uninspiring, little-loved, and now post-modernized shopping centre which creates a landmark of sorts with its spindly space-age tower (apparently based on Rotterdam's Euromast) topped by a now defunct revolving restaurant. As Joseph Sharples has described it, 'its introverted bulk not only erased Foster's 1820–22 market hall and the surrounding street pattern, but also injured the setting of St George's Hall'.[88]

The visionary quality of Shankland's planning was tempered by the involvement of Gordon Cullen. Shankland wrote of Cullen: 'Like any artist and all good urban designers, Cullen has two sides to his nature: the objective descriptive analyst of the power and magic of a place and the

[83] *Liverpool Planning Consultant's report, No. 8* ([Liverpool,] March 1963). A copy was consulted in the collection of the Martin Centre for Architectural and Urban Studies at the University of Cambridge.
[84] *Liverpool Planning Consultant's Report, No. 10* (November 1963).
[85] *Liverpool Planning Consultant's report, No. 8*, p. 14.
[86] *Liverpool Planning Consultant's report, No. 8*, p. 14.
[87] Roger Stonehouse, *Colin St John Wilson, Buildings and Projects* (London, 2007), pp. 402–25.
[88] Joseph Sharples, *Liverpool* (London and New Haven, 2004), p. 36.

personal visionary of its future.' He estimated that the planning team had directly incorporated around a third of Cullen's suggestions.[89] In line with Townscape thought, it was hoped that the segregation of systems of circulation would result in the *enclosed* forms of the traditional city, creating an amalgamation of radical means of traffic segregation and traditional urban patterns that closely resembled the advice of *Traffic in Towns*:

> The controlled relationship of all the various forms of space enclosed by buildings or containing buildings. Alleys, squares, corridor streets, riverside promenades, parks, gardens, formal paved spaces, arcades and roof gardens; this immense variety of spaces, intimate or grand, should be designed and woven together to make the fabric of this network.'[90]

Despite the vast areas of central Liverpool that were characterized as 'areas of obsolescence', which according to the planners 'must go', Shankland's approach to conservation was not as unambiguously brutal as might at first be expected.[91] Dr Quentin Hughes was brought in to advise which buildings ought to be preserved, and his recommendations became official policy in 1967. Hughes was an architect and architectural historian based at Liverpool University, whose obituaries rightly champion his book *Seaport* (1964) as 'postulating the then-unthinkable idea that Liverpool's Victorian architecture was the 19th-century equivalent of Florence's Renaissance heritage and must be preserved. It was highly influential in starting a wider national trend to counter 1960s architectural brutalism.'[92] Shankland wrote the introduction to *Seaport*, in which he stated that, 'From the start our plans for the new centre have been devised to allow the best to be kept and where possible provide a better setting for them.'[93] Shankland's approach to conservation was typical for the time, in that he saw himself as having a more preservationist ethic than earlier planners. He lamented the loss of the Bank Chambers in Cook Street, demolished in 1959 by the Bank of England, and Thomas Henry Wyatt's quadrangle, writing with apparent sensitivity that a 'city's heritage of fine buildings is, with its topography, what distinguishes it from another. Losses of this kind not only represent the loss of a loved member of the local architectural family, but they diminish the impact of the city's collective personality and its stature as a member of the family of the world's great cities.'[94]

[89] Gordon Cullen, 'Townscape: A Liverpool Notebook', *The Architectural Review,* April 1965, pp. 281–8, p. 281.

[90] Shankland, 'The Central Area of Liverpool', pp. 105–32, pp. 129–30.

[91] Shankland, *Liverpool City Centre Plan,* p. 53.

[92] Peter Elson, 'Quentin Hughes: Obituary', *The Guardian,* 17 May 2004.

[93] Hughes, *Seaport,* p. viii. [94] Hughes, *Seaport,* p. vii.

The Sunday Times picked up on the deep love for Liverpool shown by Shankland's team, reporting a breathless exchange: 'It's better than Venice . . . Take the floorscape of St George's Hall . . . the drama of the waterfront . . . the lights on the river at night.'[95] This period saw a reappraisal of the Victorian era, from the foundation of the Victorian Society in 1958 to the publication of Asa Briggs's *Victorian Cities* in 1963, a book that presented a more sympathetic view of Victorian cities in declared opposition to Lewis Mumford.[96] Shankland was at the initial meeting of the Victorian Society in 1958, although he later withdrew for fear that it would prove a threat to the William Morris Society.[97] He had been lecturing students on nineteenth-century architecture at the Architectural Association since 1957.[98] What Shankland was unable to see was that some of the more mundane fabric of the Victorian city, had it been rehabilitated, might have become valued: 'sentimentality is the enemy of understanding; Liverpool's chief inheritance from its nineteenth century is the biggest slum problem in England. Buildings have no merit because they are old or familiar.'[99] These types of buildings still had too heavy resonances. A total of 33,000 dwellings, a third of those in the inner city, were demolished by 1972, causing major social problems.[100]

A 'High Buildings Policy' was written, which noted that the 'international identity of Liverpool is inseparably linked with the views of the City from the river'.[101] Within sensitive areas, 'no high buildings will be permitted to mar important views or destroy the dominance of the landmarks', such as the Royal Liver Building and the two cathedrals.[102] In what today can be seen as prescient, Shankland seemed to predict Liverpool's future as a UNESCO World Heritage Site and tourist destination: 'Foreign visitors do not yet see Liverpool as one of Britain's main tourist attractions, the next ten years can change this. When they do come they ought to see not just what is shown [in *Seaport*] but the combined and more poignant power of the new seen and designed together with the

95 'Vision on the Mersey', *The Sunday Times*, 12 May 1963, p. 6.

96 Asa Briggs, *Victorian Cities* (London, 1963), discusses in the introduction the problems caused by traffic on the twentieth-century city as being analogous to the problems faced by congestion and disease in the nineteenth-century city. Shankland would have known Briggs through their authorship of the introductions to *William Morris: selected writings and designs* (London, 1962).

97 William Whyte, 'Founders of the Victorian Society', *Oxford Dictionary of National Biography* (2016).

98 *Universities and Left Review*, spring 1957, p. 1.

99 Hughes, *Seaport*, p. vii.

100 Hugh Wilson and Lewis Womersley, *Change or Decay: Final Report of the Liverpool Inner Area Study* (London, 1977), p. 136.

101 Liverpool Planning Department, *High Buildings Policy* (Liverpool, 1965), p. 35.

102 *High Buildings Policy*, 51.

best of the old.'[103] Shankland wrote of his 'plan for prosperity' that 'wider social and cultural objectives, concerned with the quality of life a great city should be able to offer are here put first because they are objects of vital importance but most difficult to measure and quantify and therefore too often forgotten"[104] In what appears prophetic of later arguments about the role of culture in regeneration, Shankland suggested that:

> At one end of the musical spectrum is the Philharmonic Hall and its magnificent orchestra, at the other the spectacular growth of Liverpool as the centre of popular music. A world famous Art Gallery and Library, two theatres, cinemas, the Bluecoat Arts Centre and above all the University and all it can offer, directly and indirectly are assets of incalculable value which form the nucleus of a very strong cultural and social centre.[105]

All of this, of course, reflects the influence of William Morris, but it is also strongly reminiscent of the types of arguments happening on the political Left at the time, expressed not least in Crosland's *The Future of Socialism,* about the increasing need in an affluent society for socialists to turn their attention to questions of the culture and the physical environment[106] (Fig. 4.9). As a Labour Party policy document put it, 'the emphasis will increasingly be not on jobs for all but leisure for all—leisure *and how to use it*'.[107]

The travails experienced by Shankland's plans for Liverpool are too large a subject to do justice to here.[108] The motorway achieved central-government backing in 1965, but only parts were completed. It soon became apparent that financial optimism had been spectacularly misplaced. Areas of dereliction were as often the occasion for Shankland's attention as were caused by it. Nevertheless, with very little of the plan realized, and what was built by private capital being shoddy, the Liberal Party took power of Liverpool Council in 1973 on a wave of resentment

[103] Graeme Shankland, 'Introduction', in Hughes, *Seaport*, p. viii.

[104] Graeme Shankland, *Planning Consultant's Report 10,* November 1963. See also Walter Bor, 'A question of urban identity' in *Planning and Architecture,* ed. Dennis Sharp (London, 1967), p. 28.

[105] *Planning Consultant's Report 10,* p. 30. Franco Bianchini and Michael Parkinson (eds.), *Cultural Policy and Urban Regeneration: The Western European Experience* (Manchester, 1993).

[106] Crosland, *The Future of Socialism,* p. 526. The discourse was foreshadowed by John Maynard Keynes, 'Economic Possibilities of our Grandchildren' (1930), *The Collected Writings, 9: Essays in Persuasion* (London, 1972), p. 328.

[107] Labour Party, *Leisure for Living* (London, 1959).

[108] See Chris Couch, *City of Change and Challenge: Urban Planning and Regeneration in Liverpool* (London, 2003), p. 16; and Peter Shapely 'The Entrepreneurial City: The Role of Local Government and City-Centre Redevelopment in Post-War Industrial English Cities', *Twentieth Century British History*, 22.4 (2011), pp. 498–520.

Fig. 4.9. Liverpool's central entertainment district, including a poster of a man with a Beatles moptop; *Liverpool, City Centre Plan,* p. 67. © Gordon Cullen Estate/University of Westminster Archive

over planning blight.[109] Tony Lane's observations of 1978 stress the huge divergence between the excitement of the 1960s and their results:

> The Brave New Liverpool of the 1960s was a five-year flash of public relations promotion. 'Liverpool—City of Change and Challenge' was the slogan handed down from the Town Hall. Here was a city to rival T. Dan Smith's Newcastle, a bustling, thriving, energetic city. A city that matched the immensity of its problems with a determination to eliminate them. Clear the damp, decrepit and infested housing, put an end to overcrowding with an ambitious clearance programme; speed the traffic to the new grain and container terminal in the north docks with a new inner motorway… sandblast the leavings of soot and pigeon off the old buildings; get rid of the old market hall and replace it with a shopping precinct. Scaffolding, the bulldozer, the tower crane and the ready-mix wagon, that was the Liverpool of the mid to late 60s: a frenzy of pulling down and putting up. The collapse of the property and building boom in 1973–74 was closely followed by cuts in public expenditure. The result for Liverpool, where major 'redevelopment' started later than elsewhere, was a trail of cleared sites of grassed-over rubble. Liverpool was left with the largest

[109] Lionel Brett, *The Broken Wave, the Rebuilding of England* (London, 1981), pp. 236–8; Eric Heffer, 'Planning and Politics: The Liverpool Example', *The Spectator*, 27 July 1973, p. 8. See also Heffer, *Never a Yes Man*, p. 105.

> amount of 'open-space' of any city in Britain. The decline of Liverpool is not simply statistical—it is visible. 'It looks as if it's been bombed' is a favourite local expression that does not exaggerate.[110]

The level of human suffering these failures caused was immense.[111]

BOLTON

In the north-west of England, the proximity of cities meant that redevelopment was spurred on by a feeling of competitiveness, with one councillor stating that: 'We are determined not to lag behind in the race for central redevelopment.'[112] The publicity garnered by Liverpool's plan meant, for example, that neighbouring Manchester was castigated by local businessmen for failing to produce any agreed comprehensive plan for the redevelopment of its centre, 'which just made one shudder'—especially when compared with the 'excellent city-centre redevelopment scheme' in Liverpool.[113] It was in this local context that Bolton selected Shankland as planner in 1964. As with other mill towns, such as Blackburn and Bradford, Bolton's central-area scheme was seen as part of a response to the massive contraction of the textiles industry, by giving the town a dynamic new image in the hope of attracting private investment and establishing a new economic role. Shankland was commissioned when Labour were in charge of the council, but was retained after the Tories took power.[114]

Especially when seen in the context of the sweeping plans for neighbouring Lancashire mill towns, Shankland approached Bolton with remarkable sensitivity. Shortly after his appointment, he told *The Guardian* that he appreciated Bolton's character:

> I must say that my impression of Bolton is that it is a far more interesting and nice place than one is led to believe. It has a lot of character, which is most marked, and which is very interesting. One isn't working from nothing. With a town with such a distinct personality you should try to preserve its character.[115]

[110] Tony Lane, 'Liverpool –City of Harder Times to Come', *Marxism Today,* 22 (November 1978), pp. 336–7.

[111] Wilson and Womersley, *Change or Decay*.

[112] Josephine P. Reynolds, 'Shopping in the North-West' *Town Planning Review,* 34.3 (October 1963), pp. 213–36.

[113] 'Manmade hell' in South Lancashire', *The Guardian,* 9 January 1964, p. 4.

[114] *Bolton Journal and Guardian*, 28 May 1965, p.1.

[115] 'Mr Graeme Shankland may plan for Bolton next', *The Guardian*, 4 February 1964, p. 4.

This was notably more sensitive than the views expressed by Bolton's own mayor, Harry Lucas, who stated, 'We must all face the facts that these dirty worn-out Lancashire towns have no future in their present form.'[116] The chairman of the Bolton Historical Association felt the 'plan would help to get rid of a false notion that industrial towns were second grade communities'. Ian Nairn argued that the commissioning of Shankland was 'a far-sighted thing to do, and in reward, Bolton has a lucid and practical master plan.'[117]

The town plan was presented in two phases, with the first *Bolton Draft Town Centre Map* by Graeme Shankland Associates appearing in 1964, and the second report coming a year later, this time credited to Shankland Cox. This split publication was to provide the opportunity for community engagement: 'The main reason for planning the work in two stages was to encourage the widest discussion of the proposals and the plan whilst the plan was still in draft form . . . above all from the people of Bolton.'[118] As *The Guardian* reported, there was a genuine (and for the time fairly unusual) attempt at community involvement:

> One thousand boys and girls have started work on a series of surveys to help Mr Graeme Shankland to draw up his plan for the centre of Bolton. They came from 25 schools. Yesterday teams of them began interviewing 2,400 pedestrians in the main streets about their shopping habits; and what they learn will be added to the results of other surveys of factories, offices and suburban shops.[119]

There was also a public meeting in Bolton Town Hall attended by 600 people, in which 'Mr Shankland said . . . that unless care was taken all the towns in the country would look the same in 20 years. The plan for Bolton, however, would certainly not make it resemble other towns. It would keep its character.' He also declared that he was 'less interested in producing an original plan than a good one'.[120] Nairn appreciated that 'from the tone of the present report, comments will be really welcome; this is a true attempt to interpret the town, not an autocratic imposition by the experts in London.'[121] None of this has stopped Shankland's plans for Bolton being criticized for having 'rarely involved meaningful consultation with townspeople'.[122]

[116] 'Plan: A Kiss of Life', *The Guardian,* 10 December 1964, p. 6.
[117] Ian Nairn, 'Urban Heart Surgery', *The Observer,* 7 February 1965, p. 30.
[118] Graeme Shankland Associates, *Bolton Draft Town Centre Map* ([Bolton,] 1964), p. 1.
[119] 'Schoolchildren are Helping to Plan the Town of the Future', *The Guardian,* 15 July 1964.
[120] 'Planning a Town with Character', *The Guardian,* 16 December 1964, p. 10.
[121] Nairn, 'Urban Heart Surgery'.
[122] Kevin Murray Associates, *Bolton, Local Distinctiveness Study* (Bolton, 2006).

Although car ownership in Bolton was only 70 per cent of the national average in 1964, the plan was formulated to make Bolton attractive as a shopping centre in the face of the growth of automobile use and the attendant choice offered to consumers.[123] Bolton needed to be competitive compared to the other town centres of the area, especially Manchester: 'With mobility offered by the car, town centres have to compete for shoppers.' The management of traffic was to be a central element of the plan, creating 'pedestrian precincts and squares, partly covered, in the core of the centre for safety, convenience and pleasure'.[124] This was proposed in a romantic vein, offering a sanctuary from the pollution and noise of motor-car usage in which the traditional sensations of the city would become appreciable: 'The noise of bells, band music, running water, and the buzz of human activity are all attractive and essential to a successful town centre. They should be heard and not drowned out by the roar of traffic.'[125] The report noted that there had been 184 accidents involving pedestrians and traffic during the previous three years, so that 'shopping in Bolton is needlessly dangerous'.[126] There would be elements of vertical segregation around Bridge Street, but segregation would mostly be achieved through the implementation of a pedestrian precinct, with shops being serviced from roads behind. A bus route would circle the area.

The plan was based on the idea of visually uniting three of the town's High Victorian architectural focal points, the parish church, Market Hall, and Town Hall, none of which was then on the statutory list of buildings worth preserving. 'Bolton is fortunate to have a number of fine buildings, to act as focal points, even though they do so at present in isolation. Together with the topographical features these must all be exploited.'[127] By the time of the second plan in 1965, the Flaxman chimney was also preserved as a 'fixed point' landmark, and also to provide 'historical continuity' with a Victorian industrial past. Shankland commented to *The Guardian*, 'As such chimneys become fewer, they will become clearer as landmarks and may even be regarded with sentiment as relics of another age.... The Flaxman chimney must be adapted to become the symbol of a new Bolton and not something just left over from another age.'[128] It would be important to open up vistas, so that these landmarks were visible from as many places as possible: 'it must be ensured that all these

123 *Bolton Draft Town Centre Map*, p. 22.

124 Shankland, Cox, and Associates, *Bolton Town Centre Map* ([Bolton,]1965), p. 61.

125 *Bolton Draft Town Centre Map*, p. 45.

126 *Bolton Draft Town Centre Map*, p. 22.

127 *Bolton Draft Town Centre Map*, p. 27.

128 'Mill Chimney as Symbol of the New Bolton in £20m Plan', *The Guardian*, 5 August 1965, p. 4.

landmarks can be seen from the maximum number of places in the town centre as possible. No view of a landmark should be lost through lack of care or foresight. In any of the spaces in the centre, a pedestrian should be aware of one landmark, and preferably two, giving a succession of "fixes" on his position as he moves about it.'[129] Other historical reminders were also to be placed throughout the town by 'siting in the precinct museum pieces of local origin: historic mill machinery, a tram, and the two cast-iron elephants from Chorley Street indicating Bolton's first link with Coventry'.[130]

There is also a notable Townscape element: the 'spaces in between the buildings are as important as the buildings themselves'.[131] Shankland suggested that 'No detail of the town centre is too small to warrant attention. Signs, fascias, pavings, light fittings, all these meet the eye first and set the tone of the whole town centre.'[132] Gordon Cullen again provided visual analysis, as well as beautiful illustrations.[133] They are among his most seductive. Where many of the images in the Liverpool plan had highlighted the monumental quality of the modern insertions, those of Bolton are remarkably genteel. The city's grand civic architecture is foregrounded and presented as an ensemble, while the modern insertions are politely retiring. The inhabitants mirror their elegant surroundings, and there are no cloth caps or other symbols of working class 'northernness' to be seen (Figs 4.10 and 4.11).

Three areas of comprehensive development were proposed, though Shankland stressed that Bolton did 'not require redevelopment in the town centre to a scale and size that means the demolition and rebuilding of very large segments of the centre'.[134] It was advised that in Mawdsley Street, where there was 'considerable pressure to redevelop', the 'character should not be wantonly and carelessly destroyed: some parts of it should certainly be preserved and if, in time, most of it is rebuilt, then the new Mawdsley Street should be better than the old and its character perpetuated'.[135] As far as heights were concerned, 'The Town Hall would continue to dominate the centre, and from the town park a view of the distant hills remain inviolate.'[136]

The first two phases of Shankland's plan for Bolton were largely completed, despite the fact that the economic growth rate presumed in

[129] *Bolton Town Centre Map*, p. 28.
[130] *Bolton Town Centre Map*, p. 32.
[131] *Bolton Draft Town Centre Map*, p. 28.
[132] *Bolton Draft Town Centre Map*, p. 73.
[133] *Bolton Draft Town Centre Map*, p. 78.
[134] *Bolton Draft Town Centre Map*, p. 31.
[135] *Bolton Draft Town Centre Map*, p. 33.
[136] *Bolton Draft Town Centre Map*, p. 33.

Fig. 4.10. Gordon Cullen's Bolton images emphasize the genteel. Old buildings dominate, while the new, though unashamedly modern, are retiring; *Bolton Town Centre Map*, p. 42. © Shankland Cox © Gordon Cullen Estate/University of Westminster Archive

1965 failed to materialize. In 1973 it was judged that the 'implementation of the proposals to-date has undoubtedly increased the pleasantness of the town', although it was admitted that the 'standard of the newer commercial buildings is open to criticism'.[137] Nairn returned to Bolton in 1975, and found that the 'whole square had changed completely in the last ten years. There used to be a road across the front: now it is all pedestrian as is the fashion, but, in this case, the fashion works. There are lots of seats, and

[137] R. H. Ogden, *Town Centre Map Review* ([Bolton,] 1973).

Fig. 4.11. Another image from the *Bolton Town Centre Map*, p. 36. © Gordon Cullen Estate/University of Westminster Archive

the seats are tough and durable and they are well sat on'.[138] While the 1960s additions to Bolton may be no Cullen watercolour, the impression gained today is that they are far more successful than those in most other British cities, especially those in other neighbouring mill towns. Access roads behind the precinct are, as normal, extremely depressing, but the square in front of the town hall is a magnificent set piece. The architectural additions are stone-faced and, at their worst, banal rather than brutish, and they do not impinge on the older architecture, while the Octagon Theatre realizes some of Shankland's cultural ambitions.

[138] Ian Nairn, 'The Towns Behind the Teams', *The Listener*, 21 August 1975, p. 240. For another positive reaction, see John Hudson, 'Bolton: Trotting Round the Centre', *The Guardian*, 8 June 1973, p. 25. See also Bolton and District Civic Trust, *The Buildings of Bolton* (Bolton, 1983).

THE EVOLUTION OF A RADICAL PLANNER

Shankland Cox continued to grow into a large practice with international reach. They developed a highly interdisciplinary approach to planning, employing a range of professions—covering fields including transport, landscape, economics, and sociology. The breadth of Shankland's interests enabled him to tie together these various disciplinary strands. Alongside extensive housing work (Cox's forte), the firm was especially active in the field of New Towns and town-expansion schemes, although they failed to win the Milton Keynes job. In all his later projects Shankland moved away from the architecture-led solutions of his early career, and towards plans based on intense periods of interdisciplinary research. The high point of this philosophy was the publication of *Inner London: Policies for Dispersal and Balance* (1977), a study of Lambeth written with David Jordan and the sociologist Peter Willmott for the Department of the Environment. This report identified many features of Britain's emerging inner-city problem, with its focus on racial tensions, the demand for housing, deindustrialization, and poverty to the fore. Its suggestions were small-scale but based on a deep sensitivity towards the needs and aspirations of the local population. It is a masterpiece of lucid and humane planning. It also shows that Shankland continued to move, in parallel with the culture, towards a less radical approach, advocating dispersal over renewal:

> Large-scale redevelopment in Inner London on the scale of the 1960s and early 1970s is unjustified. Such programmes were unduly expensive and socially disruptive. They often involved the destruction of adequate houses and their replacement by dwellings which were poorer value for money.[139]

He increasingly also wrote in favour of the conservation of historic buildings.[140] Nevertheless, he was no total apostate, suggesting of Jane Jacobs in 1980 that 'Her stance today is reactionary, and finally dishonest. We all know, and so does she, that some of the most important achievements of planning have only become a reality through the power of a big idea to command the resources, sacrifice and imagination of successive generations.'[141]

[139] Shankland, Willmott, and Jordan, *Inner London: Policies for Dispersal and Balance*, pp. 147–8.

[140] Graeme Shankland, 'Why Trouble with Historic Towns?' in *Conservation of Cities* (Paris, 1976), pp. 24–42.

[141] 'Confrontation in Boston: Jim Rouse v Jane Jacobs', *Architects' Journal*, 5 November 1980, p. 879. Shankland received three obituaries: 'Mr Graeme Shankland', *The Times*, 3 November 1984, p. 10; 'Obituary: Graeme Shankland', *Architects' Journal*, 28 November 1984, p. 36; John Kay, 'Graeme Shankland', *Journal of the William Morris Studies*, 6.2 (1984–5), p. 30.

Historians often see the transformations of British cities in the 1960s as primarily being the result of the delayed explosion of, in David Watkin's phrase, the 'architectural time bomb' that had been primed by Le Corbusier's paper architecture of the interwar period.[142] However, Shankland's intellectual ancestry has very little to do with Corbusianism. Rather, it was a richer amalgamation of influences encompassing Swedish architecture, William Morris, and contemporary sociology. Shankland did not merely enact fixed ideas formed and ossified in the direct aftermath of the war. His approach was an evolving one, primarily propelled by an engagement with the political concerns of the British Left in an affluent and changing Britain. Shankland's place in the history of conservation is a Janus-faced one, disrupting the neat compartmentalization of the history that sees modernism and the conservation movement as distinct entities.

Whatever the ambiguities of his approach, Shankland was undoubtedly a proponent of what William Holford described as 'the Utopian urge to reconstruct the core of the old metropolis, to bring order out of disorder, to counter sprawl by concentration, to create a symbol of efficiency—a Welfare City in a Welfare State'.[143] Nevertheless, there was a conservatism to Shankland's plans as well as a visionary quality of 'white heat' utopianism. In much of his rhetoric he was not attempting to enact revolutionary change but to react to the revolutionary changes already apparent in society. More significant than the importing of modernist continental ideas, the cultural background to Shankland's plans from the period are an accumulation of fears about the consequences of growing affluence that were widespread in the political culture of the period. It was hoped that the right kind of cities would provide a culturally rich environment which would act as a dam against the enormous changes in society that were sweeping through Britain due to rising affluence, consumerism, the motor car, and television. His plans aspired to preserve traditional urban communities, which 'people will not want to escape from—either by means of the motor car, the bottle or T.V.'[144] Shankland's approach was informed by a politically aware outlook that was meliorist and modernizing, but was simultaneously fearful about the changes affecting British society. Such a culture was not just shared by many of Shankland's professional contemporaries, but by an entire intellectual generation. Shankland's plans were carried forth on the tide of this culture.

[142] David Watkin, *A History of Western Architecture* (London, 2011), p. 609.

[143] William Holford, 'An Adventure in Architecture', *The Listener*, 12 February 1953, p.257.

[144] Shankland, 'Dead Centre–2', p. 190.

Indicative of Shankland's affinity with concurrent debates is a 1962 essay by the Labour MP Anthony Crosland. Crosland called for the 'complete physical rehabilitation' of northern cities, with their 'unsightly miles of dismal Victorian housing, schools, chapels, mills, factories and industrial debris',[145] while also advocating the retention of 'the essential *character* of the city centre—social, cultural and historical',[146] and for architectural preservation. Crosland, like Shankland, did not consider it contradictory to be simultaneously an advocate of modernization and conservation. Instead, he hoped 'we can preserve what beauty we still have left, and create a little more'.[147] Crosland's article praised the fact that Liverpool was among 'recent converts to mid-twentieth-century ideas', suggesting there was a symbiotic influence between Shankland and a wider political discourse.[148]

Shankland was a key figure in the radical rebuilding of British cities in the 1960s, but a focus on his biography also supports many of the overarching arguments of this book more generally. Firstly, for Shankland planning was an intensely political process; it is therefore unsurprising that it echoes and follows concurrent political discourse. His career, and the 1960s planning moment more generally, are therefore only explicable when understood in their full political and cultural contexts. Secondly, Shankland is indicative of the way a new appreciation of the historic fabric of cities was developed by, rather than simply in opposition to, those involved in modernist redevelopment. Chapter 5 will explore these two arguments in more depth, through a case study of another intensely political architect-planner. It will also show how the approach to cities developed by architect-planners was applied not just to industrial cities but also to historic towns.

[145] C. A. R. Crosland, 'The Use of Land and Urban Planning', in *The Conservative Enemy, A Programme of Radical Reform for the 1960s* (London, 1962), pp. 183–96, p. 184.
[146] Ibid., p. 191. [147] Ibid., p. 196. [148] Ibid., p. 195.

5

Modernism in an Old Country

Lionel Brett, an Establishment Architect-Planner

MODERNISM AND THE POLITICS OF PUBLIC SERVICE

Like Graeme Shankland, the architect-planner Lionel Brett, fourth Viscount Esher (1913–2004), espoused both modernism and preservation, being a committed modernist while also wanting to preserve many of both the social and aesthetic benefits of the traditional city. Brett fluctuated between advocating radical modernist solutions, while also attempting to leaven them with British traditions, and concerns about the environment, *genius loci*, and preservation. He was fully aware of this duality, writing in his autobiography that, 'It was these subtleties of atmosphere and problems of relationship that fascinated me about our trade. We were handling the difficult combination of a revolutionary architecture rooted in a new technology on the one hand, and on the other an historically unprecedented concern for the world we had inherited.'[1] For Brett there was, at least initially, no cognitive dissonance in attempting to hold on to both modernism and British traditions; indeed, they were mutually reinforcing. Modernist solutions were seen by Brett as the only way to achieve other, more nuanced desiderata. As with many of his generation, the Townscape movement was an influence on Brett in this respect, as it was able to teach 'a painterly delight in what exists, irrespective of its orthodoxy, it may save us from a renewal of the fits of puritan destructiveness which have so squandered our scenic capital in the past'.[2]

Brett was the only important protagonist of the post-war rebuilding of British cities to have written extensively about the experience. Martin Pawley's 1985 judgement was that he was by 'far and away the best

[1] Lionel Brett, *Our Selves Unknown* (London, 1985), p. 159.

[2] Lionel Brett, 'Two Pairs of Eyes', *The Spectator*, 17 April 1947, p. 9. This quotation comes from a review of Le Corbusier's *Vers Une Architecture*.

architect-writer in England'.[3] His writing is interesting for reasons beyond its limpid prose. He knew everyone, making his autobiography, *Our Selves Unknown,* and his history, *A Broken Wave,* something of a version of Noel Annan's *Our Age* for architecture. The thanks list of friends for *A Broken Wave* is an extraordinary roll call of the 1960s architectural establishment. As Gavin Stamp put it in a caustic review, 'The names of the members of this establishment, all so committed, so charming, all apparently friends of the author, recur like a litany throughout this book (and have, as the Index reveals, mostly managed to acquire knighthoods and peerages).'[4] Brett acted as one of the central cogs in the prosopographical machine of post-war architectural culture—making a useful case study for how modernist architecture functioned within its broader milieu—even if his planning work is less significant than Shankland's. A revealing illustration is that when Brett was President of the Royal Institute of British Architects (RIBA), his former tutor at Oxford, Richard Crossman, was Minister of Housing and Local Government. Crossman described Brett as 'my old friend', which went a long way towards oiling a mutual appreciation, so that Crossman's 'relations with the R.I.B.A. and the architects . . . got more and more friendly. (I got a letter from Lord Esher the other day saying that in their considered view I was the best Minister they had ever had.)'[5] When Brett published *Landscape in Distress* in 1965, with its 'scarifying exposure of the ineffectiveness of Oxfordshire planning', it demonstrably influenced Crossman.[6]

Whilst Brett's approach was still deeply political, it was political in a different way to that of Shankland. He was less radical than Shankland—both politically and architecturally. Throughout his career Brett remained very much a scion of the twentieth-century mandarinate, who were 'dedicated to reform in politics, social work and the civil service'.[7] To understand Brett, we need to understand the intersection between the architectural culture of modernism and this equally integral political culture of public service. In the same way that modernism alone cannot explain Shankland's approach, Brett's planning was propelled by both a culture of public service and by a commitment to British tradition. Taking

[3] Martin Pawley, 'When books become building blocks', *The Guardian*, 14 January 1985, p. 9.

[4] Gavin Stamp, 'President Disaster', *The Spectator*, 9 October 1981, p. 21. Stamp was particularly scornful of the way Brett described William Holford as 'remarkably handsome'.

[5] Richard Crossman, *The Diaries of a Cabinet Minister, Volume One, Minister of Housing 1964–66* (London, 1975), pp. 86 and 624.

[6] Ibid., p. 410.

[7] Vernon Bogdanor, 'Oxford and the Mandarin Culture: The past that is gone', *Oxford Review of Education,* 32.1 (2006), pp. 147–65. A less flattering portrait of this class can be found in Patrick Joyce, *The State of Freedom: A Social History of the British State Since 1800* (Cambridge, 2013).

a holistic biographical approach helps to resolve what initially seem to be inconsistencies and contradictions in Brett.

Through substantial journalism, letters to the press, and his involvement with a panoply of committees, including SPUR, the Civic Trust, Royal Fine Art Commission, RIBA, Council for the Preservation of Rural England, Victorian Society, and Georgian Group, he acted as an intermediary between architectural and political culture. His journalism is littered with consensus-presuming phrases such as 'of course everybody knows that the final solution is . . . ', or 'a virtually unanimous movement exists to find a solution that involves . . . ', or 'only by this means . . . '[8]—whether such a phrase was followed by mixed development at a residential density of 100 people per acre, or vertical segregation of pedestrians and traffic, the interweaving of old and new, or some other remedy. However, his journalistic output in the 1950s and 1960s is not only proselytizing, it is also attractively reflective and often highly perceptive. His writing is significantly closer to the mould of a nineteenth-century 'public moralist'[9] than it is to a blistering manifesto in the mould of Le Corbusier or Marinetti.[10]

Brett became increasingly embattled and disillusioned as the 1960s progressed, and his statements from later in the decade, and indeed his reminiscences, give an insight into what happened to the brief moment of optimism that I have so far characterized as reaching a boiling point in 1963.

BIOGRAPHICAL OVERVIEW

Brett was born into the privileged settings of the country house Watlington Park[11] in 1913, the eldest son of Oliver Brett, third Viscount Esher, and the

[8] All of these indicative examples come from Lionel Brett, 'Renewing the Cities', *The Times,* 3 July 1961, p. 4.

[9] As described by Stefan Collini, *Public Moralists, Political Thought and Intellectual Life in Britain 1850–1930* (Oxford, 1991).

[10] Alongside these written sources, this chapter makes use of Brett's plan for Portsmouth's Guildhall Comprehensive Redevelopment Area, and a better-known plan for York—which will nevertheless be presented in the new light of being the culmination of long-term ambitions. Brett has received no sustained attention from historians. He would be a deserving subject of a biography. This is not a survey of Brett's career, and I ignore some important aspects of his life and work, notably the output of his architectural practice and his persistent parallel interest in development in the countryside, which culminated in *Landscape in Distress*. The chapter limits itself to following Brett's evolving approach to city centres, his attempt to balance modernizing and preservationist instincts, and an account of the political nature of his practice.

[11] 'A neat Georgian box built c. 1755.' Brett demolished the 1911 extensions in the 1950s. See Christopher Hussey, 'Watlington Park, Oxfordshire: the home of the Hon. Lionel Brett', *Country Life*, 1 January 1959, pp. 60–3.

American heiress Antoinette Heckscher. Oliver Brett was chairman of the National Trust's executive committee for twenty-five years, chairman of the trustees of the London Museum and the Grants Committee of the Historic Churches Trust, as well as Life President of the Society for the Protection of Ancient Buildings.[12] He also bankrolled and was first chairman of the Victorian Society, despite the fact that, as his son put it, 'he intensely disliked' Victorian buildings. Lionel inherited from his father a concern with Britain's historic environment as well as a commitment to public service and committee work. Brett was a scholar and Captain of School at Eton and achieved a Congratulatory First in Modern History at New College, Oxford.[13] By the age of 17 he had already decided on a career as an architect, in defiance of the expectations that he would have a political career, his mother writing in 1934 that '*everyone* I meet who has heard about you just takes it for granted that you are cut out for public life, either in Diplomacy or the House of Commons. They all look a little dashed when I say, Oh no, he wants to be an architect.'[14] Nevertheless, Brett's background and education inculcated him with an ethos of administrative public service, or patrician *noblesse oblige* if one prefers, which he did not renounce by pursuing architecture. His decision to become an architect was motivated by a 'social as much as an aesthetic obligation'.[15] Architecture was another means with which to achieve political ends: as he put it in an interview in 1969,

> I came from a background which could have led me into either politics or architecture. Because I happened to be a visual type I chose architecture. Remember, too, that I came of age in the thirties with all that period's social conscience. If I'd gone into politics it would have been on the left. As it was, choosing architecture, I wanted to specialize in the whole environment.[16]

Throughout his career, these two aspects of his personality—between the political and his artistic faculties—would run in parallel, often working symbiotically, sometimes in conflict. It was in a sense inescapable that he would fall back on the political side of architecture, as he was, by his own account, a limited designer.

[12] 'Obituary, Viscount Esher', *The Times*, 9 October 1963, p. 15. See also Susie Harries, *Nikolaus Pevsner, The Life* (London, 2011), p. 573.

[13] For a flavour of his time at Oxford see the letter reprinted in *Our Selves Unknown*, in which he relates giving a 'slightly alarming dinner' for John Betjeman, Kenneth Clark, Maurice Bowra, and Richard Crossman. He shared a flat with Jo Grimond and John Pope-Hennessy. Brett, *Our Selves Unknown*, p. 55.

[14] Quoted in Brett, *Our Selves Unknown*, p. 53.

[15] Brett, *Our Selves Unknown*, p. 64.

[16] Kate Wharton, 'Talking to Lord Esher', *The Architect and Building News*, 19 June 1969, p. 6.

After leaving Oxford, a term at the Architectural Association left him high-mindedly disappointed ('schoolboy smut and stink bombs set the tone'). Instead, he continued his education by correspondence course, and apprenticed himself to A. S. G. Butler, a disciple of Lutyens. Brett rebelled against this milieu, another that he might have been presumed by background to have been suited to: 'a country-house architect, which I could so easily have become, was not what I wanted to be.'[17] He went on to join, as a 'disciple', the high modernist couple Aileen and William Tatton Brown. William Tatton Brown had worked with André Lurçat and Berthold Lubetkin. This was an escape into the brave new world, but only half an escape, as the only job Brett brought in was 'that classic—a new wing for my aunt Zena's wisteria-covered Queen Anne Cottage in Berkshire. This we did . . . with a flat roof and plate-glass windows. We made her a model, which she thought a sweet toy. But when she saw it full size, to her great embarrassment and misery, she had to sack me and get a builder to put on a tiled roof and Georgianize the windows. She was charming: I am sure I was intolerable.'[18]

In the late 1930s Brett was a 'paid up supporter of the Modern Movement' and a member of the MARS (Modern Architectural Research) Group (the British wing of CIAM, the International Congresses of Modern Architecture), enjoying a 'dry Martini with Chermayeff in his elegant apartment in Bayswater, a whisky with Wells Coates in his high-tech studio in Yeoman's Row, and most elevating of all, a lager with Lubetkin on the Friesian-cowskin settee in his famous Highpoint One penthouse'.[19] He qualified just before the war, by correspondence course, spending the prize money for the prestigious Ashpitel Prize on books by Le Corbusier and Lewis Mumford. He would later describe the profound effect of the 'grandly evocative' poetic vision found in these two writers, with their 'creation of the beautifully clean, invisible, magical power of electricity, spun through the air and taking the squalor out of every aspect of life'.[20]

Brett's RIBA thesis, entitled 'Modern Techniques and the English Tradition', however, showed that even in the 1930s he was developing his twin obsessions, which he would try to fuse.[21] His first two articles to appear in the architectural press were on the two major, and diametrically opposed, visionary London town-planning schemes of the war years. On

[17] Brett, *Our Selves Unknown,* p. 65.

[18] Brett, *Our Selves Unknown,* p. 65. See Berkshire Record Office, RD/E/SB6/411/1-5 for the plan.

[19] Brett, *Our Selves Unknown,* p.98.

[20] Lionel Esher, *A Broken Wave: the Rebuilding of England 1940–1980* (London, 1980), p. 30.

[21] A copy is held in the RIBA Library, XMS/711.03.

the traditionalist, beaux arts Royal Academy scheme he was damning, criticizing it for failing to recognize London's sibilantly evoked *genius loci*: 'The lover of London would find its mysteries gone . . . the curving line, the sheepy park, the piled-up asymmetrical silhouette, the secret alley and the silent square.'[22] But he was equally disparaging of the modernist MARS Plan for London, which had suggested rebuilding the capital from scratch along vertebrate spine routes of high-density development.[23] Brett described it as a 'Martian utopia', while strenuously denying he was 'for neo-anything': 'I do not think that such enormous areas, all built up in twenty years in a uniform style can be anything but dull . . . because a city is a creative evolution and not a spontaneous creation. And MARS, I think, overdo the cleaning of the slate.'[24] In both these reviews we see the embryo of Brett's approach of attempting to use modernism to solve the problems facing British cities, while accepting and working with the fact that these cities were an accumulation of history. In the paragraph which ends the review of the Academy plan, all the features of Brett's conciliatory political philosophy are already formed:

> We must recognise that compromise, which is the death of art, is the life and soul of politics and therefore of planning. After all, it is not so difficult. All that is needed is a love and understanding of what London is, and a willingness to accept rational conclusions rather than preconceptions of what it should become.

To provide a further insight into Brett's emerging philosophy, it is worth quoting at some length a 1946 article on the influence of American architect Frank Lloyd Wright (whom Brett had seen lecture at the RIBA in 1939), on current British practice in architecture and planning:

> If you have looked at some [recent British] plans you may have noticed a curious thing about them, the complete disappearance of symmetry, climax and axiality. These imaginary buildings stand (in Wright's phrase) no longer at attention but at ease. In fact, they seem to lie about on the grass like Henry Moore figures in a park on a hot afternoon. The whole cargo of Beaux Arts clichés, the focal point, the avenue, the vista, the major and minor axis, have been hurled overboard. Various converging influences have produced this

[22] Lionel Brett, 'The New Haussmann: Royal Academy Planning Committee's plans for London' in *The Architectural Review*, January 1943, pp. 23–5. Sheep were still grazed on Hyde Park. For the plan itself see *London Replanned: The Royal Academy Planning Committee Interim Report* (London, 1942).

[23] John R. Gold, 'The MARS plans for London, 1933-1942', *Town Planning Review*, 66.3 (1995), pp. 234–67.

[24] Lionel Brett, 'Doubts on the MARS plan for London: critical article', *Architects' Journal*, 9 July 1942, pp. 23–5. The reply that MARS had in fact intended to retain a Georgian square 'as a museum piece' does little to assuage one's doubts.

situation, but it was probably Wright, harping monotonously on the magic word 'organic', who lit the fuse. And incidentally, it was Wright who reminded us that it was our English landscapists of the eighteenth century who first hit upon studied informality as an answer to Versailles. What we have lost in grandeur we have gained in humanity. The planner no longer bulldozes his ruthless lines across our living cities. He weaves his way more subtly. He accepts gratefully the assistance of the ground and the queer relationship of old and new.[25]

This paragraph helps to sum up Brett's position and rhetoric. It advocates an informal approach over a beaux arts one and goes on to bolster this advocacy with reference to both a modernist precursor and British tradition—perhaps through a creative misreading of these antecedents. Lastly, it sees such a modernist approach, far from being inimical to the preservation of old buildings, instead providing an opportunity for their retention, which is beneficial to both old and new.

Brett served during the war with the Royal Artillery, becoming a major, and saw action during the invasion of France and Germany. He was mentioned in dispatches. The war, as with so many of his generation, politicized Brett further. In his autobiography, he recalled the influence of hearing Richard Crossman give a 'splendid speech' setting out the precepts of the welfare state.[26] Modernism and the politics of social justice were intimately linked for Brett: 'as those years wore on, [all of us] began to see modern architecture and "progressive" politics as inextricably interwoven.'[27] He stood, as a gesture rather than a career move, as a Beveridge Liberal in the 1945 general election, against a Tory 'well to the right of Genghis Khan'. He came third. Brett later mused that this politicization might have harmed his ability as an architect: 'Given my past life, given my present circumstances, I was becoming an ideologue and not a craftsman/builder, which every decent architect ought instinctively to be. Soon my only expertise in regard to buildings was how to blow them to pieces.'[28]

Modest about his abilities as an architect, he would rely on being partnered with talented designers, including Kenneth Boyd, Francis Pollen, and Harry Teggin.[29] One gets the sense that he was often rather underemployed. How else to explain his many other activities? Brett started on a lifelong sideline as a journalist, a writer of earnest letters to the press, and in general increasingly took on the role of an intermediary

[25] Lionel Brett, 'Work and Theories of Frank Lloyd Wright', *The Listener*, 12 December 1946, p. 838.

[26] Brett, *Our Selves Unknown*, p. 99.

[27] Brett, *Our Selves Unknown*, p. 99.

[28] Brett, *Our Selves Unknown*, p. 99.

[29] Esher, Lionel Gordon Baliol Brett (4 of 13), National Life Stories, Architects' Lives. British Library. See Alan Powers, *Francis Pollen* (London, 1999).

between architectural culture, the Establishment, and the general public: 'I had become something of a pundit, addressing the stage army of the good all over the place and endlessly churning out improving pieces in the architectural press and in the Sundays, weeklies, monthlies etc.'[30]

During a brief spell working with Clough Williams-Ellis (a lifelong friend, Brett would build a house at Williams-Ellis's fantastical village of Portmeirion, where he wrote the Shell Guide to *North Wales*[31]), he gained planning experience working on frustrated plans for Littlehampton, Weston-super-Mare, and (with planner Patrick Abercrombie) Redditch. They shared an office with Abercrombie, then at the peak of his fame due to the publication of his wartime plans for London, and Brett cited him as an important influence.[32] During this time he gained a planning qualification, again by correspondence course. He took over the family seat at Watlington in 1947, where he would set up an architectural office, with Kenneth Boyd running the London arm (Fig. 5.1). Brett broke Watlington up into flats, using the dining room as a drawing-office.[33] He intended it to have a communal atmosphere based on Frank Lloyd Wright's studio and estate Taliesin, although one suspects that at times it must have felt rather more feudal to the other participants. He described the set-up as having 'the charming but risky tendency to appeal to architectural dropouts, intellectuals and early-day hippies'.[34]

On the basis of what seems today remarkably scant experience, in 1949 Brett was appointed architect-planner of Hatfield New Town, the smallest of the first generation of New Towns, with a projected population of only 26,000. His tenure at Hatfield was marred by the fact that during a storm, on 3 November 1957, the roofs were blown off fifty houses, for which Brett was liable for half the damages, along with the contractors, Wimpey. As Brett sadly put it in his autobiography, the incident was 'probably the only thing widely known about my architectural career'. He only escaped bankruptcy after his father 'sold off some of the family silver'.[35]

More importantly for Brett's intellectual development were the frustrations, both intellectual and practical, at having to work within the constraints of a New Town project. He looked jealously at the modernist

[30] Brett, *Our Selves Unknown,* p. 106.

[31] Elisabeth Beazley and Lionel Brett, *North Wales* (London, 1971).

[32] Esher, Lionel Gordon Baliol Brett (5 of 13), National Life Stories, Architects' Lives. British Library.

[33] Christopher Hussey, 'Watlington Park, Oxfordshire - II: the home of the Hon. Lionel Brett', *Country Life,* 8 January 1959, pp. 60–3, p. 62.

[34] Brett, *Our Selves Unknown,* p. 105.

[35] Esher, Lionel Gordon Baliol Brett (5 of 13), National Life Stories, Architects' Lives. British Library.

Fig. 5.1. Watlington Park country house in 1959. The pavilions were added by Brett. An inflated version of the cliché of modernist architects living in nice Georgian houses? © Country Life Archive

mixed development schemes being carried out by the London County Council Architects Department.[36] But any attempt to achieve such development in the New Towns was stymied by a mixture of 'red tape, lack of funds, engineering restrictions, consumer's conservatism, inefficient organization'.[37] Guidelines were especially irksome, as they had been 'written against a Garden City background and never envisaged architects wanting to build any tighter'.[38] An architect working in the New Towns was hindered by the need for a 'spacious pattern of sewers, services, cables, standards, improvement lines, sight lines, verges and footpaths prising his buildings apart and enforcing a suburban density, or on the other hand the universal demand for concrete lamp-standards, kerbs, seats, refuse bins, television aerials, overhead cables, front fences, turning-circles and uniform road widths'.[39] With this unromantic catalogue of subtopian

[36] Lionel Brett, 'Ten Million Private Dreams', *The Listener*, 6 October 1955, p. 539.

[37] Lionel Brett, 'Failure of the New Towns?', *The Architectural Review*, August 1953, pp. 119–20.

[38] Brett, 'Failure of the New Towns?'

[39] Lionel Brett, 'Post-war housing estates: critical appraisal of aesthetic qualities', *The Architectural Review*, July 1951, pp. 16–26.

obligations to deal with, the New Town architect-planner was unable to be an art-architect but was, rather, a mere unglamorous committee man: 'For we live in an over professionalized country, in which too many people (and I write as one) are employed keeping an eye on each other, and drinking in the taxpayer's time eternal cups of unsweetened tea at eternal conferences.'[40]

At Hatfield, therefore, Brett 'became immersed in a fight to raise densities, taking Old Hatfield's cosy Church Street as model of the feeling we ought to aim at. I failed, of course. The suburban—indeed the rustic—dream held sway in that part of the world.'[41] Although he wrote a spirited letter of defence after Gordon Cullen's and J. M. Richards's famous 1953 attack on the New Towns, he did not disagree with their fundamental critique.[42] Because the 'suburban ideal has dominated the scene', the New Towns, though they were 'tolerable and occasionally even delightful in design, respectable in quantity, unique in the world in spaciousness, [they have] yet quite failed to add up to a civilized environment'.[43] Or putting it more bluntly, 'nobody would ever want to paint a picture in Harlow or Bracknell'.[44] The Ghyllgrove Estate in Basildon, designed with Kenneth Boyd, and built at 22.4 dwellings per acre, was the scheme that came closest to Brett's ambitions, but was still a long way from the modernist ideal.[45]

THE SOCIETY FOR THE PROMOTION OF URBAN RENEWAL AND THE ROYAL FINE ART COMMISSION

The perceived failure of the first generation of New Towns in the 1950s would provide a stimulus for Brett's renewed appreciation of the problems of city-centre redevelopment emerging into the 1960s, as it had with Shankland. As Brett put it, 'My own exit from the world of the New Towns coincided, as it happened, with a public need to divert attention from them to the state of the inner cities.'[46] This move, reinforcing the political side of Brett's nature, was fortified by a realization of his inadequacies as an architect: 'Both my limitations and my ambitions pointed

[40] Lionel Brett, letter to *The Architectural Review*, August 1953, pp. 119–20.
[41] Brett, *Our Selves Unknown*, p. 107.
[42] Brett, 'Failure of the New Towns?', pp. 28–32.
[43] Lionel Brett, 'Ten Million Private Dreams', *The Listener*, 6 October 1955, p. 539.
[44] Lionel Brett, 'A Swing of the Pendulum', *The Listener*, 5 September 1957, BRL/1/3.
[45] Gordon Cullen, 'Description of the ideas behind Ghyllgrove, Basildon', *The Architectural Review*, October 1957, p. 226.
[46] Brett, *Our Selves Unknown*, p. 148.

me towards the problems of cities, the dilemmas of planning, the politics of architecture. The decision was inevitable and I never regretted it.'[47] In part the move was galvanized by a letter from Graeme Shankland to the council of the Architectural Association, in which he stressed that 'the need at the moment is for the planned large-scale redevelopment of our existing cities', as it was here that 'we have had least success in our post-war physical planning and architecture'.[48] Brett wrote to Shankland that the letter proved the 'need for a propaganda body to close the gap between technician and man in the street'.[49] Brett found a suitable outlet for this ambition in the Society for the Promotion of Urban Renewal (SPUR), for which he would serve as chairman. SPUR was founded in 1958, growing out of an initiative of the Association of Building Technicians.[50] Brett was a good consensus figurehead for the group, many of whom were, like Shankland, on the far Left and therefore politically suspect.[51] The group was set up with the purpose of changing the direction of policy away from dispersal and New Towns towards the renewal of existing areas in cities. Behind this policy agenda was a deeply romantic undercurrent stressing the benefits of urban life, which intended, in Brett's own proselytizing words, 'to affirm that cities were worth living in—that there was a quality about urban life which was better than suburban life and different from rural life'.[52]

As with Shankland's contemporaneous pronouncements about Hook, Brett's rhetoric at SPUR was informed by a belief in the social benefits of compact development over suburban expansion, which was encouraged by a fear of what was understood, through a rather snobbish lens, as an Americanized admass culture of television and what it was doing to social cohesion. One can also hear the echo of Brett's early mentor Clough Williams-Ellis's pronouncements of the interwar period:[53]

> In suburban life everyone did what he or she wanted without thought for the total result; this was uncivilized and barbarous. It led to standardization in ways of living, as opposed to the variety and individuality of urban and rural living. There were other social implications, such as the menace of television,

[47] Brett, *Our Selves Unknown*, p. 148.

[48] British Architectural Library (hereinafter BAL), Extract from a letter to the council of the AA from Mr Graeme Shankland dated 18th November, 1956. BrL/39/3.

[49] BAL, Lionel Brett to Graeme Shankland, 19 July 1957, BrL/39/3.

[50] For a full history of SPUR see John Gold, 'A SPUR to action?: The Society for the Promotion of Urban Renewal, "anti-scatter" and the crisis of city reconstruction, 1957–1963', *Planning Perspectives* 27.2 (2012), pp. 199–223.

[51] Gold, 'A SPUR to action?', p. 205.

[52] LMA, Brett, 'Urban redevelopment Report of a meeting held at the Housing Centre on 4.2.1959', ACC/1888/152 SPUR A.7b.

[53] Clough Williams-Ellis, *England and the Octopus* (London, 1928).

> which kept people apart, as opposed to the group amusements and entertainments of the city.[54]

A feature of Brett's rhetoric about city-centre renewal, which does not occur in Shankland's, is that the move away from the city is related by him to a general spirit of post-imperial decline:

> The idealism which drives the Russian tractors across Siberia and the American bulldozers through blighted cities, the energy which is recreating Pittsburgh and the Ruhr, transforming China, enriching Canada, haven't been concentrated upon any physical improvement here since 1889, when the Forth Bridge was complete.[55]

Discussing a 'truly mind-stretching' scheme by fellow SPUR member Derrick Childs, Brett wrote: 'At last here is the *scale* of thinking we need, taken for granted in other countries but quite alien to the mental Lilliput we have settled into since we ceased to be an imperial power.'[56]

There was a fissure in SPUR between those for whom renewal was synonymous with large-scale radical comprehensive redevelopment and those with a more holistic view, which foreshadowed the complete disavowal of radical renewal of later in the decade; although both sides of this divide attacked dispersal, some thought this was better achieved through rehabilitation than renewal. Housing consultant Elizabeth Denby led the most stinging attack on radical renewal, writing to Brett to complain about the fact that SPUR focused 'almost exclusively on renewal'.[57] Brett, as might be expected, fell somewhere between the two poles. The romantic aim of rediscovering the beneficial aspects of urban life was in Brett's hands very much to the fore. A 1959 piece about the group in

[54] LMA, Brett, 'Urban redevelopment Report'.

[55] BAL, manuscript 'The Coffin', *c.*1956, Brl/1/3.

[56] BAL, Lionel Brett, Letter to *Architects' Journal*, 17 Jan. 1962, Brl/1/1.

[57] BAL, Letter Elizabeth Denby to Brett, 8 June 1959, Brl/4/1. It is worth quoting Denby's policy-group paper on the issue at length, because it is unusually blistering for so early a date: '"Comprehensive redevelopment" is the generally accepted method of regenerating a dilapidated or worn-out area. This policy seems to me to be short-sighted as well as wrong. All British towns are the growth of centuries. They enshrine local history. They represent the activities, successes, hopes and failures, work and play of the citizens for many generations. The result is "flavour and character", though neither the flavour nor the character may appeal at first sight to any but the citizens themselves. Thus shipbuilding, the cotton, the pottery, the mining towns give a very different impression to a visitor when he visits them by himself than when he is shown around by some old resident. There is of course no doubt whatever that many very large areas of British industrial development need regenerating, but it is my strong conviction that this must be done sensitively with and not for or against the citizens themselves.' Elizabeth Darling, '"The star in the profession she invented for herself": a brief biography of Elizabeth Denby, housing consultant', *Planning Perspectives*, 20 (July 2005), pp. 271–300; LMA, Elizabeth Denby,'SPUR policy group, Paper II part 2, c. 1959', ACC/1888/152 SPUR A.7b.

The Architectural Review even eschews the radical implications behind the label SPUR, preferring instead 'the Environmentalists': '"rebuild," "renew," "re-create," are words I avoid in this context, since they imply varying degrees of condescension to places many of which are thick with character, guarded by the wry affection of many people, and short only on imaginative leadership.'[58] This article took the theme of SPUR, the feeling of 'impatience that the official policy of decentralization to new towns, necessary though it has been, should now take second place to the rebuilding of old ones', but added to it the romantic celebration of urban life and *genius loci*, in line with *The Architectural Review*'s agenda: 'You can search town-planning from Hadrian to Abercrombie and you won't find a theorist or practitioner who saw that the essence of cities was their continuity, complexity and dramatic contrast of old and new.'[59] This was not, yet, a disavowal of the modernist methods of improving cities, but, as will be seen, aiming these methods at a new set of desiderata.

Although it is doubtful whether SPUR significantly contributed to the change of policy direction (their exhibition 'Better Towns for Better Living' was a flop),[60] the Society was wound down on 31 December 1963, as the growing wave of city-centre redevelopment made its advocacy appear redundant.[61] By 1963 urban renewal was kicking off. But SPUR's more nuanced agenda, as it was formulated by Brett, of reinvesting in a romantic idea of urban life and of cultivating such wispy but crucial concepts as 'character', was lost when the rhetoric of renewal was adopted by developers. Brett later said that SPUR was disbanded when 'the words "urban renewal" acquired purely commercial connotations'.[62]

We can best follow Brett's growing disillusionment with the way city-centre redevelopment schemes were panning out through his involvement with the Royal Fine Art Commission (RFAC), of which he was a member from 1951 to 1969. The RFAC had been established in 1927 to advise and monitor changes to the built environment.[63] The organization had come to embody much of Brett's attitude in corporate form. They summed up their approach in a 1962 report as follows:

> The choice is not, as seems to be thought in some influential circles, between progressive, scientific, forward looking development schemes on the one

[58] Lionel Brett, 'The Environmentalists', *The Architectural Review*, May 1959, p. 303.

[59] Ibid.

[60] As a reviewer put it, 'This exhibition . . . has been described as illiterate in its presentation. But in fact you would have to be very literate indeed to decipher some of the appalling jargon in this expensively-mounted display.' *The Spectator*, 17 July 1959, p. 19.

[61] Gold, 'a SPUR to action?', p. 216.

[62] Lionel Brett, 'Reply', *Architects' Journal*, 28 April 1982, p. 38.

[63] A. J. Youngson, *Urban development and the Royal Fine Art Commissions* (London, 1990).

> hand, and sentimental living in the past on the other. It is the duty of any civilised community, while taking full advantage of technological progress in the renewal of its fixed assets, to keep a sense of continuity by preserving and indeed cherishing the more important physical landmarks from its past.[64]

Despite the involvement of non-modernist figures like the poet John Betjeman and the traditional architect Raymond Erith, the RFAC, when it came to planning philosophy, closely followed the centre ground of modernist orthodoxy in the early 1960s. Their 1960 report echoes other documents of that date in stating the need for comprehensive planning, horizontal and vertical pedestrianization, as well as the need for 'full collaboration from the outset between traffic engineers and architect-planners'.[65] But even if these pronouncements were identical to the advice coming from central government, the RFAC stated that the guidance on public–private partnership in the first two planning bulletins was 'much more lenient' than their own position.[66] They deplored 'the present tendency of many local authorities to invite developers to submit three-dimensional planning proposals as part of the tendering process, with little or no guidance from the Planning Authority, who are responsible for safeguarding the long-term interests of the area and should not be allowed to shirk their responsibilities in this way'.[67]

Brett was on a subcommittee of the RFAC, alongside fellow architects Frederick Gibberd and Sir Leslie Martin, looking for the 'the best method for the Commission to deal with questions of central area redevelopment generally'.[68] In 1963 they considered schemes for Aylesbury, Cirencester, Crewe, Gloucester, Hereford, Liverpool, Salisbury, and Worcester. It was Worcester and Gloucester that caused concern, as 'too much was left to the developer'.[69] A tipping point was the story of the redevelopment of Worcester's Lychgate, which Brett described, referencing Jane Jacobs, as having been 'swamped in cataclysmic floods' and was a national scandal.[70] Worcester had enthusiastically embraced a scheme by Shingler and Risdon, for Western Properties Ltd, which obliterated much of the city's medieval street pattern just to the north of the cathedral. As Worcester Alderman E. J. Whitt later boasted, 'rather than keep at bay the "enemy at

64 *Eighteenth Report of the Royal Fine Art Commission*, September 1960–August 1962, p. 7.

65 *Seventeenth Report of the Royal Fine Art Commission*, September 1959–August 1960, p. 8.

66 TNA, '1959–1963 Central Area Redevelopment Schemes', BP2/248.

67 *Eighteenth Report of the Royal Fine Art Commission*, p. 5.

68 TNA, '1959–1963 Central Area Redevelopment Schemes', BP2/248.

69 TNA, Note from 4 September 1963, BP2/248.

70 See 'The Developers', n.d. but *c.*1964; review of Brian Whitehouse, *Partnerships in Property*. Brl/1/4; James Lees Milne, 'The Ruin of Our Cities', *The Sunday Times*, 20 September 1964, p. 13; and Council for British Archaeology, *Historic Towns* (1965).

the gates"—the property developers—the city has admitted them as friends and advisers using their skill and expertise, albeit guided and controlled.'[71] But with no qualified town planner, only a borough engineer, and no development plan, the last part of this statement could hardly be said to be true. To speed the process, roof tiles had been removed on listed buildings 'just where the gutter pipe has coincidentally fractured'.[72] Apart from eventually agreeing to reduce the scale of the scheme's tower down to at least the level of the ridge of the cathedral's nave, Worcester's local-authority bigwigs emphatically ignored what they saw as 'criticism by those "itinerant architects and planners" whose sole object... seemed to be the maintenance of Worcester as a museum piece'.[73] The Ministry of Housing and Local Government (MHLG) also tried to curb the scheme, sending chief architect Cleeve Barr to try and improve it, but as Evelyn Sharp wrote to the RFAC, 'I'm afraid there is not much hope of doing more with a scheme which has got as far as this.'[74] All in all, it was 'A sad story!'[75]

Brett's deep distaste for the commercialization of the agenda of urban renewal is evidenced in a 1963 article, in which he wrote a stingingly accurate parody of the way developers invested in the tropes and phraseology of modernism:

> 'Skyscraper flats, spacious shopping malls and a drive-in bank are among the features proposed by the Developers. New retail premises will line a landscaped pedestrian piazza and motorists will find ample accommodation in multi-storey garages adjacent to the Inner Ring Road. Conveniently grouped with the Civic Hall and Public Library, the new Council Offices will take the form of an 11-storey tower block rising from a podium. The historic Chequers Inn, part of which dates back to the fifteenth century, will be preserved and incorporated in the new development.' The heart sinks, even though this is what we asked for, more or less.[76]

It was not only that the language of redevelopment had become clichéd; the results too were grisly, even at this early date before the rebuilding had really got into its stride:

[71] W. R. Young, 'The Changing Face of a Thriving City', *Birmingham Post*, 19 June 1967.

[72] Geoffrey Moorhouse, 'The Sack of Worcester', *The Guardian*, 28 November 1964, p. 7.

[73] TNA, Quoted in 'The Changing Face of a Thriving City'. For a full history of RFAC's efforts at Worcester, see the letter from Godfrey Samuels to Lionel Brett, 4 December 1964, BP 2/284. J. Vilagrasa and P. Larkham, 'Post-war redevelopment and conservation in Britain: Ideal and reality in the historic core of Worcester', *Planning Perspectives,* 10 (1995), pp. 149–72.

[74] TNA, Letter from Evelyn Sharp to Godfrey Samuels, 7 August 1962, BP 2/284.

[75] TNA, Letter from Godfrey Samuels to Lionel Brett, 4 December 1964, BP 2/284.

[76] Lionel Brett, 'Doing without Utopia', *The Architectural Review*, July 1963, pp. 9–11.

> For people who have travelled and used their eyes, stock solutions, even if they unquestionably derive from the masters of the modern movement, and whether they are enunciated by faceless development companies or by gormless planning officers, are no longer acceptable. We prefer the slums.[77]

It was not unusual among modernists to look askance at the results of 1960s development, whether it was a result of disappointed expectations or that idealism had been hijacked by commercialism.[78] The disjunction of modernist theory and its shoddy practice did not set Brett on a course away from the modernist solutions of comprehensive planning, traffic management, and segregation. At Worcester it was the lack of a comprehensive scheme prepared by a planner that had been the problem.

Brett took the Buchanan Report very seriously—Buchanan was 'the sword of the spirit'.[79] It invigorated his thinking for the rest of the decade. He was quick to come to the defence of the profession's commitment to Buchanan-style solutions when Ian Nairn launched a broadside against them: 'Nairn may debunk "pedestrian precincts," and of course we are all sick of the word already.... But the fact remains that total motorisation confronts us with a revolutionary situation and we are fortunate to possess a technique, over-simplified and vulgarized as it inevitably is, which could handle the crisis if we could only afford to deploy it.'[80] He argued that Nairn would 'find his best allies among the architects he derides' in trying to care for towns and attack 'what the developers have done to some of them in the last few years'.[81] Brett, unlike Nairn by this date, was still juggling the two instincts of the radical and the preservationist:

> At the back of Nairn's mind, of course, is the best of English instincts—the attachment to organic growth rather than revolution, to the pieces-by-pieces replacement of old towns rather than their 'comprehensive' redevelopment. Yet here, too, as elsewhere, he settles for a half truth. For half our cities *are* tragically squalid and unworthy, and need the boldness of mind that created Edinburgh New Town and Bath and Regent's Park.[82]

In the right situation, Brett argued, vertical segregation was 'of course the final answer', although characteristically he argued that 'the pedestrian deck could be given the glamour of something new, which has always been the best possible disguise for the recapture of something old'.[83]

[77] Ibid., p. 11.

[78] See also Walter Bor, 'A question of urban identity', in *Planning and Architecture,* ed. Dennis Sharp (London, 1967).

[79] BAL, Lionel Brett, manuscript 'Architecture in the Sixties', n.d. [1969], BRL/1/4.

[80] Viscount Esher, 'Where Ian Nairn goes wild', *The Observer,* 20 February 1966, p. 30.

[81] Ibid. [82] Ibid.

[83] Lionel Brett, 'Renewing Our Cities', *The Times*, 3 July 1961; Lionel Brett, 'Into Reverse', *The London Magazine,* March 1964, pp. 65–7, p. 66.

Nevertheless, Brett was one of the few people to see past the visions of multidimensional cityscapes of *Traffic in Towns*. He saw *Traffic in Towns* as a solution to the problems he had been wrestling with. Talking at the RIBA conference in Glasgow in 1964, Brett took as his subject 'Preservation after Buchanan'. This sets out many of the principles that would inform his planning work at Portsmouth and York. The talk started with a nice distillation of Brett's dual-mindedness: '"What am I doing coming up from the South to talk about preservation in a city whose people obviously need a new city, a fresh start?" After 24 hours, I felt myself thinking: "This is a great city. It is entirely built of stone, better than we can begin to do now. We must preserve it." I'm afraid you are going to find this split mind running through most of this paper.'[84] Taking as his cue Buchanan's study of Norwich, Brett argued that for the half dozen or so historic cities which 'represent our version of the European urban tradition at its best' radials should stop before the core, 'ending normally in a ring of multi-storey car parks linked by some sort of inner circular road', while inside the core there should be a total ban on commuters' and visitors' cars. He suggested, as Konrad Smigielski had for Leicester, that an electric rickshaw service should be developed to serve 'elderly people and invalids and heavily laden shoppers'. This all pretty much foreshadows the approach Brett would apply at York four years later. The article is also interesting for warning of the risk of 'regeneration degenerating into eviction and class war', in the same year that Ruth Glass coined the term 'gentrification'.

Brett's pronouncements of the mid-1960s accord with my earlier presentation of the period as being one in which the brief economic optimism when grand plans were formulated quickly appeared unfeasible. As Brett reminisced, 'We now look back on the 1960s as a decade of unprecedented and probably unrepeatable prosperity, creativity and high living. In fact its middle years were marked by mismanagement and the usual "cuts", always first felt in architecture.'[85] His inaugural address as president of the RIBA in 1965 set out his frustrations that the solutions offered by the Buchanan Report, even in the flagship example of Martin and Buchanan's plan for Whitehall, would probably never be implemented: 'I find it hard to accept the fact that we are the first civilization which has known quite clearly what it needed to do, wanted passionately to do it, possessed all the techniques to do it, but been physically incapable of the necessary effort. It sounds like some extraordinary psychosomatic disease... The gap between planning theory and

84 Viscount Esher, 'Preservation after Buchanan', *RIBA Journal*, June 1964, pp. 1075–80.
85 Brett, *Our Selves Unknown*, p. 154.

planning investment is now so wide that to close it will need some urgent and hard re-thinking at both ends: both the theory and the investment policy will have to be overhauled.'[86] The gap between planning theory and planning practice is one this chapter itself needs to cross, as we go from Brett's pronouncements to his two plans for Portsmouth and York.

PLANNING WORK, MOSTLY PORTSMOUTH

After leaving Hatfield, Brett was mostly occupied with adding to rural villages, and was appointed as architect-planner of the Cadogan Estate. Brett suggested a red-brick tower of middle-class flats 'on the axis of Hans Place', and the bridging of the street at the top and bottom ends of Cadogan Place: 'under these bridge buildings you would enter a unified and noble space on the scale of the Palais Royal.'[87] The forty-year redevelopment plan proposed a 70 per cent increase in residential units, with no increase in office space.[88] Brett's firm only built two projects for Cadogan. First was an elegant office block, with black glass on an anodized aluminium framed rising from an exposed concrete base, at 190–192 Sloane Street (1963–5), with an internal layout based on the LCC's scissor maisonette (Fig. 5.2).[89] Second was a dull, dark red brick block of flats with boxed-out bay windows at 82 Sloane Street, where Brett owned the penthouse flat.[90] Behind was a terrace of mews houses at Pavilion Road. Both of these projects show a concern for local context, not through the imitation of style, but through such devices as respecting the original building line.[91] The building at 190–192 Sloane Street, for example, has its upper floors cantilevered out, with 'Harriet Street to be widened while still maintaining the original building line for the upper floors'.[92] Nevertheless, these buildings came as a shock to Earl Cadogan, and the firm was summarily dismissed: 'Cadogan himself hated Modernism, didn't realize

[86] 'Inaugural address of the RIBA President, the Viscount Esher, given at the RIBA on 19 October 1965', *RIBA Journal*, November 1965, pp. 529–33, p. 533.

[87] Brett, *Our Selves Unknown*, p. 159.

[88] BAL, 'Draft, 190/192 Sloane Street, 53 Lowndes Square and 3 & 5 Harriet Walk', BRL/29/2.

[89] This was listed in 1995; the primary designer was Harry Teggin. See https://historicengland.org.uk/listing/the-list/list-entry/1272552.

[90] Praised for its sensitivity in Roy Worskett, *The Character of Towns* (London, 1969), p. 195.

[91] For my account of the way architects of this period approached historical context (including a brief discussion of Brett's building for Exeter College, Oxford), see Otto Saumarez Smith, 'A Strange Brutalist "Primitive Hut": Howell, Killick, Partridge and Amis's Senior Combination Room at Downing College, Cambridge', *Twentieth Century Architecture 11* (London, 2013), pp. 148–65.

[92] '190 Sloane Street', 16 November 1965, BRL/31/1.

Fig. 5.2. No. 190–192 Sloane Street, London SW1. © Historic England

that when he got me, as a fellow aristocrat, that he was going to get modernism, and was horribly shocked at the first building we did.'[93]

Brett was also brought in as a consultant for Abingdon-on-Thames. The market town had a scheme for a pedestrian precinct (Bury Street) on the site of the former cattle market, submitted by Second Covent Garden Property Co. Ltd. It was to be designed by Messrs Fewster and Partners, with Geoffrey Beard of the Oxford Architects Partnership as the consultant architect. The precinct culminated in the Market Square, dominated by the magnificent English baroque County Hall. The scheme had involved the demolition of the Corn Exchange of 1886 and Queen's Hotel of 1864, two buildings 'of which nothing good can be said... quite

[93] Esher, Lionel Gordon Baliol Brett (7 of 13), National Life Stories, Architects' Lives. British Library.

unbelievably joyless', according to Pevsner.[94] But the point of juncture between the precinct and Market Place presented an awkward architectural problem: Beard had been 'striving for the creation of a bold, if not dramatic, new building while at the other extreme the developers' architects have their eye on the functional economic aspects'.[95] The council had decided that 'the general desire that such replacements should be pleasant but unobtrusive. In other words there is no room for two masterpieces in our small Market Place.'[96] But when the plans were published, they provoked a storm of controversy, including a stinging piece in the *Oxford Mail*,[97] and the RFAC complained. Brett precluded rebuilding in a Georgian style, and advised a building with a zigzagging roof, which currently looks rather peculiar now that it has itself been Georgianized—rather less successfully than the more banal modernist frontages of the rest of the precinct. As an ameliorative public-relations job, though, it was deemed a success at the time: 'it was by bringing in Lord Esher that the Council finally silenced the "Oxford Mail" whose attacks came close to holding up the scheme altogether.'[98]

Brett was appointed by Maidenhead Borough Council in July 1961 to produce a 'three dimensional phased master plan for the redevelopment of the town centre'.[99] This was submitted in 1962, and proposed a ring road, enabling the High Street (where pavements were then only 4 feet [1.2 metres] wide) to be pedestrianized and paved wall-to-wall. The scheme was presented to the Council and amended in the light of criticism from the Chamber of Commerce and the Civic Society. A plan of 1966, not authored by Brett, summed up its features as:

1) Improved shopping facilities concentrated in pedestrian precincts;

2) A multifold of off-street car parking; and

3) The segregation of different types of traffic and all traffic from shoppers—a principle since advocated in the Buchanan Report.[100]

In 1963 Lionel Brett's firm was appointed to give advice on the redevelopment of 38 acres (15.4 hectares) of central Portsmouth, in an area dominated by the grand neoclassical Guildhall (1890, by William

[94] Nikolaus Pevsner, *Berkshire* (London, 1966), p. 56. A record of Abingdon before the demolition can be found at http://www.aeolian-hall.myzen.co.uk/abingdon%20destruction.html, which shows that the Corn Exchange was in fact rather jolly.

[95] Abingdon Archives, Letter from Town Clerk, to B Watkin, 8 October 1964, CRS/56(a).

[96] Ibid. [97] 'Yet Another Bad Plan', *Oxford Mail*, 22 September 1964, p. 6.

[98] Abingdon Archives, Letter from Town Clerk to Mr Parry, 11 March 1965, CRS/19/62.

[99] *Maidenhead Central Area Redevelopment Scheme, an outline of proposals* (1966).

[100] Ibid.

Hill).[101] This was following an interview, in which Sir Hugh Casson and Geoffrey Jellicoe were also considered.[102] Brett's firm would later become architects for the Civic Offices, which were only completed in 1976, by Harry Teggin. The area had suffered extensive damage during the Blitz, with 40 per cent of the buildings destroyed and the Guildhall itself gutted. Nothing had happened since, and the area suffered planning blight, so that 'donkeys still grazed on wasteland a few yards from its great Corinthian portico', while heavy traffic passed directly in front of the steps.[103]

Brett's scheme was third in a line of post-war plans for the area. Nothing had come of an approved plan for the Civic Centre of 1948 by T. L. Marshall, which would have been in a stiff formal style somewhat reminiscent of Plymouth's contemporary post-Blitz renewal.[104] In 1960 the Commercial Road (Portsmouth) Property Investment Co. Ltd submitted an egregious £5 million scheme, with a vast traffic roundabout in front of the Guildhall, while all the normal jamboree of shopping precinct, offices, car parks, and a twenty-storey hotel tower rising from a podium and dwarfing the Guildhall were squashed into an inadequately small area to the north of the site. The developers advertised that their 'aim is to produce a completely integrated residential, social and shopping centre in a vivid, imaginative and comprehensive architectural conception, which they say, would be far in advance of anything which has so far been done'.[105] The Council enthusiastically approved it, reporting that it would add £100,000 to the rates.[106] Portsmouth's archives do not relate what happened to this scheme. At any rate, sense prevailed that the city needed some disinterested professional advice and Brett was appointed in June 1963 to 'advise on the redevelopment of the Guildhall Redevelopment Area and to act as consultant co-ordinator of the Architects and Engineers who will be responsible for the constructional works to be executed in the said area'.[107] His first consultant's report was submitted in March 1964,

[101] Hill also designed Bolton Town Hall. Brett noted the similarities of his approach and Shankland's in the two areas. Lionel Esher, *The Continuing Heritage* (London, 1982), p. 109.

[102] 'Lionel Brett for Portsmouth's centre', *Architect and Building News,* 10 July 1963, p. 46.

[103] A total of 20,000 vehicles, including 2,500 buses as well as 6,400 cycles on a typical August day in 1961.

[104] T. L. Marshall, *New Civic Centre for Portsmouth* (1948). See also 'Proposed Civic Centre for city of Portsmouth', *Official Architect*, February 1959, pp. 78–85.

[105] 'New Look', *Portsmouth Evening News*, 3 March 1960, Portsmouth Record Office.

[106] 'Portsmouth says "yes" to "Wonderful Plan for Guildhall"', *Portsmouth Evening News*, 12 April 1961.

[107] Portsmouth Record Office (PRO), Brett and Pollen, *Guildhall Redevelopment Area Consultant's Report Number 1* (1964).

and was accepted in principle by the council, forming the basis for *City of Portsmouth Development Plan, Amendment no. 1*, submitted and approved by MHLG in 1967. A second, more detailed report was produced in 1970. In 1967 Pevsner described the area as 'just a formless meeting of roads with desolate dreary buildings'. But he went on to predict that Brett's scheme would give the city what it needed: 'For the first time since it became a big city in the middle of the C19 Portsmouth will obtain a civic heart worthy of its status and importance.'[108]

The first report was 'a general appreciation of the historical, functional and aesthetic aspects of the city centre and a first approach to the guiding lines which should determine its reconstruction'.[109] Brett started by describing the area, in a way which separated the values of the Guildhall's Victorian architecture from its Victorian surroundings: 'Portsmouth's civic centre thus dates, as could be expected, from the great days of British naval expansion, and equally from the worst days of British town-planning. The awkward siting of the Guildhall jammed up against the railway, and the failure to give it a decent setting, are characteristic of the period.'[110] Equally characteristic of its own period was Brett's plan, which aimed to improve the Guildhall's 'environment' through pedestrianization (as often, too tightly conceived, although this was decided by the traffic engineer before Brett's appointment), and the creation of a half-picturesque, half-formal setting of respectful buildings in a modern idiom, and generally 'embodying such Victorian architecture as survived', as Brett put it in *Our Selves Unknown*.[111]

As Brett pointed out, the whole scheme started with the Guildhall: 'The Guildhall was the most important feature of the area and [the] proposals were designed to accentuate this building and to create a vista that would achieve this purpose'[112] (Figs 5.3, 5.4, and 5.5). Brett's elevation of the Guildhall to such a central position in the civic design aspect of his plan was not unusual in the schemes of post-war architect-planners. His approach at Portsmouth bears strong comparison with earlier plans, such as William Holford's plan for the area around St Paul's (of which Brett was an avid champion)[113] or Walter Bor's plan for the Tower Hill

[108] Nikolaus Pevsner, *Buildings of England: Hampshire and the Isle of Wight* (London, 1967), p. 446.

[109] BAL, Guildhall Area Redevelopment, Report no. 2 draft (1970), Brl/40/2.

[110] Brett and Pollen, *Guildhall Redevelopment Area Consultant's Report Number 1.*

[111] Brett, *Our Selves Unknown,* p. 109.

[112] Lionel Brett, speaking at a meeting, 31 December 1964, with owners and occupiers of premises within the Guildhall Redevelopment Area. BRL/39/3.

[113] BAL, Lionel Brett, letter to *the Times*, 16 April 1956, Brl/4/1.

Fig. 5.3. Model of Portsmouth, from *Plan for Portsmouth Central Area* (Portsmouth, 1970). Reproduced with the permission of Michael Brett.

Precinct West.[114] Brett himself pointed out the similarity with Shankland's plan for Bolton, which was also centred on a town hall by William Hill.[115]

The area contained 'a scatter of small shops and banks, two substantial Victorian office buildings, (to which two modern blocks have recently been added) several public houses, a small cinema and a late Victorian theatre with a splendid interior now given over to bingo and wrestling. Facing St Michael's Road is a harmonious group of Victorian buildings, of which only St. Andrew's Presbyterian church and its manse are likely to survive for long.'[116] St Andrew's did not survive, but Brett would campaign, eventually successfully, to keep the Theatre Royal—although the creation of a new Townscape-style cobbled setting for it, 'Theatre Square',

114 Percy Johnson Marshall, *Rebuilding Cities* (London, 1965), p. 290.
115 Esher, *The Continuing Heritage*, p. 109.
116 Brett and Pollen, *Guildhall Redevelopment Area Consultant's Report Number 1.*

Fig. 5.4. Perspective of the proposal for Guildhall Square, from *Plan for Portsmouth Central Area* (Portsmouth, 1970). Reproduced with the permission of Michael Brett and Portsmouth County Council.

never occurred (Fig. 5.6).[117] The more mundane Victorian fabric was discarded with little fuss.

As Pevsner had noted, Portsmouth lacked 'a central core which is both unmistakable and worthy of [its] size and importance'.[118] The concentration of three major 'traffic generators' in the area—the Guildhall itself, the railway station, and the shopping area—was 'incompatible with pedestrian access to the Guildhall or with the creation of a usable civic space in front of it'. Brett therefore proposed diverting Commercial Road away from the area, to produce 'an "environmental area" ideal in size and easy to handle in terms of both access and architecture', served by multistorey car parks

[117] Brett, *Our Selves Unknown*, p. 161.
[118] Brett and Pollen, *Guildhall Redevelopment Area Consultant's Report Number 1.*

Fig. 5.5. Perspective of the proposal for Theatre Square, from *Plan for Portsmouth Central Area* (Portsmouth, 1970). Reproduced with the permission of Michael Brett and Portsmouth County Council.

Fig. 5.6. Perspective of the view from the service road to the rear of Civic Offices, from *Plan for Portsmouth Central Area* (Portsmouth, 1970). Reproduced with the permission of Michael Brett and Portsmouth County Council.

for 2,600 cars. This was, therefore, a classic example of applying Buchanan principles to redevelopment, as was the discussion about how to achieve segregation:

> The next question to consider is the method to be adopted with in the area for the segregation of vehicles from pedestrians. The area is clearly too large and contains too many important buildings entered at ground level to allow a comprehensive multi-level system with vehicle circulation and parking at ground level and pedestrian circulation on a deck above. The converse solution (i.e. rooftop parking) would be open to serious amenity objection in the immediate vicinity of the Guildhall... It is therefore proposed to concentrate the bulk of the car parking in two 3-deck garages immediately adjacent to the perimeter roads, one on the east and one on the west side of the civic centre.

With multilevel segregation out of the question, the project would create a pedestrian precinct:

> These service roads are planned to delimit an island within an island, on which stands the Guildhall itself, the new civic offices, the Technical College, Theatre Royal, Health Clinic and a number of new commercial premises. Pedestrians enter this inner precinct by various routes and levels.

There is a notable Townscape element to the scheme. Each of the approaches to the square would have its own atmosphere, so that every 'route that a pedestrian can take should be visualized and designed as "a rewarding experience"'.[119] The most romantically picturesque of these was what Brett called 'the Mall':

> This approach (which I refer to as the Mall) is informal in character, varied in width and slightly bent so that the whole façade of the Guildhall bursts into view as one rounds the bend. The eye would be drawn round this bend from either direction by the curved front of the student's hostel building.

In creating this oblique approach, Brett later said he had in mind the approach to St Paul's from Ludgate.[120] Happily, this rather effete idea was actually borne out in the completed project, although one wonders how many notice it as anything but an irritation that the Guildhall is semi-obscured by the bronzed windows of the civic offices and the cylindrical backside of the library (Portsmouth Architect's Department do Frank Lloyd Wright's Guggenheim in a provincial brutalism). *The Architectural Review*, however, appreciated that Brett's multiple entrance points had

[119] 'From the Rubble of the Old', *Hampshire Telegraph*, 23 July 1970, Portsmouth Record Office.

[120] Brett, *Our Selves Unknown*, p. 161.

granted the square a scenographic and theatrical quality: 'The theatrical feel of this gathering of architectural elements is hard to deny.... The convergence upon the square of stage-like points of entry. "Enter Local Government officers, bottom left, carrying files... Enter Royal Marines, band playing, front right... Enter crowd of poly students over bridge at back of stage, yelling abuse... and so on."'[121]

As Brett put it in the second report, a mix of uses was crucial:

> It is therefore most important to keep alive the existing mixed uses of the old Commercial Road, with a theatre, shops, offices, cafes and pubs. This applies equally to the central space in front of the Guildhall, which must be designed primarily for liveliness and must avoid an excessively 'civic' feeling.

When the plan was first submitted, *The Times* wrote that a 'Continental atmosphere will be created by open air cafes and shops with canopies'.[122] This would be the hardest ambition to achieve, and the council ignored the intention that 'the south-facing ground stories of these buildings should contain restaurants or cafes with tables spilling out into the square in summer',[123] and filled these spaces with offices.

On the issue of height, Brett stressed that none of the new buildings should exceed that of the Guildhall, although he nevertheless proposed, for buildings not fronting streets, that seven storeys would 'give the civic centre a big-city scale which will make it conspicuous because this scale is notably absent from the rest of the city'. When it came to aesthetics, Portsmouth did not have a strong enough local character to dictate the architectural approach needed:

> The general architectural character of the centre cannot, as in older cities, be inspired by traditional local materials or building types. In so far as the Victorians and Edwardians gave Portsmouth an individual stamp, it tended to a pleasant amateurishness, with a lavish use of multi-coloured faience, giving the older parts that survive the sort of character that cannot be reproduced. Everything therefore depends on each new building being good of its kind. What we must also avoid is the tired old glass and concrete clichés of contemporary office building design.[124]

The use of reflective bronzed glass in Teggin's final project, itself a cliché by the 1970s, fitted in with a long running belief of Brett's that such architecture could best offset fine architecture of the past: 'A seventeenth-

[121] A. D. G. Smart and Lance Wright, 'Portsmouth Pomp', *The Architectural Review,* February 1977, pp. 89–100, p. 100.
[122] 'Continental Touch for Portsmouth', *The Times,* 9 April 1964.
[123] Brett and Pollen, *Guildhall Redevelopment Area Consultant's Report Number 1.*
[124] *Guildhall Area Redevelopment, Report no. 2 draft* (1970), Brl/40/2.

century church or an eighteenth-century terrace, overborne by ten stories of neo-Georgian windows in a red cliff, is overwhelmed and lost. But seen in its chiselled delicacy against a grid of glass and steel it is as vivid as a figure drawing on squared paper or as a plant on a trellis.'[125] Even if this sounds eccentric on paper, at Portsmouth the reflection of the Guildhall in the bronzed glass creates a genuinely appealing effect, partly because the volume is broken up and it is not just a direct reflection of a curtain wall.

A meeting with local businessmen and shopkeepers on 31 December 1964 saw Brett's plan attacked, as so many of these schemes were. A Mr Aldridge 'considered that the proposals were designed to glorify the civic centre, irrespective of the existing traders', while a Mr Middleton 'could not help but come to the conclusion that the Council was going to demolish a great many valuable buildings in the Guildhall Square area south of the Guildhall Square, mainly for architectural effect'.[126] Brett pointedly made it clear that, in the months following Wilson's Labour victory, his plans had nevertheless 'been made for the type of partnership between the City Council and private enterprise, as envisaged by the last [i.e. Conservative] Government'. Still, Brett described his role as a counter to the developer's plans, of the type that had been submitted at Portsmouth in 1960:

> Cities were being encouraged to plan for themselves so that the situation did not arise where private developers had demolished large sections of City Centres to suit their own purposes without any knowledge or understanding of a City's problems. The City Council were trying to think for themselves and to formulate clear policies so that when the time came a development scheme prepared on behalf of the City could be carried out as planned.[127]

The scheme was finally brought to fruition in 1976 by Teggin and Taylor. The *Architects' Journal* considered that 'Portsmouth has achieved a space worthy of any city in Europe. It is, at last, urbane. We shall probably never achieve the like again in our lifetime.'[128] But they also complained of 'a dead belt of as yet unresolved and lifeless roadworks', necessitated by the pedestrianization—a perennial problem of pedestrian precincts. Less complimentary was SAVE Britain's Heritage, which picked it as one of three projects (alongside London's Victoria Street and Liverpool University) to illustrate what was wrong with contemporary planning practice, in its report 'Concrete Jerusalem', republished in *New Society*. It lambasted

[125] BAL, 'Business and Beauty', (n.d., 1963?), BRL/1/1.

[126] BAL, 'Meeting, 31st December 1964, with owners and occupiers of premises within the Guildhall Redevelopment Area. BRL 39/3.

[127] Ibid.

[128] 'Portsmouth Gets a Heart', *Architects' Journal*, 24 November 1976, pp. 960–70.

'Pompey's failed heart surgery'. This was especially damning in lamenting the 'decline of places to shop, eat and drink' that had existed before redevelopment, and it quoted a 1975 inspector's report that 'Time has shown that without the retention of existing buildings to house specialist shops and small restaurants and entertainment facilities of all kinds, the Guildhall will be lifeless.'[129] The Portsmouth Civic Society pointed out the effect of this, especially at night: 'use of the Square tends to fall off when the offices are closed and there is little evening use of it as a through route—it can be frightening and is definitely not a place to linger.'[130] These attacks seem inordinate today, and the times I have visited, the square has appeared a happy mixture of old and new, the grand and the informal. On a summer day, there were even the hoped-for tables spilling out into the square, courtesy of a coffee van. Portsmouth's City Architect robustly defended the scheme, stating that even in 1977 there were 'tremendous evenings last summer, with the square filled by thousands of people, with food and drink stalls set up and music and dancing'. They, rather charmingly, argued that it did 'on a more modest scale for Portsmouth what St Mark's Square does for Venice'.[131]

Portsmouth remains without a satisfactory centre, but clearly benefits from the thickening-up that is provided by the Civic Centre, although an increased mixed use of shops and restaurants, as Brett intended, would no doubt improve the area. It comes into its own for occasions, from graduation day at the university to naval parades. The problem is how tightly conceived it is—the pleasures of the pedestrian precinct a pyrrhic victory far outweighed by the four-lane ring road, named Winston Churchill Avenue, and all the urban mess it causes.

YORK

Brett's plan for York was one of four conservation studies that had been commissioned by Minister of Housing and Local Government Richard Crossman in 1966.[132] They were in response to the disastrous

[129] Marcus Binney, Timothy Cantell, and Gillian Darley, 'Pompey's Failed Heart Surgery', *New Society*, 23/30 Dec 1975, pp. ix–xi, p. x Previous occupancy comprised ten public houses, seven restaurants, two tobacconists, two confectioners, two car-hire firms, an antique dealer, a betting shop, a car showroom, an outfitters, a photographer, a house furnishers, and an optician. In 1976 this was reduced to five pubs and a snack bar.

[130] *The Portsmouth Society City Centre Report*, January 1977, Portsmouth Record Office.

[131] W. W. Worden, 'Letter', *New Society* (10 February 1977), pp. 296–7.

[132] See also Colin Buchanan, *Bath, A Study in Conservation* (London, 1968); G. S. Burrows, *Chichester, A Study in Conservation* (London, 1968); and Donald Insall, *Chester, A Study in Conservation* (London, 1968).

consequences of redevelopment seen in historic cities such as Worcester. After initial niceties, the York plan opens with a radical modernist bang, with a quote from Dutch architect and theorist Aldo van Eyck: 'This much is certain: the town has no room for the citizen—no meaning at all—unless he is gathered into its meaning. As for architecture; it need do no more than assist man's homecoming.'[133] The plan attempts to use many of the textbook solutions of 1960s planning, such as traffic management and separation of incompatible uses, but applying them to the problems of conservation in a historic town, while—and this is a central point of the plan—also pushing for the SPUR ideal of returning life to the centre of cities:

> It should now go without saying that the main object of the exercise is to make the walled city liveable again. It must be emphasised that the essence of conservation is continuing economic use, and that the great majority of the best secular architecture in York was built for living in and is still eminently liveable, given the right environment. The exodus from city centres which has been a feature of the last half century has been due not to any love of commuting but to a revulsion from the dirt, noise and congestion that invaded them in the Victorian era, and that more than cancelled out the convenience of living in them. If the invaders could be ejected, the balance would at once swing the other way.[134]

The opening chapters lay out the city's illustrious history, followed by an account of the problems facing it. The history section recalls Thomas Sharp's plans for cathedral cities of the 1940s, including those for Durham, Salisbury, and Exeter—with their mixture of topography, anecdote, and history. The ultimate source for the way the plan is set out is Patrick Geddes's exhortation to make a survey and analysis before planning. The description of 'York today' is realized in classic Townscape style, attempting to perceive 'the life and personality' of places, and is sensitive to such things as sudden 'complete changes of scene', the 'splendid variety of middle-distance features', and 'character and potentiality'.[135] But there is some recognition of the limitations of this aesthetic approach, and the section ends with the argument:

> So far we have looked at the city as a kind of stage-set. Now it is time to bring in the actors. A city is not a work of art. It is shaped by human activities, and in turn shapes them, and nobody has ever been able to analyse or order them precisely enough to achieve a fully controlled townscape. But we must do our best to understand them, because our plans will fail to work if we study a town as a mere arrangement of streets and buildings.

[133] Viscount Esher [Lionel Brett], *York, A Study in Conservation* (London, 1968).
[134] Ibid., p. 49. [135] Ibid., pp. 13–23.

The report criticizes the Stonebow House development, a mini-megastructure realized in a corporate, brutalist style, with a tower rising out from a podium deck used for car parking, and a supermarket below (Wells, Hickman, and Partners, 1964), whose 'visual characteristics are sufficient commentary on the national loss of touch which has led to the need for this Report'.[136] Nevertheless, the recommendations of the plan for York, especially when viewed in the context of Brett's long-term intellectual development, can be seen to be very much within the mainstream of 1960s planning thought, although the familiar weapons are used for different aims. For a 'study in conservation' Brett pushed what is commonly understood as conservation into the background. The plan set out five objectives:

> 1. That the commercial heart of York should remain alive and able to compete on level terms with its neighbour cities, new or old.
>
> 2. That the environment should be so improved by the elimination of decay, congestion and noise that the centre will become highly attractive as a place to live in for families, for students and single persons, and for the retired.
>
> 3. That land use which conflict with these purposes should progressively be removed from the walled city.
>
> 4. That the historic character of York should be so enhanced and the best of its buildings of all ages so secured that they become economically self-conserving.
>
> 5. That within the walled city the erection of new buildings of anything but the highest architectural standards should cease.[137]

Traffic remained by 'far the greatest obstacle to the rehabilitation of the historic core . . . [with] its familiar accompaniment of noise, smell, congestion and visual intrusion'.[138] The traffic objectives set out in the report are classic Buchanan, in both advice and terminology. They involve excluding traffic from environmental areas, trying to rid the city of cross-town traffic and of uses which generated excessive traffic, and the creation of a pedestrian network while also enabling vehicular access for servicing. The plan suggests a residents' permit system and the banning of on-street parking for all but residents' cars. Nevertheless, it eschews full-scale pedestrianization, arguing that 'York lives by its trade of one sort or another, and trade is strangled without accessibility.'[139] As Buchanan had advised, the York plan balanced the needs of accessibility with the damage inflicted on the environment by this accessibility. The plan is

[136] Ibid., p. 7. It has recently been reclad. [137] Ibid., p. 41.
[138] Ibid., p.49. [139] Ibid., p. 58.

unusually restrictive of traffic, coming down firmly on the side of 'the environment, on which York's fortunes, must finally depend',[140] rather than access: 'Unquestionably this is the one department where some curtailment of existing freedoms in the general interest is inevitable in York as elsewhere.'[141]

The section on conservation is as much about creating the prerequisites by which buildings would be looked after as about the actual bricks-and-mortar process: 'We now know that it is useless to preserve old buildings unless we preserve with (or restore to them) a setting which encourages their appropriate use.' This involved a reawakened appreciation of the benefits of that much maligned figure in early 1960s planning, the small shopkeeper: 'While the big stores and offices are the main agents of destruction of old buildings, the "quality" stores, boutiques and specialized shops are some of their most effective guardians, and are in a position to spend more money on them than most private owners.'[142] New buildings were advised to 're-interpret the York tradition in 20th century terms'. The plan is reticent about what this might mean, but the illustrations and plans show that this was envisioned as being low-rise blocks arranged in picturesque and dense clusters, often, as at Swinegate, using their ground floor for garages. In perspectives they are shown with various modish features, such as mono-pitched roofs and boxed-out windows in the manner of Howell, Killick, Partridge, and Amis.

DISILLUSIONMENT

If the York plan goes some way to suggesting that a self-defining modernist like Lionel Brett was able to slide effortlessly towards new, more conservation-orientated aims, such a narrative is belied by Brett's intense disillusionment at the end of the 1960s. In 1969 Brett wrote an article which lucidly summed up the philosophy of the past decade—of which he had been a central advocate—and the way it now seemed pathetically inadequate:

> In places of all sizes, Traffic was public enemy No. 1, and Buchanan was the sword of the spirit. His clear analysis leading inescapably to clear courses of action commanded universal assent and in record time became the Bible of the Borough engineer. 'Environmental areas' were delimited where pedestrians were to have absolute priority, and up and down the country commercial developers put on white sheets and provided, at what seemed to be

[140] Ibid., p. 58. [141] Ibid., p. 58. [142] Ibid., p. 77.

> an actual profit to the municipality, brand-new multi-storey car parks and shopping precincts where the house-wife was going to be absolutely happy in her nursery of consumer durables. That it is impossible to sum up the conventional wisdom in any other tone than irony must already have given the show away. For the truth is that the sixties, which saw the good intentions of the fifties put into effect, were a decade of disenchantment . . . it was only too painfully obvious that the welfare-state generation had failed, except in a few odd corners, to deliver the goods.[143]

This failure was not just one of failure to implement, but was visible and writ large in the appalling modern development in city centres: 'in the city centres and the historic towns, where it showed, modern architecture seemed both monotonous and gimmicky, the lumpish offspring and peculiarly unpleasant liaison between faceless planning officers and the wide boys of the real estate world.'[144] In his 1970 book *Parameters and Images* Brett fired a splenetic broadside against the whole parade of post-war development:

> We hate not only what the builders are doing in the country but what the architects are doing in the towns. We hate civic centres and shopping precincts and car parks and the absence of car parks. We dread highway improvements and landscaping, public conveniences and public sculpture and municipal murals.[145]

By 1970 Brett had set out a new philosophy, which totally abandoned the radical rhetoric of reconstruction in favour of a philosophy of quietist restraint:

> Ninety-nine times out of a hundred the architect should see himself as contributing a brushstroke or two to a collective work of art and science which changes with every contribution, rather than as sole author of an isolated statement in a static environment. The raw material of his design will be the perennial parameters . . . but his analysis of them and the resulting synthesis will be crude and lifeless unless informed by love, that is to say by an affectionate understanding of what human beings have tried to do there in the past . . . you have to work with the grain, stroke the animal down-fur, set up no image that fails to take hold in the user's imagination.[146]

In 1970 Brett left the world of architecture to become Rector of the Royal College of Art. This was partly motivated by a falling-out with his partner, Harry Teggin, who Brett later complained was beastly to his friend the

[143] Brett, 'Architecture in the Sixties'. [144] Brett, 'Architecture in the Sixties'.
[145] Lionel Brett, *Parameters and Images* (London, 1970), p. 151.
[146] Ibid., p. 111.

architect Geoffrey Jellicoe.[147] There was also little work to go round between the five or so private planning consultancy firms in Britain, because cities were beginning to build up their own internal planning departments.[148] A deeper reason why Brett left architecture was that he had become both disillusioned and embittered. Furthermore, his new quietist philosophy was a tough one for an ambitious practising architect or planner. He threw in the towel.

In 1973 Hugh Casson grouped Brett with Ian Nairn, Jane Jacobs, and Nan Fairbrother as one of the figures who had pointed the way forward.[149] If we just had Brett's writing, it might not be so surprising to see him in this company, as an outsider figure dismantling modernist orthodoxies. He was certainly an astute commentator, and devoted his life to improving the environment. That he was a practitioner as well as a critic makes him a much more difficult figure to unambiguously celebrate than these other figures—but that he could inhabit both roles suggests that we need to revise our understanding of the period in a way which sees it as both messier and less polarized. A study of Brett suggests that the Manichaean narrative of modernists versus conservationists has been damagingly limiting.

It is clear that Portsmouth was lucky to have Brett's planning expertise rather than the scheme by Commercial Road (Portsmouth) Property Investment Co. Ltd, and that Worcester would have had a happier outcome had some of Brett's approach at York been applied. His approach and philosophy could easily be criticized as being rarefied from ordinary life, and he had at best a rather woolly, paternalist conception of those he was planning for. In his fight with the Portsmouth shopkeepers, they were proved right. Nevertheless, he was a long way from the bigoted planner of popular conception. He won many small victories in tempering the more egregious brutalities of 1960s development. Brett is interesting beyond the facts of his individual biography. He helps us to see modernism and the rise of the preservation movement as linked phenomena rather than in dialectical conflict. Brett gives an insight into how these processes could be seen as naturally concomitant in the 1950s, but were in increasingly uncomfortable alliance through the 1960s, breaking apart by 1970, primarily under the sheer weight of the awfulness of development.

[147] Esher, Lionel Gordon Baliol Brett (9 of 13), National Life Stories, Architects' Lives. British Library.

[148] Although to a lesser extent than Shankland Cox and Llewelyn-Davies, Weeks, Forestier-Walker & Bor, Brett did go down the route of international consultancy, and his last plan was for Caracas from 1975.

[149] Sir Hugh Casson, 'One man's formula for overcoming a nation's disenchantment', *The Times*, 27 February 1973, p. 2.

His rhetorical stance and approach were often sensitive, and could even occasionally be lyrical, but they proved inadequate under external pressures—a fact Brett was only too aware of. He articulated better than anyone the experience of disillusionment that happened with near unanimity. As he wrote in 1982,'The "consensus", and its later collapse, was that of a whole intellectual generation'.[150] The next, concluding Chapter 6 will explore this collapse further.

[150] Lionel Brett, 'Reply', *Architects' Journal*, 28 April 1982, p. 38.

6

The Trajectory of Central-Area Redevelopment

> At times it did not seem possible that a mere idea could have become so concrete, that it could be employing so many men, so many cement mixers and bulldozers, so much cement, so many bricks. But there they all were as evidence. . . . So this was what people complained about when they complained about the ruination of city centres. How right they were. It was monstrous, inhuman, ludicrous. It was just as well that the country had gone bankrupt, that property developers had collapsed and that Len was in jail. This was no improvement: this was an environmental offense as bad as a slag heap.
>
> Margaret Drabble, *The Ice Age* (1977)

I

The approach that Brett and Shankland share was not some aberration among 1960s planning culture, but can be broadly taken as indicative of the mainstream. It is therefore unhelpful to see them as part of some alternative strand of modernism, set up against an inflexible mainstream.[1] Rather, modernism accounted for only part of a complex hinterland of motivating influences. So where does the narrative of the dogmatic Corbusians coming to Britain come from? A biographical approach is helpful here: for architects beginning to practise around the end of the war, those demonstrably obsessed with 'Corbu' (James Stirling, Alison and Peter Smithson, Bill Howell and John Partridge, Colin St John Wilson being famous examples—although they too would develop critiques of Corbusier) went on to become the art architects of the 1960s, most influential in the universities and mass housing schemes, and with

[1] As in Colin St John Wilson, *Other tradition of modern architecture: The uncompleted project* (London, 2007) and countless other books about modernist architects.

scant influence on approaches to existing city centres. An architect just would not go on to get a planning qualification if they did not have some sort of holistic, humanist, *Architectural Review*-inflected vision. Chamberlin, Powell, and Bon (notably Joe Chamberlin) were unusual in inhabiting both worlds and both domains of influence.

What became of this planning culture? Aside from the abovementioned move towards a more holistic conception of cities and therefore a broader account of what was to be preserved, the changes were fourfold. The first was that the long battle to train more architect-planners and to build up internal planning departments was beginning to show fruit. This forced the five or so planning consultancy firms (Shankland Cox; Buchanan and Partners; Llewelyn-Davies, Forestier-Walker, Weeks and Bor; Wilson and Womersley; Brett) to move to doing consultancy jobs abroad, often through former colonial networks.[2] Although we might regret the relative lack of colour in the more bureaucratic planning conducted under the aegis of a planning office, this was nevertheless generally a happy occurrence, since so many of the worst catastrophes of city-centre redevelopment happened when local authorities did not have the internal wherewithal to steer it.

The second development was that planners were eschewing the romantic language of urbanity and high density that had charged much planning discourse in the early 1960s. This can be seen most clearly in the further round of New Town and town expansion schemes from the mid-1960s, which were commissioned by the Ministry of Housing and Local Government from private consultants drawn from the usual suspects among radical planners.[3] The most famous of these, for what would become Milton Keynes, gives a sense of how the planning profession was itself shifting away from the romantic ideal of high-density planning towards a more open and dispersed ideal.[4] It was a remarkably rapid volte-face, which reflects the influence of a strand of ideas coming from the USA,

[2] Guy Ortolano, 'Exporting Britain's New Towns', talk given at the 'Transformation of Urban Britain since 1945' conference, Centre for Urban History at the University of Leicester, 9–10 July 2013.

[3] D. A. Bull, 'New Town and Town Expansion Schemes: Part I: An Assessment of Recent Government Planning Reports', *Town Planning Review*, July 1967, pp. 103–14. See Shankland Cox and Associates, *Expansion of Ipswich* (London, 1966); Colin Buchanan and Partners, *South Hampshire Study* (London, 1966); Wilson and Womersley, *Expansion of Northampton* (London, 1966); Wilson and Womersley, *Northampton, Bedford, North Bucks Study* (London, 1966); John H. D. Madin and Partners, *Dawley: Wellington: Oakengates* (London, 1966), the towns which would become Telford; The Welsh Office, *A New Town for Mid-Wales* (London, 1966); Richard Llewelyn-Davies, John Weeks, Robert Forestier-Walker, and Walter Bor, *A New City* (London 1966).

[4] Terence Bendixson and John Platt, *Milton Keynes, Image and Reality* (Cambridge, 1992).

especially those of urban theorist Melvin Webber.[5] These plans saw community not in terms of people's propinquity, to use the jargon phrase of the period, but saw emerging forms of transport and communications as creating new and richer possibilities for 'voluntary association'. I suspect it has something to do with planners realizing their relative impotence and deciding to plan with the flow rather than against it. Flexibility was a keynote of these plans, a recognition of the impossibility of predicting where the rapid changes affecting society would end up. A celebrated expression of this strain of ideas was Reyner Banham, Paul Barker, Peter Hall, and Cedric Price's 'Non-Plan: an experiment in freedom' of 1969.[6] However, a flavour of these new ideas can be tasted even in Colin Buchanan's 1966 plan for South Hampshire, which totally abandons the celebration of urbanity and the attack on suburbia found in *Traffic in Towns* only three years earlier:

> It may be argued that what we have proposed is nothing more nor less than a 'sprawl' or a 'suburbia'. We would reject those terms in as much as they contain various innuendoes, but there is no doubt we are suggesting a dispersed, but structured and landscaped city with a new kind of urban texture. We have little doubt that this will meet the tastes and desires arising from trends in education, leisure and mobility, far more realistically than any notions of concentrating large numbers of people into high density flats for the sake of saving an insignificant amount of agricultural land, or in pursuit of some purely architectural concept.[7]

The third switch was the divorce and subsequent extreme drifting apart of those in power and the avant-garde. It was a very brief moment when such apparently practical and responsible people as civil servants, developers, and politicians made a brief junction with the most radical ideas.[8] The 'walking cities' of Archigram might be seen as comment enough on the fact that the avant-garde was itself moving in the opposite direction from practical applicability.

The fourth change was the fact that architecture ceased to be the dominant profession in planning. Shankland's later career is indicative of a move away from a physical, towards a broader, more social approach, which increasingly took in issues beyond the built environment and

[5] Mark Clapson, *Anglo-American Crossroads, Urban Research and Planning in Britain, 1940–2010* (London, 2010).

[6] Reyner Banham, Paul Barker, Peter Hall, and Cedric Price, 'Non-Plan: an experiment in freedom', *New Society*, 20 March 1969.

[7] *South Hampshire Study*, p.107.

[8] Douglas Murphy, *Last Futures: Nature, technology and the end of architecture* (London, 2016) is a good guide to the late stage of techno-utopian modernism.

subsequently relied on expertise from a range of disciplines. Planning documents from the United States were making a similar journey in this period.[9] A related development was the growth of systems planning, which overrode the articulate, visionary, and romantic planning documents of the early 1960s and replaced them with a diagrammatic scientism. Plans from the later 1960s tend to shift planning away from design disciplines and towards the social sciences, especially economics.[10] A cost-analysis approach certainly doused the Buchanan Report with cold water.[11] Terence Bendixson, in a defence of Buchanan, argued that what such cost-analysis approaches had 'failed to grasp is that sweeping social policies are not adopted or rejected on grounds of cost but because they strike an emotional chord and become a political necessity'.[12] One planner at least lamented the loss of the old design-led discipline, as can be seen in Konrad Smigielski's 1973 broadside against it:

> There is no public opposition because no one can understand it. Fooled by computers and by cost benefit analysis, planners have been led away from the design of cities and the countryside – their true role.[13]

II

Although the high point in the movement to radically redevelop cities had already passed by the mid-1960s, there is no obvious date to mark the crash of city-centre redevelopment—indeed it was a drawn-out process, with a further orgy of construction during the 'Barber Boom' of the early 1970s.[14] It is obvious, though, that the accumulating sense of disillusionment was increasingly palpable, and that the crisis of disenchantment enunciated by Brett was part of a widespread phenomenon, which Peter Hall has gone as far as to describe as a 'national nervous breakdown'.[15] There are so many manifestations of such a switch that it is tempting to

[9] See NY City Planning Commission, *Plan for New York City, 1969* (New York, 1969).

[10] H. W. E. Davies 'The Planning System and the Development Plan', in *British Planning: 50 Years of Urban and Regional Policy,* ed. Barry Cullingworth (London, 1999), p. 53.

[11] See D. J. Reynolds, *Economics, Town Planning and Traffic* (London, 1966), pp. 60–97.

[12] Terence Bendixson, 'Doomed', *The Spectator*, 4 November 1966, p. 18.

[13] 'Planner Errant Takes a Tilt', *Architects' Journal*, 4 April 1973, p. 789. See also J. L. Womersley, 'Prospects and Pitfalls', *Yorkshire Architect,* November/December 1969, pp. 198–200.

[14] For a fictional treatment of this moment, see Margaret Drabble, *The Ice Age* (London, 1977).

[15] Peter Hall, *Cities of Tomorrow* (London, 1988), p. 346.

discuss it in terms of zeitgeist. Revelations about murky corruption surrounding property speculation, brought to light through the conviction in 1974 of the architect John Poulson and Newcastle politician T. Dan Smith, further tarnished the reputation of Britain's city-centre schemes.[16] The explosion at Ronan Point tower block in 1968, and the subsequent revelations about poor construction of modern buildings, formed a further symbolically charged moment in a concatenation of crises that appeared to beset modernist buildings.

Many schemes that had first been forged in the white heat of economic optimism nevertheless continued to grind into realization, often enacted in a vulgarized and diluted form under the increased imperatives of financial stringency. Development takes a long time. When Pevsner visited Lancashire—one of the epicentres of city-centre redevelopment—for the two volumes of the *Buildings of England* series on that county in 1969, there was still almost nothing to be seen except for construction sites and the embryonic promise of 'great changes'.[17] The *Daily Mirror*'s 1967 feature 'Boom City', in which readers wrote in to boast of their booming cities, captures the sense of the excitement it was still possible to experience when these eruptions of construction were still in progress.[18] Here is an example from Sheffield: 'Just pause along any of the main shopping centres and you will hear Sheffield booming. The constant roar of traffic, the passage of crowds of people and noise of building construction will tell you this. It is the boom of expansion.'[19]

An insight into the later vicissitudes suffered by redevelopment schemes can be gained from *City Centre Redevelopment*, a 1973 book cataloguing the 'major changes which have taken place in five city centres [Coventry, Birmingham, Leicester, Liverpool, and Newcastle] since the war, and particularly in the last ten years'.[20] Konrad Smigielski was the most wryly articulate: a 'walk through Leicester today would give an impression that the city has undergone a recent bombardment by enemy action... The public is bewildered and critical about these changes. Elderly ladies write rude letters to me: "Why do you hate Leicester? Why are you

[16] Peter Jones, 'Re-thinking corruption in post-1950 urban Britain: the Poulson affair, 1972–6', *Urban History*, 39.3 (2012); Ewan Harrison, '"Money spinners": R. Seifert & Partners, Sir Frank Price and Public-Sector Speculative Development in the 1970s', *Architectural History*, 61 (2018), pp. 259–80.

[17] Nikolaus Pevsner, *Buildings of England: South Lancashire* (London, 1969), p. 64. See also the same volume, p. 56.

[18] Selina Todd, 'Phoenix Rising: Working Class Life and Urban Reconstruction, c. 1945–1967', *Journal of British Studies*, 54.3 (2015), pp. 679–702, pp. 698–701.

[19] Letter from Mrs Elizabeth Cannings, *Daily Mirror*, 12 January 1967.

[20] John Holliday, ed., *City Centre Redevelopment* (London, 1973), p. 1.

destroying this once gracious city?" '[21] This attitude was expressed during a defence of his tenure as planner of Leicester!

The dubious honour for being the last 1960s city-centre scheme to be completed goes to Wood Green Shopping City, designed by Sheppard Robson for Haringey Council in partnership with Electricity Supply Nominees and Unilever. It uses 3 million bricks, over a 14-acre (5.7-hectare) site, to house a convoluted layer cake of 500,000 square feet (46,450 square metres) of shopping space, a 70-stall market hall, car parking for 1,500 cars and, on top of it all, an incongruous village of 201 pitched-roofed houses and flats. It was only completed in 1981. Large-scale projects of this sort experienced major construction delays because of inflation and strike action in the construction industry.[22] Wood Green is the last of the megastructures.[23] The plan was formulated following the amalgamation of Tottenham, Wood Green, and Hornsey in 1965.[24] Wood Green was to be reinvented as a 'Heart for Haringey', one of a number of new suburban centres intended to counteract the magnetic pull of Central London.[25] Plans were published from 1966, and though they were criticized by MHLG for being too grandiose, the council held on to the 1960s vision with an unusual tenacity. As was recognized on its completion, 'Shopping City can be seen as one of the last of the ambitious town-centre redevelopments of the 1960s, and after many delays, redesigns and other development problems it was finally completed in the harsher economic climate of the 1980s.'[26] The chartered surveyor for the scheme, Harry Lucas, described the scheme in a way which highlights how totally inappropriate it appeared in the very different world of the early 1980s. Shopping City had been built...

> in keeping with many town centre redevelopment schemes of the 1960s, designed to reshape our challenge for new prosperity and the motor car. They now appear too grandiose with their over provision of multi-storey car parks, segregated pedestrian vehicular traffic and organization of activities on multiple levels... Such a project takes a long time to come to fruition and the world has suffered various upheavals during its gestation period. It would

[21] Ibid., p. 135.

[22] Alan Powers, *Britain, Modernist Architecture in History* (London, 2007), p. 204.

[23] See Otto Saumarez Smith, 'Robinson College, Cambridge, and the Twilight of a Collegiate Modernism, 1974-81', *Architectural History,* 55 (2012), pp. 369–402, for another modernist project completed in the new cultural climate of the early 1980s. The Barbican was completed in 1982, 'stillborn whilst the rest of the world had moved on', as one scathing reviewer put it. Lance Knobel, 'Barbican Arts Centre', *The Architectural Review*, October 1981, pp. 238–52.

[24] For my fuller account of Shopping City, see http://www.c20society.org.uk/botm/wood-green-shopping-city-london/.

[25] Haringey Archives, 'Origins of the Scheme', 'Haringey Central Area' (n.d., 1978–9).

[26] Robert K. Home, *Wood Green Shopping City* (London, 1984), p. 4.

be easy, given the benefit of hindsight, to assume that one might now tackle this sort of job in a different way.[27]

III

Looking at the way politicians thought about architectural production may not provide us with any particularly profound insights into buildings themselves, but it can nevertheless help us to understand not just something about the history of taste but about the way modernist architecture was able to articulate ideas about British identity, the future, and about Britain's relationship with the world. Richard Crossman's assiduously kept diaries during his tenure at the Ministry of Housing and Local Government are an illuminating source for following the shifting outlook from enthusiasm towards disillusionment that occurred over modernist solutions. A particularly revealing entry describes a visit to Cumbernauld New Town on 14 February 1965. Cumbernauld was the only New Town designated in the 1950s, and as such was an important incubator for a range of planning ideas, mixing both the social and the aesthetic, that were influential in the city-centre rebuilding of cities. These ideas can be summed as being: a use of radical forms which nevertheless adheres to an anti-suburban and basically traditional idea of society; a push for increased densities expressed rhetorically through the desire for 'urbanity'; the use of a tough aesthetic; and planning for full automobile ownership through total segregation of pedestrians and motor traffic.[28] Crossman found Cumbernauld thrilling: 'a fascinating variety of modern houses. Up-and-down houses, vertical houses, and everything, including the churches, fitting into the style, everything done in a tremendously austere, exhilarating, uncomfortable style.'[29] The *Sunday Times* architectural correspondent, 'Atticus', wrote an article about Crossman's visit. According to Atticus, Crossman's visit marked…

> an important development in the debate (or perhaps battle is a better word) between two apparently irreconcilable groups of people who want to determine the character of our future towns and cities: the garden city planners (or water colour school as their enemies call them) who like their new towns

[27] Quoted in Home, *Wood Green Shopping City*, p. 2.

[28] A density of 70–80 persons to the acre, rising to 100–200 near the centre. Hugh Wilson, *Cumbernauld New Town, Preliminary Planning Report, First Addendum Report* ([Cumbernauld], 1959), p. 9.

[29] Richard Crossman *The Diaries of a Cabinet Minister Vol 1. Minister of Housing 1964–66* (London, 1974), p. 158.

> bosky, diffuse and full of nice little houses nice little people want, and the city-in-a-garden planners (or arrogant, intellectual, theorizing high density madmen as their enemies call them) who think a town should be planned first of all as a *town*, tightly packed, many storied, and visually exciting.[30]

According to Frederic Osborn, the leading propagandist for the first Garden City group, this article had 'escalated a border incident into a nuclear war'.[31] Osborn had long been waging a solitary campaign against what he called the 'city addict, whether a writer of attractive mixtures of topography, history and anecdote, or an architectural student captivated by the fashion for visual "urbanity"'.[32] The war had already been lost as far as central government was concerned, at least if Crossman's private secretary Dame Evelyn Sharp's virulent comments at Cumbernauld are anything to go by:

> We have an overcrowded island, we need good solid hard towns. High density planning is the only way. I know that most people, if asked, opt for the detached house and garden. But even if people don't think they want the kind of housing that makes sensible, effective towns they come to like them once they live in it.[33]

Crossman noted that Atticus had hit the nail on the head in this article: 'I thought Atticus this morning in the *Sunday Times* was extremely apposite when he pointed out that this was the kind of thing which Dame Evelyn and I are excited about, in contrast to the cosy garden suburb atmosphere of Stevenage or Harlow or Basildon.'[34] Atticus had drily suggested that 'It's not surprising that Cumbernauld and Crossman should get on well together. They have similar personalities and similar prejudices. Both are brilliant, handsome and according to their critics, uncomfortable to live with.'

As the relationship between Crossman and Brett suggests, Crossman was able to fit effortlessly in with what might be regarded as the architecture and planning establishment. His enthusiasm could be unbounded.

[30] Atticus, *The Sunday Times,* 14 February 1965, p. 9.

[31] Hertfordshire Archives, Letter from Osborn to General Sir Gordon MacMillan, chairman of the Cumbernauld Development Corporation, 19 April 1965, CDEFJO/2/44. See also 'Report of Talk by Sir Frederic Osborn at a conference of the Scottish National Housing and Town Planning Council at Pebbles on 3rd of March, 1966', *The Scotsman,* 11 March 1966.

[32] Peter Self, *Cities in Flood, The Problems of Urban Growth* (London, 1957), p. xiv.

[33] Atticus, *The Sunday Times,* 14 February 1965, p. 9.

[34] Crossman, *Diaries of a Cabinet Minister Vol 1*, pp. 158–9. It is worth quoting some of the following discussion as reported by Crossman: '"Wouldn't that help Laing, the builders?" "Of course it would" said Oliver, "and it would help Oldham too." "Well why don't we do it?" "It depends on the Minister."'

For example, when seeing Oliver Cox's project for Oldham, developed while Cox was Deputy Chief Architect at MHLG, he overflowed: 'Why shouldn't we assume that instead of doing one little bit of the centre of Oldham we should use the whole 300 acres... Let's see one piece of central redevelopment that really works.'[35] MHLG's appointment of Cumbernauld's head architect, Hugh Wilson, to reorganize the architectural side of the department was a strong indication of the government's commitment to the Cumbernauld style of planning. Crossman was greeted by the planning profession enthusiastically; as Percy Johnson Marshall put it after hearing Crossman's inaugural lecture to the Town Planning Institute, 'At last, it seemed to me, we had a politician in Parliament who understood our problems; and this made me feel really extraordinarily exhilarated.'[36]

Privately, though, Crossman had doubts, when visiting Welwyn the next week, he found 'it charming and I am sure that it is a delightful place to live in. The Dame of course is contemptuous. She loves Cumbernauld. I also like Cumbernauld as architecture, but I see that the vast majority of British people would probably prefer to live in Welwyn with its red bricks and its North Oxford lilac.' Worse than such aesthetic worries were fears about what was happening in city-centre redevelopment, that it just wasn't good enough, a widely felt sentiment. Crossman lamented, 'As I go round the country... I am getting used to being shown the most magnificent plans in the council offices and then feeling a sense of anti-climax when I walk outside and see the actual buildings going up.'[37] In Wigan he made the prescient prediction: 'I am afraid they have built a Wigan that in 2000 will look as bad as the old 1880s Wigan looks in the eyes of the 1960s.'[38] Crossman was aware of the inadequacy of using urban renewal to truly renew deindustrialized townscapes—the problem that was only too obvious in Blackburn. Deindustrialization was a word and concept that would only gain wide currency in the 1970s, but as a condition it was already a stark and visible fact in many cities.[39] This struck Crossman forcefully on a visit to Stoke-on-Trent, where he, if only to himself, entertained the

[35] Crossman, *Diaries of a Cabinet Minister Vol 1.*, p. 81.

[36] TNA, 'Planning Advisory Group, Papers Circulated', HLG136/142.

[37] Richard Crossman, 'Planning Policies of the Government' *Town Planning Institute Journal*, 1965, pp. 206–7.

[38] Crossman, *Diaries of a Cabinet Minister Vol 1.*, p. 341.

[39] For the etymology of the word see Bert Altena and Marcel van der Linden, *De-Industrialization: Social, Cultural, and Political Aspects* (Cambridge, 2002), p. 7.

managed decline of industrial cities, which almost became official policy in Thatcher's Britain:[40]

> As I was driving through [Stoke-on-Trent] I suddenly felt, 'Here is this huge, ghastly conurbation of five towns [*sic*] – what sense is there in talking about urban renewal here? Other towns have a shape, a centre, some place where renewal can start, perhaps a university. But if one spent billions on this ghastly collection of slag heaps, pools of water, old potteries, deserted coal mines, there would be nothing to show for the money.' There is nothing in Stoke except the worst of the industrial revolution, and the nicest of people... When it was over I felt even more strongly that it was impossible to revive Britain without letting such places as Stoke-on-Trent decline. Indeed, I began to wonder whether it wasn't really better to let it be evacuated: renewal is an impossibility, or alternatively a fantastic waste of money.[41]

IV

In a mixed economy, where the money for the radical transformations of cities was going to come from, unless it was from developers, had always been ambiguous. What is more, in the years after 1963 economic confidence very quickly began to appear increasingly naive, as the country lurched from one economic crisis to the next, which was made impossible to ignore by the devaluation crisis of 1967. The whole project of radical reconstruction was based on an economic optimism that, as the 1960s progressed, became ever harder to sustain. Furthermore, the planning of the early 1960s was little prepared to combat two of the problems that would become increasingly paramount: how to give cities a new role in the face of deindustrialization, and how to help those in inner-city areas left behind in the general trend towards greater affluence. Cities were subsequently increasingly understood as sites of crisis rather than of opportunity.

As the 1960s moved towards the 1970s, deindustrialization and the sharp decline of jobs were increasingly blamed on the processes of urban modernization, especially because of the removal of smaller firms in clearance schemes.[42] The feeling that urban modernism had actually exacerbated, or even created, Britain's economic and social woes was an

[40] Joerg Arnold, '"Managed Decline"? Merseyside and the Politics of the Thatcher Administration', paper given at Urban Societies in Europe since 1945 conference, 6/7 September 2013, University of Leeds.

[41] Crossman, *Diaries of a Cabinet Minister Vol 1,* p. 151.

[42] Christopher Booker, 'Shoring up disaster', *The Spectator,* 2 October 1976, p. 15. Alistair Kefford, 'Disruption, destruction and the creation of the "inner cities": the impact of urban renewal on industry, 1945–1980', *Urban History,* 43.3 (2016).

important feature of a set of worries centred on the term 'inner city' and its role in the disavowal of urban modernism.[43] The growth of the term 'inner city', imported from American discourse and introduced into government policy by the 1966 Local Government Act, was a sign of the growing awareness of an alternative set of problems. Following the Commonwealth Immigration Act of 1962, the inner ring around city centres had increasingly been inhabited by new immigrant communities, who clustered in areas often suffering planning blight. If one wants a single exemplar of the way modernist solutions no longer seemed adequate, then the three Inner Area Studies published in 1977 are a strong candidate. Lambeth was tackled by a team led by Shankland alongside Peter Willmott, Liverpool by Wilson and Womersley, and Birmingham by Llewelyn-Davies, Weeks, Forestier-Walker, and Bor.[44] These were all men who had been at the forefront of radical renewal, but if this continuity in personnel suggests a continuity in approach with an earlier period, this is belied by the contents of the reports, which foreground the failures of the post-war period and disavow modernist approaches and radical forms—as the Lambeth study argued, 'the traditional remedies were no longer adequate'.[45]

To put it rather broadly, in the early 1960s city-centre plans had been created for the beneficiaries or future beneficiaries of affluence, people who, like the architects themselves, were envisaged as 'young professionals, likely to have a taste for Mediterranean holidays, French food and Scandinavian design'.[46] This was linked to the Croslandite ideal that a more equitable and 'civilized' society could be built on the basis of increased economic growth. Planners focused on the needs of those emerging into affluence, with very little concept that some would be left behind. There was an element of wish fulfilment in all this, as it was exactly in those cities which were being left relatively behind in the move towards mass affluence that the planners most resoundingly celebrated the new world, so that Walter Bor could say of Liverpool, 'Car ownership is

[43] For my fuller account of this issue, see Otto Saumarez Smith, 'The inner city crisis and the end of urban modernism in 1970s Britain', *Twentieth Century British History*, 27.4 (2016), pp. 578–98.

[44] Graeme Shankland, Peter Willmott, David Jordan, *Inner London: Policies for Dispersal and Balance* (London, 1977); Hugh Wilson and Lewis Womersley, *Change or Decay: Liverpool Inner Area Study* (London, 1977); Llewelyn-Davies, Weeks, Forestier-Walker, and Bor, *Unequal City: Final Report of the Birmingham Inner Area Study* (London, 1977). In a similar vein, see Robert Matthew, Johnson-Marshall & Partners (for the Department of the Environment), *New Life in Old Towns: Two Pilot Studies on Urban Renewal in Nelson and Rawtenstall Municipal Boroughs* (London, 1971).

[45] Shankland et al, *Inner London*, p. 2.

[46] Chamberlin, Powell & Bon, *Barbican Redevelopment* (London, 1959).

rising, travel is becoming more popular, new patterns of recreation are emerging.'[47] Well yes, but significantly less than in the rest of England and on shaky foundations. Before what has been called the 'rediscovery of poverty' in the later 1960s, planning discourse mirrored political discourse in that it tended to ignore problems of poverty.[48] There is a presumption that all would eventually share in the fruits of growth. Ruth Glass, unusually early, noted the way Britain's 'gleam of affluence' hid sections of society, using a quote from Bertolt Brecht's *Threepenny Opera* to make the point:

> There are those who are in darkness
> And there are others in the light
> And sure one sees those in brightness
> Those in darkness are out of sight.'

A single yet striking and indicative example of the way that some needs—needs not intertwined with a narrative of expanding affluence and modernization—were forgotten by 1960s planning can be seen in the strange blind spot towards the possibility that cycling could be a valid alternative to car usage. Though Buchanan himself saw the motor car as a 'mixed blessing', before the oil crisis of 1973 it was rare to see the expansion of private car ownership as anything but a beneficial thing, an enabler of social enfranchisement, and a 'symbol of spreading prosperity'.[49] Physical mobility was intimately linked with social mobility. As the planners for Glasgow's inner motorway put it, 'We believe that this mobility does enlarge the life of the ordinary citizen to a greater degree than any other single invention of the 20th Century.'[50] The fact that Glasgow had one of the lowest car-ownership levels in the country was irrelevant. Any attempt to curb or restrict the use of cars was commonly referred to as defeatist in plans[51]: 'Some people say we ought to ban cars from our cities, relying upon passes for essential cars and upon public transport. I believe that this kind of talk is quite unreal and wishful thinking.'[52]

[47] Walter Bor, 'Liverpool Interim Planning Policy, Statement' (Liverpool, 1965), p. 59.

[48] Ken Coates and Richard Silburn, *Poverty: The Forgotten Englishmen* (Nottingham, 1983).

[49] *Change and Challenge: Next Steps in Town and Country Planning* (London, 1962), p.7

[50] Scott and Wilson, Fitzpatrick and Partners, *Report on a Highway Plan for Glasgow* (Glasgow, 1965), p. 65.

[51] See *Cumbernauld New Town Planning Proposals –First Revision* ([Cumbernauld],1959), p. 5.

[52] Ernest Doubleday, 'Traffic in a Changing Environment' *Official Planning and Architecture* (July, 1960), p. 311.

Cycling, on the other hand, is treated blithely, if at all. Buchanan mentions techno-gizmos such as jetpacks, hovercraft, helicopters, and conveyor belts as 'possible substitutes for the motor car', but the bicycle was forgotten and the possibility of cycle tracks dismissed as 'very expensive, and probably impracticable'.[53] Cycles receive similarly scant, or non-existent, treatment in the other planning manuals or overviews of the period.[54] At Hook, it was felt that 'In view of the considerable possibility that non-powered bicycles will virtually disappear except for their use by children, only a limited system of independent cycle tracks is proposed.'[55] Geoffrey Jellicoe wrote that cycling was 'an anachronism in the modern world'.[56] This was all despite the fact that, in a survey of six towns near London in 1957, 35 per cent of the journeys to work were by bicycle, while even in the new town of Crawley, where no provision whatsoever had been made for cyclists, it was found that 25 per cent of journeys were made by this means.[57]

V

Economic optimism provided the intellectual fuel propelling the confidence behind attempts to restructure city centres. The fact that the hoped-for growth failed to materialize had the effect of limiting more radical approaches to city centres. Alongside the loss of economic confidence, there was also the emergence of a train of thought that questioned the very supposition that economic growth was a benevolent force in itself. That this development of scepticism about economic growth might itself be tied to a disillusionment about the perceived failures of city-centre redevelopment can be shown by one of the earliest and most powerful declarations of such a position, E. J. Mishan's *The Costs of Economic Growth*. This book constantly returns to 'the dereliction of the city' as one of the prime examples where the devastating cost of economic growth had not been taken into account. Mishan even set out a parable in which a culture inundated with cars is switched to a culture inundated with firearms, making a well-aimed polemical point against the Buchanan

[53] Colin Buchanan, *Traffic in Towns* (London, 1963), p. 65.

[54] Wilfred Burns, *New Towns for Old* (London, 1963), p. 133; John Tetlow and Anthony Goss, *Homes, Traffic and Towns* (London, 1968); *The Pedestrian in the City*, ed. David Lewis (London, 1965); Peter Hall, *London 2000* (London, 1963).

[55] LCC, *The Planning of a New Town* (London, 1961).

[56] Geoffrey Jellicoe, *Motopia* (1961), p. 19.

[57] Paul Ritter, *Planning for Man and Motor* (Oxford, 1963), p. 52.

Report.[58] Modernism and meliorism were being allied, and both disavowed, in a way which mixed the aesthetic, the political, and the social, and foreshadowed much of the language used to talk about architecture of this period over subsequent decades:

> Certainly if we cannot do better than the present assortment of engineering monstrosities – from which, for monumental folly, the palm must be handed to the architects of the Elephant and Castle Centre – we had best call a halt to further building. Indeed, if we were emancipated enough to ignore the strong religious feelings about 'progress', and to recognize that the new was the enemy of the excellent, a good case could be made for a programme of removing the postwar crop of eye-sores, and replacing them by an older and more intimate style of architecture.[59]

Such language would become an increasingly common way of talking about the architecture of the 1960s, good and bad. The architecture of the 1960s often served as a proxy for the whole gamut of post-war meliorist, state-led, top-down progressivism—whether such attacks originated from a left- or right-wing perspective.[60] Although the disavowal of urban modernism occurred across the political spectrum, the issue was particularly crucial for many on the New Right during the 1970s, and the rejection of modernism was often proclaimed as exemplary of the failure of state intervention per se.[61]

The endemic and extravagant disgust attached to concrete was always going to produce its antithesis in fashion, especially after decades of overblown castigation. The architecture of the 1960s is now fashionable. I expect this is in part a natural generational changing of taste, buoyed by a degree of *épater les bourgeois*, but there is also a strong political edge to it. I recognize myself as being part of a generation born after the glory days of the welfare state which looks back on the physical remains of this vanished

[58] E. J. Mishan, *The Costs of Economic Growth* (London, 1966), p. 127: The chief features of his plan are based on what he aptly calls 'pistol architecture', and include provision for no-shooting precincts fenced high with steel, the construction of circular and wavy road designs to increase the difficulties of gun-duelling, the erection of high, shatterproof glass screens running down the centres of roads to prevent effective cross-firing.... Every progressive journalist pays tribute to the foresight and realism of the plan B and makes much of the virtues of 'pistol architecture', the architecture of the future. Alas, the government begins to realize that any attempt to raise taxes to implement the plan B would start a revolution. So the plan is quietly shelved.

[59] Mishan, *The Costs of Economic Growth*, pp. 111–12.

[60] For example, Colin Ward, *An Anarchist Approach to Housing* (London, 1976) and David Watkin, *Morality and Architecture: the Development of a Theme in Architectural History and Theory from the Gothic Revival to the Modern Movement* (London, 1977).

[61] Roger Scruton, 'The architecture of Stalinism', *Cambridge Review*, 97 (26 November 1976), pp. 36–41; Patrick Hutber, *The decline and fall of the middle class and how it can fight back* (London, 1977); Keith Joseph, *A bibliography of freedom* (London, 1980), p. 20.

era with nostalgia for a lost idealism. The writer Owen Hatherley has been the pioneer of this approach. The architecture of the post-war period is now commonly celebrated for its social idealism and revolutionary zeal. These values are set up in opposition to those of the corporate architecture that has come since. One can easily sympathize with this vantage point: never has Ernő Goldfinger's Alexander Fleming House, a building originally occupied by the Ministry of Health and designed by an architect of intense social commitment, appeared nobler than now that it is in the shadow of the Strata tower, winner of the 2010 Carbuncle Cup—a building that has been dubbed 'the gillette shaver', which I am not alone in seeing as a bullying symbol of crass commercialism, gentrification, and neo-liberal capitalism. But to get a holistic image of the post-war period, one needs to remember also some of the other less appealing buildings in Elephant and Castle: the shopping centre, the roads, and the underpasses. It is these kinds of structures this book has been about. It is a complex story with its share of both idealism and crassness, and one that doesn't neatly fit into a polemic.

Bibliography

ARCHIVES

Abingdon Archives
Bolton Archives History Centre
British Library, National Sound Archive, London
Conservative Party Archive, Bodleian Library, Oxford
Haringey Archive Centre
Hertfordshire Archives and Local Studies
Imperial College Archives
Islington Local History Centre
Lancashire Archives, Preston
Leicestershire Archives, Leicester
London Metropolitan Archives (LMA)
London School of Economics Archives
The National Archives, Kew (TNA)
Oxfordshire History Centre
Percy Johnson-Marshall Archives, University of Edinburgh
Portsmouth Record Office
The Record Office for Leicestershire, Leicester and Rutland
RIBA Drawings and Archive Collection
Tower Hamlets Local History Library and Archives

PERIODICALS

Architects' Journal
Architects' Year Book
Architectural Association Journal
Architectural Design
The Architectural Review
Architecture and Building (London)
The Blackburn Times
Bolton Journal and Guardian
Building Design
Daily Worker
The Economist
Encounter
The Guardian (Manchester Guardian)
The Illustrated London News
Journal of the Town Planning Institute
The Listener
The London Magazine

New Left Review
New Society
New Statesman (and Nation)
The Observer
Official Architecture and Planning
Official Architecture and Planning Year Book
Private Eye
RIBA Journal
Socialist Commentary
The Spectator
The Sunday Times
The Times
The Times Literary Supplement
Town and Country Planning
Town Planning Institute Journal
Town Planning Review
Twentieth Century
Universities and Left Review

PUBLICATIONS

Abercrombie, Patrick, *Sheffield: A Civic Survey and Suggestions Towards a Development Plan* (Liverpool, 1924).

Abercrombie, Patrick, *County of London Plan* (London, 1943).

Abercrombie, Patrick, *Town and Country Planning* (Oxford, 1943).

Abercrombie, Patrick, *Greater London Plan 1944* (London, 1945).

Abercrombie, Patrick, *A Plan for the City and County of Kingston Upon Hull* (London and Hull, 1945).

Adams, Thomas, *Regional Plan of New York and Its Environs* (New York, 1931).

Aitchison, Matthew, 'Townscape: Scope, Scale and Extent', *Journal of Architecture*, 17 (2012), pp. 621–42.

Aldous, Tony, *Battle for the Environment* (London, 1972).

Aldous, Tony, *Goodbye Britain?* (London, 1975).

Aldous, Tony, *Tackling Dereliction* (London, 1984).

Allan, John, *Lubetkin: Architecture and the Tradition of Progress* (London, 1992).

Amery, Colin and Cruickshank, Dan, *The Rape of Britain* (London, 1975).

Annan, Noel, *Our Age: A Portrait of a Generation* (London, 1990).

Appleyard, Brian, *The Pleasures of Peace: Art and Imagination in Post-War Britain* (London, 1989).

Bale, Tim, *The Conservatives Since 1945: The Drivers of Party Change* (London, 2012).

Ballon, Hilary and Jackson, Kenneth T., eds, *Robert Moses and the Modern City: The Transformation of New York* (New York, 2007).

Banham, Reyner, *Theory and Design in the First Machine Age* (London, 1960).

Banham, Reyner, *The New Brutalism: Ethic or Aesthetic* (London, 1966).

Banham, Reyner, 'Revenge of the Picturesque: Architectural Polemics, 1945–1965', in *Concerning Architecture, Essays on Architectural Writers*, ed. John Summerson (London, 1968).

Banham, Reyner, *Los Angeles: The architecture of the four ecologies* (London, 1971).

Banham, Reyner, *Megastructure, Urban Futures of the Recent Past* (London, 1976).

Barker, Paul ed., *Arts in Society* (Nottingham, 2006).

Barker, Paul, *The Freedoms of Suburbia* (London, 2009).

Barr, Cleve, *Public Authority Housing* (London, 1953).

Beattie, Derek, *A History of Blackburn* (Lancaster, 2007).

Bendixson, Terence, *Without Wheels: Alternatives to the Private Car* (Bloomington, 1975).

Bendixson, Terence, *Instead of Cars* (London, 1977).

Bendixson, Terence, *The Peterborough Effect: Reshaping a City* (Peterborough, 1988).

Bendixson, Terence and Platt, John, *Milton Keynes, Image and Reality* (Cambridge, 1992).

Benn, Anthony Wedgwood, *The Regeneration of Britain* (London, 1965).

Benn, Tony, *Out of the Wilderness: Diaries 1963–1967* (London, 1987).

Benn, Tony, *Years of Hope: Diaries, Papers and Letters 1940–1962* (London, 1994).

Bernoulli, Hans, *Die Stadt und ihr Boden* (Zurich, 1949).

Black, Lawrence, *The Political Culture of the Left in Affluent Britain* (London, 2003).

Black, Lawrence, '"Making Britain a Gayer and More Cultivated Country": Jennie Lee, The Creative Economy and 1960s Cultural Revolution', *Contemporary British History*, 20.3 (2006), pp. 29–48.

Black, Lawrence, 'The Lost World of Young Conservatism', *Historical Journal*, 51.4 (2008), pp. 991–1024.

Black, Lawrence, *Redefining British Politics: Culture, Consumerism and Participation, 1954–1970* (Basingstoke, 2010).

Black, Lawrence, and Pemberton, Hugh, eds, *An Affluent Society? Britain's Post-War 'Golden Age' Revisited* (Aldershot, 2004).

Booker, Christopher, *The Neophiliacs: Revolution in English Life in the Fifties and Sixties* (London, 1969).

Booker, Christopher, *The Seventies: Portrait of a Decade* (London, 1980).

Booker, Christopher and Green, Candida Lycett, *Goodbye London: An Illustrated Guide to Threatened Buildings* (London, 1973).

Bor, Walter, *Liverpool Interim Planning Policy, Statement* (London, 1965).

Bor, Walter, 'A Question of Urban Identity', in *Planning and Architecture*, ed. Dennis Sharp (London, 1967).

Bor, Walter, *The Making of Cities* (Aylesbury, 1974).

Boyd Whyte, Iain, ed., *Man-Made Future: Planning, Education and Design in Mid-Twentieth century Britain* (London, 2007).

Brack, Harry, *Building for a New Society* (London, 1964).

Brett, Lionel, *Landscape in Distress* (London, 1965).

Brett, Lionel [Viscount Esher], *York, A Study in Conservation* (London, 1968).
Brett, Lionel, *Parameters and Images* (London, 1970).
Brett, Lionel, *The Broken Wave, the Rebuilding of England* (London, 1981).
Brett, Lionel, *The Continuing Heritage: The Story of the Civic Trust* (London, 1982).
Brett, Lionel, *Our Selves Unknown* (London, 1985).
Brett, Lionel and Pollen, Francis, *Guildhall Redevelopment Area Consultant's Report Number 1* (Portsmouth, 1964).
Brett, Lionel and Pollen, Francis, *Plan for Portsmouth Central Area* (Portsmouth, 1970).
Briggs, Asa, *Victorian Cities* (London, 1963).
Briggs, Asa, *Michael Young: Social Entrepreneur* (Basingstoke, 2001).
Bristol City Centre Policy Report 1966 (Bristol, 1966).
Brittain-Catlin, Timothy, *Leonard Manasseh & Partners* (London, 2011).
Brittain-Catlin, Timothy, *Bleak Houses, Disappointment and Failure in Architecture* (Cambridge, MA, 2014)
Brome, Vincent, *Aneurin Bevan* (London, 1953).
Browne, Kenneth, *West End: Renewal of a Metropolitan Centre* (London, 1971).
Bruegmann, Robert, *Sprawl, a Compact History* (Chicago, 2005).
Buchanan, Colin, *Mixed Blessing: The Motor in Britain* (London, 1958).
Buchanan, Colin, *Traffic in Towns* (London, 1963).
Buchanan, Colin, *Traffic in Towns, A Study of the Long Term Problems of Traffic in Urban Areas* (London, 1963).
Buchanan, Colin, 'Britain's Road Problem', *Geographical Journal*, 130.4 (1964), pp. 470–8.
Buchanan, Colin, *No Way to the Airport* (London, 1981).
Buchanan, Colin, and Partners, *Cardiff Development and Transportation Study* (Cardiff, 1966).
Buchanan, Colin, and Partners, *Bath, A Study in Conservation* (London, 1968).
Buchanan, Colin, and Partners, *North East London* (London, 1970).
Bullock, Nicholas, 'Plans for Post-War Housing in the UK: The Case for Mixed Development and the Flat', *Planning Perspectives*, 2.1 (1987), pp. 71–98.
Bullock, Nicholas, 'Fragments of a Post-War Utopia; Housing in Finsbury 1945–51', *Urban Studies*, 26.1 (1989), pp. 46–58.
Bullock, Nicholas, 'Ideals, Priorities and Harsh Realities: Reconstruction and the LCC, 1945-51', *Planning Perspectives* 9.1 (1994), pp. 87–101.
Bullock, Nicholas, *Building the Post-War World Modern Architecture and Reconstruction in Britain* (London and New York, 2002).
Burns, Wilfred, *British Shopping Centres* (London, 1960).
Burns, Wilfred, *Newcastle Development Plan Review* (Tyne and Wear Archives, 1963).
Burns, Wilfred, *New Towns for Old, the Technique of Urban Renewal* (London, 1963).
Burns, Wilfred, *Newcastle, a Study in Replanning at Newcastle Upon Tyne* (London, 1967).
Burns, Wilfred, *Personal reflections on the changing planning system* (Cambridge, 1983).

Cadman, David, 'Property Finance in the UK in the Post-War Period', *Land Development Studies,* 1.2 (1984), pp. 61–82.
Calder, Barnabas, 'Brutal Enemies? Townscape and the "hard" moderns', in *Alternative Visions of Post-War Reconstruction: Creating the Modern Townscape,* ed. Pendlebury, John et al. (London, 2014).
Calder, Barnabas, *Raw Concrete: The Beauty of Brutalism* (London, 2016).
Campbell, John, *Roy Jenkins* (London, 2014).
Campbell, Louise, *Twentieth Century Architecture and its Histories* (London, 2000).
Campbell, Louise, Thomas, Jane, and Glendinning, Miles, *Basil Spence: Buildings and Projects* (London, 2012).
Caro, Robert, *The Power Broker: Robert Moses and the Fall of New York* (New York, 1975).
Carolin, Peter, 'Sense, sensibility and tower blocks: the Swedish influence on post-war housing in Britain', in *Twentieth Century Architecture,* 9, *Housing the Twentieth Century Nation* (London, 2008), pp. 98–112.
Carolin, Peter and Dannatt, Trevor, eds, *Architecture, Education and Research: the Work of Leslie Martin: Papers and Selected Articles* (New York, 1996).
Carroll, Rutter, *Ryder and Yates* (London, 2009).
Carter, C. J., *Innovations in Planning Thought and Practice at Cumbernauld New Town 1956–62, Occasional Paper no. 15* (Dundee, 1983).
Castle, Barbara, *Diaries, 1964–70* (London, 1990).
Catterall, Peter, ed., *The Macmillan Diaries* (London, 2003).
Chamberlin, Powell, and Bon, *Barbican Redevelopment 1959: Report to the Court of Common Council of the Corporation* (London, 1959).
Chamberlin, Peter, Powell, Geoffry, and Bon, Christoph, *University of Leeds Development Plan* (Leeds, 1960).
Chamberlin, Peter, Powell, Geoffry, and Bon, Christoph, *Proposal for Redevelopment in the Central Part of Weston-Super-Mare* ([London,] 1961).
Change and Challenge: Next Steps in Town and Country Planning (London, 1962).
Cherry, Gordon E., *Evolution of British Town Planning* (London, 1974).
Cherry, Gordon E., *A History of British Town Planning* (Leighton Buzzard, 1974).
Cherry, Gordon E., *Holford, a Study in Architecture Planning and Civic Design* (London, 1986).
Cherry, Gordon E., *Town Planning in Britain Since 1900* (Oxford, 1996).
Clapson, Mark, *Invincible Green Suburbs, Brave New Towns: Social Change and Dispersal in Post-War England* (Manchester, 1998).
Clapson, Mark, *Anglo-American Crossroads, Urban Research and Planning in Britain, 1940–2010* (London, 2010).
Cohen, Jean Louis, *Architecture in Uniform: Designing and Building for the Second World War* (New Haven and London, 2011).
Coleman, Alice, *Utopia on Trial: Vision and Reality in Planned Housing* (London, 1991).
Colquhoun, Ian, *RIBA Book of British Housing* (London, 2008).
Conn, Stephen, *Americans against the city* (Oxford, 2014).
Le Corbusier, *The Radiant City* (London, 1964).

Council for British Archaeology, *Historic Towns* (London, 1965).
Council for British Archaeology, *The Erosion of History* (London, 1972).
Covent Garden Community Association, *Keep the Elephants Out of the Garden* (London, 1977).
Crinson, Mark, 'The Uses of Nostalgia: Stirling and Gowan's Preston Housing' *Journal of the Society of Architectural Historians*, 65.2 (June 2006), pp. 216–37.
Crinson, Mark, *Stirling and Gowan: Architecture from Austerity to Affluence* (London and New Haven, 2012).
Crinson, Mark, *Alison and Peter Smithson* (London, 2018).
Crosland, Anthony, *The Future of Socialism* (London, 1956).
Crosland, Anthony, *The Conservative Enemy, A Programme for Reform for the 1960s* (London, 1962).
Crosland, Susan, *Tony Crosland* (London, 1982).
Crossman, Richard, *Labour in the Affluent Society* (London, 1960).
Crossman, Richard, *The Diaries of a Cabinet Minister Vol 1. Minister of Housing 1964–66* (London, 1974).
Crossman, Richard, *The Diaries of a Cabinet Minister Vol. 2, 1966–1968* (London, 1976).
Cullen, Gordon, *The Concise Townscape* (London, 1961).
Cullingworth, Barry, ed., *British Planning: 50 Years of Urban and Regional Policy* (London, 1999).
Cullingworth, J. B., *Restraining Urban Growth: the Problem of Overspill* (London, 1960).
Cullingworth, J. B., *New Towns for Old: the Problem of Urban Renewal* (London, 1962).
Curtis, William, *Modern Architecture Since 1900* (London, 1996).
Curtis, William, *Denys Lasdun: Architecture, City, Landscape* (London, 1994).
Dannat, Trevor, *Modern Architecture in Britain* (London, 1959).
Darling, Elizabeth, 'Kensal House: The Housing Consultant and the Housed', in *Architecture and Design in the 1930's,* ed. Susannah Charlton, Elain Harwood, and Alan Powers (London, 2007).
Darling, Elizabeth, *Re-Forming Britain: Narratives of Modernity before Reconstruction* (London, 2007).
Davenport-Hines, Richard, *An English Affair: Sex, Class and Power in the Age of Profumo* (London, 2013).
Davis, John, 'From GLC to GLA: London Politics from Then to Now', in *London From Punk to Blair* (London, 2003), 109–16.
Davis, John, '"Simple Solutions to Complex Problems": The Greater London Council and the Greater London Development Plan, 1965-1973', in *Civil Society in British History. Ideas, Identities, Institutions* (Oxford, 2003), pp. 249–74.
Davis, John, 'Macmillan's Martyr: the Pilgrim Case, the "Land Grab" and the Tory Housing Drive, 1951–9'. *Planning Perspectives,* 23 (2008).
Decker, Thomas, ed., *The Modern City Revisited* (London and New York, 2000).
Delafons, John, *Politics and Preservation: a Policy History of the Built Heritage, 1882–1996* (London, 1997).

Delafons, John, 'Reforming the British planning system 1964–5: the Planning Advisory Group and the genesis of the Planning act of 1967', *Planning Perspectives,* 13.4 (1998), pp. 373–87.

Dennison, Edward, *McMorran and Whitby* (London, 2009).

Dunleavy, Patrick, *The Politics of Mass Housing in Britain, 1945–75: Study of Corporate Power and Professional Influence in the Welfare State* (Oxford, 1981).

Durant [Glass], Ruth, *Watling: a Social Study* (London, 1939).

Elkin, Stephen L., *Politics and Land Use Planning; The London Experience* (Cambridge, 1974).

Erten, Erdem, '*Shaping the Second Half Century: The Architectural Review, 1947–1971*', diss., Massachusetts Institute of Technology (2004).

Erten, Erdem, 'Thomas Sharp's Collaboration with H. de C. Hastings: the Formulation of Townscape as Urban Design Pedagogy', *Planning Perspectives,* 24 (2009), pp. 29–49.

Fairbrother, Nan, *New Lives, New Landscapes* (London, 1970).

Fairbrother, Nan, *The Nature of Landscape Design* (London, 1974).

Fleetwood-Hesketh, Peter, *Murray's Lancashire Architectural Guide* (London, 1955).

Foot, Michael, *Aneurin Bevan 1897–1960* (London, 1997).

Forty, Adrian, 'Being or Nothingness: Private Experience and Public Architecture in Post War Britain', *Architectural History,* 38 (1995), pp. 25–35.

Forty, Adrian, *Words and Buildings: A Vocabulary of Modern Architecture* (London, 2004).

Forty, Adrian, *Concrete and Culture: A Material History* (London, 2012).

Frampton, Kenneth, *Labour, Work and Architecture: Collected Essays on Architecture and Design* (London, 2012).

Fraser, Murray and Kerr, Joe, *Architecture and the Special Relationship, The American Influence on Post-War British Architecture* (London, 2007).

Friedman, Alice T., *American Glamour and the Evolution of Modern Architecture* (London and New Haven, 2010).

Galbraith, J. K., *The Affluent Society* (London, 1958).

Gans, Herbert, *The Levittowners: Ways of Life and Politics in a New Suburban Community* (New York, 1967).

Gans, Herbert, *People and Plans* (New York, 1968).

Gibberd, Frederick, *Town Design* (London, 1953).

Gibberd, Frederick, *Harlow, the Story of a New Town* (Stevenage, 1980).

Gibberd, Frederick and Bainbridge, C. S., *Plan for St Pancras* (London, 1947).

Giedion, Sigfried, 'The Need for a New Monumentality', in *New Architecture and City Planning* (New York, 1944).

Giedion, Sigfried, *Space, Time and Architecture* (Cambridge, MA, 1967).

Gilmour, Ian, *Whatever Happened to the Tories: the Conservatives since 1945* (London, 1998).

Glass, Ruth, *London, Aspects of Change* (London, 1964).

Glass, Ruth, 'The Mood of London', in *London: Urban Pattern* (London, 1973).

Glass, Ruth, *Clichés of Urban Doom and Other Essays* (Oxford, 1989).

GLC Architects Department, *Woolwich-Erith, A Riverside Project* (London, 1966).

GLC Architects Department, *Covent Garden Area Draft Plan* (London, 1968).

GLC Architects Department, *Covent Garden's Moving, Covent Garden Area Draft Plan* (London, 1969).

GLC Architects Department, *Covent Garden: The Next Step: The Revised Plan for the Proposed Comprehensive Development Area* (London, 1970).

Glendinning, Miles, *Rebuilding Scotland: The Postwar Vision 1945–1975* (East Linton, 1997).

Glendinning, Miles, 'The Conservation Movement: A Cult of the Modern Age', *Transactions of the Royal Historical Society*, 6.13 (2003), pp. 359–76.

Glendinning, Miles, *Modern Architect: the Life and Times of Robert Matthew* (London, 2008).

Glendinning, Miles, *The Conservation Movement: A History of Architectural Preservation, Antiquity to Modernity* (London, 2013).

Glendinning, Miles and Muthesius, Stefan, *Tower Block: Modern Public Housing in England, Scotland, Wales and Northern Ireland* (New Haven and London, 1994).

Gold, John R., *Experience of Modernism, Modern Architects and the Future City, 1928–53* (London, 1997).

Gold, John R., 'Modernism and Reconstruction: Architects, Networks and Plans', *Planning Perspectives*, 19 (2004), pp. 333–8.

Gold, John R., 'York: A Suitable Case for Conservation', in *Twentieth Century Architecture 7: The Heroic Period of Conservation* (London, 2004), pp. 88–98.

Gold, John R., 'The Making of a Megastructure: Architectural Modernism, Town Planning and Cumbernauld's Central Area, 1955-75', *Planning Perspectives*, 21.2 (April 2006), pp. 109–31.

Gold, John R., *The Practice of Modernism: Modern Architects and Urban Transformation 1954–1972* (London, 2007).

Gold, John R., 'Modernity and Utopia', in *Compendium of Urban Studies*, ed. P. Hubbard, T. Hall, and J. R. Short (London, 2008).

Gold, John R., 'A SPUR to action: the Society for the Promotion of Urban Renewal, 'anti-scatter' and the crisis of reconstruction', *Planning Perspectives*, 27:2 (2012), pp. 199–223.

Goldhagen, Sarah, 'Something to Talk About: Modernism, Discourse, Style', *Journal of the Society of Architectural Historians*, 64.2 (2005), pp. 144–67.

Goldhagen, Sarah and Legault, Rejean, eds, *Anxious Modernisms: Experimentation in Postwar Architectural Culture* (Cambridge, MA, 2000).

Gorham, Maurice and Dunnett, H. McG., *Inside the Pub* (London, 1950).

Goss, Anthony, *British Industry and Town Planning* (London, 1962).

Goss, Anthony, *The Architect and Town Planning: a Report Presented to the Council of the RIBA* (London, 1965).

Goss, Anthony, *Industry on Humberside; Growth and Potential* (Kingston-upon-Hull, 1967).

Goss, Anthony and Tetlow, John, *Homes Towns and Traffic* (London, 1965).

Graeme Shankland Associates, *Bolton Draft Town Centre Map* (London, 1964).

Gregory, Terrance et al., *City of Coventry Review Plan 1966, Analysis and Written Statement* (Coventry, 1967).

Grindrod, John, *Concretopia: A Journey Around the Rebuilding of Post-War Britain* (London, 2013).

Gunn, Simon, 'The Rise and Fall of British Urban Modernism: Planning Bradford 1945–1970', *Journal of British Studies,* 48:3 (2010).

Gunn, Simon, 'The Buchanan Report: Environment and the Problem of Traffic in 1960s Britain', *Twentieth Century British History,* 22.4 (2011), pp. 521–42.

Gunn, Simon, 'Beyond Coketown: The Industrial City in the Twentieth Century', in *Industrial Cities: History and Future,* ed. Clemens Zimmerman (Frankfurt, 2013).

Gunn, Simon, 'People and the Car: the Expansion of Automobility in Urban Britain, *c.*1955–70', *Social History,* 38.2 (2013), pp. 220–37.

Gunn, Simon, 'Konrad Smigielski and the planning of post-war Leicester', in *Leicester: A Modern History* (Lancaster, 2016), pp. 267–91.

Halcrow, Morrison, *Keith Joseph: a Single Mind* (London, 1989).

Hall, Peter, *London 2000* (London, 1963).

Hall, Peter, 'The Buchanan Report', *Geographical Journal,* 130.1 (1964), pp. 125–8.

Hall, Peter, *The Containment of Urban England* (London, 1973).

Hall, Peter, *London 2001* (London, 1989).

Hall, Peter, *Cities of Tomorrow* (London, 2002).

Hall, Peter, 'The Buchanan Report 40 Years On', *Proceedings of the ICE - Transport,* 157.1 (London, 2004), pp. 7–14.

Halsey, A. H., *No Discouragement* (London, 1996).

Hancock, Tom, *Chester Castle Precinct* ([Chester,] 1966).

Hanna, Erika, *Modern Dublin, Urban Change and the Irish Past, 1957–1973* (Oxford, 2013).

Hanna, Erika, 'Don't make Dublin a Museum': Urban heritage and Modern architecture in Dublin, 1957–71', *Past and Present,* 226.10 (2015), pp. 349–67.

Harwood, Elain, 'Post-War Landscape and Public Housing', *Garden History,* 28.1 (2000), pp. 102–16.

Harwood, Elain, 'Lansbury', in *Festival of Britain,* ed. Elain Harwood and Alan Powers (London, 2001).

Harwood, Elain, *A Guide to Post War Listed Buildings* (London, 2003).

Harwood, Elain, *Chamberlin, Powell and Bon* (London, 2012).

Harwood, Elain, *Space Hope and Brutalism* (London, 2015).

Harwood, Elain and Powers, Alan, eds, *Twentieth Century Architecture 6, The Sixties* (London, 2002).

Harwood, Elain and Powers, Alan, eds, *Twentieth Century Architecture 7: The Heroic Period of Conservation* (London, 2004).

Harwood, Elain and Powers, Alan, eds, *Twentieth Century Architecture 9, Housing the 20th Century Nation* (London, 2008).

Harwood, Elain and Powers, Alan, eds, *Twentieth Century Architecture 10, The Seventies* (London, 2012).

Harwood, Elain, Powers, Alan, and Saumarez Smith, Otto, eds, *Twentieth Century Architecture 11: Oxford and Cambridge* (London, 2013).

Hatherley, Owen, *Militant Modernism* (London, 2009).
Hatherley, Owen, *A Guide to the New Ruins of Great Britain* (London, 2011).
Hatherley, Owen, *A New Kind of Bleak: Journeys Through Urban Britain* (London, 2013).
Hayes, Nicholas, *Consensus and Controversy: City Politics in Nottingham 1945–1966* (Liverpool, 1996).
Heathcote, David, *Barbican Penthouse Over the City* (London, 2004).
Hebbert, Michael, 'The City of London Walkway Experiment', *Journal of the American Planning Association*, 59.4 (1993), pp. 433–50.
Hebbert, Michael, 'Re-enclosure of the Urban Picturesque: Green-Space Transformations in Postmodern Urbanism', *Town Planning Review*, 79.1 (2008), pp. 31–59.
Heffer, Eric, *Never a Yes Man* (London, 1991).
Heller, Gregory L., *Ed Bacon: Planning Politics and the Building of Modern Philadelphia* (Philadelphia, 2013).
Hennessy, Peter, *Whitehall* (London, 1989).
Hennessy, Peter *Never Again: Britain 1945–1951* (London, 1992).
Hennessy, Peter *Muddling Through: Power, Politics and the Quality of Government in Post-War Britain* (London, 1997).
Hennessy, Peter *The Prime Minister: The Office and its Holders Since 1945* (London 2001).
Hennessy, Peter, *Having it so Good* (London, 2006).
Higgott, Andrew, *Mediating Modernism, Architectural Cultures in Britain* (London, 2007).
Higgs, Leslie, *New Town: Social Involvement in Livingston* (Glasgow, 1977).
Hilberseimer, Ludwig *Großstadtarchitektur* (Stuttgart, 1924).
Hoggart, Richard, *The Uses of Literacy: Aspects of Working-Class Life with Special Reference to Publications and Entertainments* (London, 1957).
Holden, Charles and Holford, William, *Reconstruction in the City of London* (London, 1947).
Holford, William, *Cambridge Planning Proposals: a Report to the Town and Country Planning Committee of the Cambridge City Council* (Cambridge, 1950).
Holford, William, *Corby New Town* (Corby, 1952).
Holford, William, *Piccadilly Circus Future Development—Proposals for a Comprehensive Development* (London, 1962).
Holford, William, 'Preservation and Prejudice', the Lord Bossom lecture in the House of Commons' (Beckenham, 1970).
Hollamby, Edward, *Lambeth Central Hill Development* (London [,1967?]).
Hollamby, Edward, *Waterloo: Draft Planning Strategy* (London, 1975).
Holliday, John, ed., *City Centre Redevelopment* (London, 1973).
Home, Robert K. *Wood Green Shopping City* (London, 1984).
Hughes, Michael, ed., *The Letters of Lewis Mumford and Frederic J. Osborn, A Transatlantic Dialogue, 1938–70* (Bath, 1971).
Hughes, Quentin, *Seaport: Architecture and Townscape in Liverpool* (London, 1962).

Insall, Donald, *Thaxted; An historical and architectural survey for the County of Essex* (Chelmsford, 1966).
Insall, Donald, *Chester, A Study in Conservation* (London, 1968).
Jackson, Anthony, *The Politics of Architecture: A History of Modern Architecture in Britain* (London, 1970).
Jacobs, Jane, *The Life and Death of American Cities* (New York, 1961).
Jeffreys, Kevin, *Anthony Crosland: A New Biography* (London, 1999).
Jenkins, Roy, *The Labour Case* (London, 1959).
Jerram, Leif, *Streetlife, The Untold History of Europe's Twentieth Century* (Oxford, 2011).
Johnson-Marshall, Percy, *Rebuilding Cities* (London, 1966).
Jones, Peter, 'Re-thinking corruption in post-1950 urban Britain: the Poulson affair, 1972–6', *Urban History*, 39.3 (2012).
Judt, Tony, *Post War, A History of Europe Since 1945* (London, 2010).
Kadleigh, Sergei, *High Paddington, a Town for 8000 people* (London, 1952).
Kefford, Alistair, 'Disruption, destruction and the creation of "the inner cities": the impact of urban renewal on industry, 1945–80', *Urban History*, 44.3 (2017), pp. 492–515.
Kefford, Alistair, 'Housing the citizen-consumer in post-war Britain: The Parker Morris Report, affluence and the even briefer life of social democracy', *Twentieth Century British History*, 29.2 (2017), pp. 225–58.
Klemek, Christopher, 'Placing Jane Jacobs in a Transatlantic Urban Conversation', *Journal of the American Planning Association*, 73.1 (2007), pp. 49–67.
Klemek, Christopher, *The Transatlantic Collapse of Urban Renewal, Postwar Urbanism from New York to Berlin* (Chicago, 2011).
Klose, Dietrich, *Multi-Storey Car Parks and Garages* (London, 1965).
Knight, Timothy et al., *Let Our Cities Live* (London, 1960).
Kruse, Kevin M. and Sugrue, Thomas J., eds, *The New Suburban History* (Chicago, 2006).
Kuper, Leo, *Living in Towns* (London, 1953).
Kynaston, David, *Austerity Britain, 1945–1951* (London, 2008).
Kynaston, David, *Family Britain, 1951–1957* (London, 2010).
Kynaston, David, *Modernity Britain: Opening the Box, 1957–1959* (London, 2013).
Kynaston, David, *Modernity Britain: A Shake of the Dice, 1959–1962* (London, 2014).
Labour Party, *Leisure for Living* (London, 1959).
Labour Party, *Signposts for the Sixties* (London, 1961).
Laing, Stuart, *Representations of Working-Class Life 1957–1964* (Basingstoke, 1986).
Lancashire and Merseyside Industrial Development Association, *A Guide to Merseyside* (Manchester, 1964).
Lancashire and Merseyside Industrial Development Association, *The Decline of the Cotton and Coal Mining Industries of Lancashire* (Manchester, 1967).
Lancaster, Osbert, *From Pillar to Post, the Pocket Lamp of Architecture* (London, 1938).
Lawrence, Jon, 'Class, 'affluence' and the study of everyday life in Britain, c. 1930–64', *Cultural and Social History*, 10.2 (2013) pp. 273–99.

Lawrence, Peter L., *Becoming Jane Jacobs* (Philadelphia, 2016).
LCC Architects Department, *The Planning of a New Town* (London, 1961).
Ling, Arthur, *The Reconstruction of Warsaw* (London, 1951).
Ling, Arthur, *Runcorn New Town* (Runcorn, 1967).
Lewis, David, ed., *The Pedestrian in the City* (London, 1965).
Llewelyn-Davies, Richard, Weeks, John, Forestier-Walker, Robert, and Bor, Walter, *A New City* (London 1966).
Llewelyn-Davies, Richard, Weeks, John, Forestier-Walker, Robert, and Bor, Walter, *Unequal City: Final Report of the Birmingham Inner Area Study* (London, 1977).
Lock, Max, *Reconstruction in the Netherlands: an Account of a visit to post-war Holland by members of the Town Planning Institute* (London, 1947).
Lock, Max and Partners, *Salisbury, The Redevelopment of the City Centre* (London, 1963).
Lodge, David, *Changing Places* (London, 1975).
Loft, Charles, *Government, the Railways and the Modernization of Britain: Beeching's Last Train* (London, 2006).
Logie, Gordon, *The Urban Scene* (London, 1954).
Logie, Gordon, *Lion Yard Cambridge* (Cambridge, 1965).
London Dockland Study Team, *Docklands Redevelopment Proposals for East London, Volume One –Main Report* (London, 1973).
Low, Nicholas, 'Centrism and the Provision of Services in Residential Areas', *Urban Studies,* 12.2 (1975).
Lowe, Rodney, 'The Rediscovery of Poverty and the Creation of the Child Poverty Action Group, 1962–68', *Contemporary British History,* 9.3 (1995), pp. 602–11.
Lubbock, Jules, *The History of Taste: Politics of Architecture and Design in Britain, 1550–1960* (London and New Haven, 1995).
Lutyens, Edwin et al., *London Replanned* (London, 1942).
MacEwan, Malcolm, *Crisis in Architecture* (London, 1974).
MacEwan, Malcolm, *The Greening of a Red* (London and Concord, 1991).
Madin, John H. D. and Partners, *Dawley: Wellington: Oakengate* (London, 1966).
Mandler, Peter, 'John Summerson (1904–1992): the Architectural Critic and the Quest for the Modern', in *After the Victorians: Private Conscience and Public Duty in Modern Britain,* ed. Pedersen, Susan and Mandler, Peter (London, 1994).
Mandler, Peter, 'New Towns for Old' in *Moments of Modernity: Reconstructing Britain 1945–1964* (London and New York, 1999).
Marriott, Oliver, *The Property Boom* (Abingdon, 1989).
Martin, Leslie, *Whitehall: A Plan for the National and Government Centre* (London, 1963).
Mass, Sarah, 'Commercial heritage as democratic action: Historicizing the 'Save the Market' campaigns in Bradford and Chesterfield, 1969–76', *Twentieth Century British History,* 29.3 (2017), pp. 459–84.
Matthew, Robert, *Belfast Regional Survey and Plan* (Belfast, 1962).

Matthew, Robert, Johnson-Marshall, Percy, and Partners, *Salford, Ellor Street Redevelopment* (Edinburgh, 1963).

Matthew, Robert, Johnson-Marshall and Partners (for Department of the Environment), *New Life in Old Towns: Two Pilot Studies on Urban Renewal in Nelson and Rawtenstall Municipal Boroughs* (London, 1971).

Meacham, Standish, *Regaining Paradise, Englishness and the Early Garden City Movement* (New Haven and London, 1999).

Meller, Helen, *Patrick Geddes: Social Evolutionist and City Planner* (London, 1993).

Meller, Helen, *Towns, Plans and Society in Modern Britain* (Cambridge, 1997).

Mellor, Leo, *Reading the Ruins: Modernism, Bombsites and British Culture* (Cambridge, 2011).

Meredith, Jesse, 'Decolonizing the New Town: Roy Gazzard and the Making of Killingworth Township', *Journal of British Studies*, 57 (2018), pp. 333–62.

Ministry of Housing and Local Government, *The Density of Residential Areas* (London, 1952; repr. 1959).

Ministry of Housing and Local Government, *Design in Town and Village* (London, 1953).

Ministry of Housing and Local Government, *Residential Areas: Higher Densities* (London, 1962).

Ministry of Housing and Local Government, *Town Centres: Approach to Renewal* (London, 1962).

Ministry of Housing and Local Government, *Town Centres: Cost and Control of Redevelopment* (London, 1963).

Ministry of Housing and Local Government, *Town Centres: Current Practice* (London, 1963).

Ministry of Housing and Local Government, *Development Plan Maps* (London, 1964).

Ministry of Housing and Local Government, *Parking in Town Centres* (London, 1965).

Ministry of Housing and Local Government, *The Deeplish Study: Improvement Possibilities in a District of Rochdale* (London, 1966).

Moran, Joe, 'Crossing the road in Britain, 1931–1976', *The Historical Journal*, 49.02 (2006), pp. 477–96.

Moran, Joe, 'Early Cultures of Gentrification in London, 1955–1980', *Journal of Urban History*, 47.4 (2007), pp. 101–21.

Moran, Joe, '"Subtopias of Good Intentions": Everyday Landscape in Postwar Britain', *Cultural and Social History*, 4.3 (2007).

Moran, Joe, *On Roads, a Hidden History* (London, 2009).

Moran, Joe, 'Imagining the Street in Post-war Britain', *Urban History*, 39 (2012), pp. 166–86.

Morrison, Kathryn, *English Shops and Shopping: an Architectural History* (London and New Haven, 2004).

Multiple Shops Federation, *The Planning of Shopping Centres* (London, 1963).

Mumford, Eric, *CIAM Discourse on Urbanism* (Cambridge, 2000).

Mumford, Eric, *Defining Urban Design: CIAM Architects and the Formation of a Discipline, 1937–69* (London and New Haven, 2009).

Mumford, Eric and Sarkis, Hashim, *Josep Lluis Sert: The Architect of Urban Design, 1953–1969* (London and New Haven, 2008).

Mumford, Lewis, *The Culture of Cities* (London, 1938).

Mumford, Lewis, *The Highway and the City* (London, 1964).

Munby, D. L. *Industry and Planning in Stepney* (London, 1951).

Murphy, Douglas, *Last Futures: Nature, technology and the end of architecture* (London, 2016).

Murray, Irena and Osley, Julian, *Le Corbusier and Britain, an Anthology* (London, 2009).

Muthesius, Stefan, *The Postwar University, Utopianist Campus and College* (New Haven and London, 2000).

Nairn, Ian, *Outrage* (London, 1955).

Nairn, Ian, *Counter Attack Against Subtopia* (London, 1956).

Nairn, Ian, *Modern Buildings in London* (London, 1964).

Nairn, Ian, *Nairn's London* (London, 1966).

Nairn, Ian, *Britain's Changing Towns* (London, 1967).

Nash, Logan, 'Middle-Class Castle Constructing Gentrification at London's Barbican Estate', *Journal of Urban History*, 39.5 (2013), pp. 909–32.

National Chamber of Trade memorandum, *The Plight of Displaced Independent Traders* (London, 1963).

Norwich City Planning Department, *Foot Streets in Four Cities—Düsseldorf, Essen, Cologne, Copenhagen* (Norwich, 1966).

Nottingham County Planning Department, *Newark, Action for Conservation* (Nottingham, 1968).

Ogden, R. H., *Town Centre Map Review* ([Bolton,] 1973).

O'Hara, Glen, *From Dreams to Disillusionment: Economic and Social Planning in 1960s Britain* (London, 2006).

Opher, Philip, *Architecture and Urban Design in Six British New Towns* (Oxford, 1981).

Orlans, Harold, *Stevanage: A Sociological Study of a New Town* (London, 1952).

Ortolano, Guy, 'Planning the Urban Future in 1960s Britain', *Historical Journal*, 54.2 (2011), pp. 477–507.

Osborn, Frederic J. and Whittick, Arnold, *New Towns: Their Origins, Achievements and Progress* (London, 1977).

Pass, David, *Vallingby and Farsta, From idea to reality* (Cambridge, 1973).

Pendlebury, John, 'Alas Smith and Burns? Conservation in Newcastle upon Tyne City Centre 1959-68', *Planning Perspectives*, 16 (2001), pp. 114–41.

Pendlebury, John, 'Conservation and Regeneration: Complementary or Conflicting Processes? The Case of Grainger Town, Newcastle Upon Tyne', *Planning Practice and Research*, 17.2 (2002), pp. 145–58.

Pendlebury, John, 'Planning the Historic City: Reconstruction Plans in the United Kingdom in the 1940s', *Town Planning Review*, 74.4 (2003), pp. 371–94.

Pendlebury, John, 'Reconciling History with Modernity: 1940s Plans for Durham and Warwick', *Environment and Planning B: Planning and Design*, 31.3 (2004), pp. 331–48.

Pendlebury, John, 'The Modern Historic City: Evolving Ideas in Mid-20th Century Britain', *Journal of Urban Design*, 10.2 (2005), pp. 253–73.

Pendlebury, John, *Conservation in the Age of Consensus* (London, 2008).

Pendlebury, John, 'The Urbanism of Thomas Sharp, *Planning Perspectives*, 24.1 (2009), pp. 3–27.

Pendlebury, John, Erten, Erdem, and Larkham, Peter J., *Alternative Visions of Post-War Reconstruction, Creating the Modern Townscape* (London, 2014).

People and Cities (Report of the 1963 London conference organized by the British Road Federation in association with the Town Planning Institute) (London, 1963).

Pevsner, Nikolaus, *Pioneers of the Modern Movement from William Morris to Walter Gropius* (London, 1936).

Pevsner, Nikolaus, *The Englishness of English Art* (London, 1956).

Pevsner, Nikolaus, *Visual Planning and the Picturesque* (Los Angeles, 2010).

Pimlott, Ben, *Harold Wilson* (London, 1992).

Poulson, John, *Southport Town Centre Map* (Pontefract, 1964).

Powell, Kenneth, *Powell and Moya* (London, 2009).

Power, Anne, *Hovels to High Rise* (London, 1993).

Powers, Alan, *Frances Pollen: Architect, 1926–1987* (London, 1999).

Powers, Alan, *Britain: Modern Architectures in History* (London, 2007).

Powers, Alan, 'Exhibition 58: Modern Architecture in England at Moma, 1937', *Architectural History*, 56 (2008), pp. 277–98.

Powers, Alan, *Aldington, Craig and Collinge* (London, 2009).

Price, Frank, *Being There* (Leicester, 2002).

Ramsden, John, *The Winds of Change: Macmillan to Heath, 1957–1975* (London, 1996).

Rasmussen, Steen Eilar, *London, The Unique City* (London, 1937).

Reisman, David, *The Lonely Crowd* (New Haven, 1952).

Reynolds, Josephine P., 'Shopping in the North-West', *Town Planning Review*, 34.3 (October 1963), pp. 213–36.

Rice, Ian, '"Ziggurats for Bureaucrats": Sir Leslie Martin's Whitehall Scheme', *Architectural Research Quarterly*, 8 (2004).

Richards, J. M., *Modern Architecture* (London, 1940).

Richards, J. M., *The Castles on the Ground: The Anatomy of Suburbia* (London, 1973).

Ritter, Paul, *Planning for Man and Motor* (Oxford, 1963).

Roberts, John, *Pedestrian Precincts in Britain* (London, 1981).

Robinson, Andrew, *The Man Who Deciphered Linear B: The Story of Michael Ventris* (London, 2002).

Rowe, Colin, *As I Was Saying: Texas, Pre-Texas, Cambridge* (Boston, 1996).

Rowe, Colin and Koetter, Fred, *Collage City* (Cambridge, MA, 1976).

Royal Commission on the distribution of the Industrial Population, *Report* (London, 1940).

Royal Institute of British Architects, *Towards a Better London: A Report on the Greater London Development Plan* (London, 1970).
Rudberg, Eva, *Sven Markelius; Architect* (Stockholm, 1989).
Saint, Andrew, *Towards a Social Architecture* (London and New Haven, 1987).
Saint, Andrew, '"Spread the People": The LCC's Dispersal Policy, 1889–1965,' in *Politics and the People of London, The London County Council 1889–1965*, ed. Andrew Saint (London, 1989).
Saint, Andrew, *A Change of Heart: English Architecture Since the War* (London, 1992).
Sampson, Anthony, *The Anatomy of Britain* (London, 1962).
Sampson, Anthony, *The Anatomy of Britain Today* (London, 1965).
Samuel, Raphael, *Theatres of Memory Vol. 1: Past and Present in Contemporary Culture* (London, 1994).
Samuel, Raphael, *Island Stories: Unravelling Britain, Theatres of Memory vol. 2* London, 1998).
Samuel, Raphael *The Lost World of British Communism* (London, 2006).
Sandbrook, Dominic, *Never Had it so Good: A History of Britain from Suez to the Beatles* (London, 2005).
Sandbrook, Dominic, *White Heat, A History of Britain in the Swinging Sixties* (London, 2006).
Saumarez Smith, Otto, 'Robinson College, Cambridge, and the Twilight of a Collegiate Modernism, 1974–81', *Architectural History,* 55 (2012), pp. 369–402.
Saumarez Smith, Otto, 'Graeme Shankland. A Sixties Architect-Planner and the Political Culture of the British Left', *Architectural History*, 57 (2014), pp. 393–422.
Saumarez Smith, Otto, 'Central Government and Town Centre Redevelopment', *Historical Journal,* 58.1 (March, 2015), pp. 217–44.
Scott, Keith, *Shopping Centre Design* (London, 1989).
Seabrook, Jeremy, *City Close Up* (London, 1971).
Self, Peter, *Cities in Flood; the Problem of Urban Growth* (London, 1957).
Shankland, Graeme, 'Ownership, Patronage and Architecture', in *Contemporary Problems of Land Ownership* (London, 1962).
Shankland, Graeme, *Liverpool City Centre Plan* (Liverpool, 1965).
Shankland, Graeme, *Our Secret Economy: the Response of the Informal Economy to the Rise of Mass Unemployment* (London, 1980).
Shankland, Graeme, Willmott, Peter, and Jordan, David, *Inner London: Policies for Dispersal and Balance* (London, 1977).
Shankland Cox, and Associates, *Bolton Town Centre Map* ([Bolton,] 1965).
Shankland Cox Associates, *Social Survey, Childwall Valley* (Liverpool, 1967).
Shankland Cox Associates, *Winsford Plan, Proposals for Town Expansion* (Chester, 1967).
Shankland Cox Associates, *Ipswich Draft Basic Plan* (London, 1968).
Shankland Cox Associates, *The Planning of Isfahan* (London, 1968).
Shankland Cox Associates, *Deeside planning Study: Consultants Report to the Secretary of State for Wales* (Liverpool, 1970).

Shankland Cox Associates, *La Vie dans un Grand Ensemble: Étude de l'Habitat au Puits-la-Marlière en Banlieue Nord de Paris* (Pontoise, 1971).
Shankland Cox Associates, *Woodley and Earley Master Plan* (London, 1971).
Shapely, Peter, *The Politics of Housing: Power, Consumers and Urban Culture* (Manchester, 2007).
Shapely, Peter, 'The Entrepreneurial City: The Role of Local Government and City-Centre Redevelopment in Post-War Industrial English Cities', *Twentieth Century British History*, 22.4 (2011), pp. 498–520.
Shapely, Peter, 'Civic Pride and Redevelopment in the Post-War British City', *Urban History*, 39:02 (2012), pp. 310–28.
Shapely, Peter, 'Governance in the Post-war City: Historical Reflections on Public-Private Partnerships in the UK', *International Journal of Urban and Regional Research*, 37.4 (2013), pp. 1288–304.
Sharr, Adam and Thornton, Stephen, *Demolishing Whitehall: Harold Wilson, Leslie Martin and the Architecture of White Heat* (London, 2014).
Sharp, Thomas, *Town and Countryside* (London, 1932).
Sharp, Thomas, *Town Planning* (London, 1940).
Sharp, Thomas, *Cathedral City, A Plan for Durham* (London, 1945).
Sharp, Thomas, *Exeter Phoenix* (London, 1946).
Sharp, Thomas, *Georgian City; A Plan for the Preservation and Improvement of Chichester* (Brighton, 1949).
Sharp, Thomas, *Newer Sarum: A Plan For Salisbury* (London, 1949).
Sharp, Thomas, *English Panorama* (London, 1950).
Sharp, Thomas, *Design in Town and Village* (London, 1953).
Sharp, Thomas, *Town and Townscape* (London, 1968).
Simmie, J. M., *Citizens in Conflict: Sociology of Town Planning* (London, 1974).
Skeffington Committee, *People and Planning: Report of the committee on public participation in planning* (London, 1968).
Smigielski, Konrad, *Market Area Leicester, Report of the City Planning Officer* (Leicester, 1963).
Smigielski, Konrad, *Leicester Traffic Plan* (Leicester, 1964).
Smigielski, Konrad, *Self-supporting Co-operative Village at Stanford Hall, Nottinghamshire* (Coalville, 1978).
Smith, T. Dan, *An Autobiography* (Newcastle upon Tyne, 1970).
Smithson, Alison and Smithson, Peter, *Ordinariness and Light, Urban Theories 1952–60 and their application in a building project 1963–70* (London, 1970).
Smithson, Alison and Smithson, Peter, *The Charged Void: Architecture* (London, 2002).
Smithson, Alison and Smithson, Peter, *The Charged Void: Urbanism* (London, 2004).
Stamp, Gavin, *Britain's Lost Cities* (London, 2007).
Stamp, Gavin, *Lost Victorian Britain: How the Twentieth Century Destroyed the Nineteenth Century's Architectural Masterpieces* (London, 2013).
Stamp, Gavin, 'Anti-Ugly Action', *AA Files* 70 (2015), pp. 76–88.
Steel, Robert and Slayton, William, *Urban Renewal, Proposals for Britain and Experience in America* (London, 1965).

Stonehouse, Roger, *Colin St John Wilson, Buildings and Projects* (London, 2007), pp. 402–25.

Sutcliffe, Anthony and Smith, Roger, *Birmingham 1939–1970* (Oxford, 1974).

Swenarton, Mark, 'Politics versus Architecture: the Alexandra Road Public Enquiry of 1978-81', *Planning Perspectives*, 29.4 (2004), pp. 1–23.

Swenarton, Mark, 'Geared to Producing Ideas, With the Emphasis on Youth: the Creation of the Camden Borough Architect's Department under Sydney Cook', *Journal of Architecture*, 16.3 (2011), pp. 387–414.

Swenarton, Mark, 'Developing a New Format for Urban Housing: Neave Brown and the Design of the Alexandra Road Estate', *Journal of Architecture*, 17.6 (2012), pp. 873–1007.

Swenarton, Mark, 'Politics, Property and Planning: Building the Brunswick, 1958-74', *Town Planning Review*, 84.2 (2013), pp. 197–226.

Swenarton, Mark, Avermaete, Tom, and van den Heuvel, Dirk, eds, *Architecture and the Welfare State* (Abingdon, 2014).

Sykes, A. J. M., Livingsone, J. M., and Green, M., *Cumbernauld 67* (Glasgow, 1967).

Taylor, Nicholas, *The Village in the City* (London, 1973).

Taylor, Nigel, *Urban Planning Theory Since 1945* (London, 1998).

Thorpe, D. R., *Alec Douglas-Home* (London, 1996).

Thorpe, D. R., *Eden: The Life and Times of Anthony Eden, first Earl of Avon 1897–1977* (London, 2003).

Thorpe, D. R., *Supermac; The Life of Harold Macmillan* (London, 2011).

Tiratsoo, Nicholas, *Reconstruction, Affluence and Labour Politics: Coventry 1945–1960* (London, 1990).

Todd, Selina, 'Phoenix Rising: Working Class Life and Urban Reconstruction, c. 1945–1967', *Journal of British Studies*, 54.3 (2015), pp. 679–702.

Tomlinson, Jim, 'Conservative Modernization, 1960–64: Too Little too Late?', *Contemporary British History*, 11.3 (1997), pp. 18–38.

Tomlinson, Jim, 'De-industrialisation not decline: A new meta-narrative for post-war British history', *Twentieth Century British History*, 27.1 (2016), pp. 76–99.

Tripp, Alker, *Town Planning and Road Traffic* (London, 1942).

Tripp, Alker, *Road Traffic and its Control* (London, 1950).

Trystan Edwards, Arthur, *Good and Bad Manners in Architecture* (London 1924).

Trystan Edwards, Arthur, *Modern Terrace Housing; Researches on High Density Housing* (London, 1946).

Trystan Edwards, Arthur, *Towards Tomorrow's Architecture* (London, 1968).

Tyrwhitt, J., Sert, J. L., and Rogers, E.N., eds, *The Heart of the City: Towards the Humanization of Urban Life* (London, 1952).

Warburton, Nigel, *Ernö Goldfinger: the Life of an Architect* (London, 2003).

Ward, Colin, ed., *Vandalism,* (London, 1973).

Ward, Colin, *Housing: An Anarchist Approach* (London, 1976).

Ward, Colin, *When We Build Again Lets Have Housing that Works!* (London, 1985).

Ward, Colin, *Talking Houses: Ten Lectures* (London, 1990).

Ward, Colin, *Welcome Thinner City: Urban Survival in the 1990s* (London, 1990).

Ward, Colin, *New Town, Home Town: The Lessons of Experience* (London, 1993).

Ward, Pamela, *Conservation and Development in Historic Towns and Cities* (Newcastle upon Tyne, 1968).

Ward, Stephen V., 'Public–Private Partnerships', in *British Planning: 50 Years of Urban and Regional Policy,* ed. B. Cullingworth (London, 1999), pp. 232–49.

Ward, Stephen V., 'Thomas Sharp as a Figure in the British Planning Movement', *Planning Perspectives,* 23.4 (2008), pp. 523–33.

Ward, Stephen V., 'Soviet Communism and the British Planning Movement: Rational Learning or Utopian Imagining?', *Planning Perspectives,* 2.4 (2012), pp. 499–524.

Watkin, David, *Morality and Architecture: the Development of a Theme in Architectural History and Theory from the Gothic Revival to the Modern Movement* (London, 1977).

Weiler, Peter, 'The Rise and Fall of the Conservatives' "Grand Design for Housing", 1951–64', *Contemporary British History,* 14.1 (2000), pp. 122–50.

Whitehouse, Brian P, *Partners in Property* (London, 1964).

Whyte, William, 'The Modernist Moment at the University of Leeds', *Historical Journal,* 51.1 (2008), pp. 169–93.

Whyte, William, 'The Englishness of English Architecture: Modernism and the Making of a National International Style, 1927–1957', *Journal of British Studies,* 48 (2009), pp. 441–65.

Whyte, William, *Redbrick: A social and architectural history of Britain's civic universities* (Oxford, 2015).

Wildman, Charlotte, 'Urban Transformation in Liverpool and Manchester, 1918–1939', *Historical Journal,* 55.1 (2012), pp. 119–43.

Williams-Ellis, Clough, *England and the Octopus* (London, 1928).

Williams-Ellis, Clough, *Britain and the Beast* (London, 1937).

Williams-Ellis, Clough, *Architect Errant* (London, 1971).

Willmott, Peter, *Family and Class in a London Suburb* (London, 1960).

Willmott, Peter, *The Evolution of a Community: a Study of Dagenham after Forty Years* (London, 1963).

Wilson, Harold, *The New Britain: Labour's Plan* (Harmondsworth, 1964).

Wilson, Hugh, *Cumbernauld New Town, Preliminary Planning Report* (Glasgow, 1958).

Wilson, Hugh, *Cumbernauld New Town, Preliminary Planning Report, First Adendum Report* (Glasgow, 1959).

Wilson, Hugh, *Cumbernauld New Town, Preliminary Planning Report, Second Adendum Report* (Glasgow, 1962).

Wilson, Hugh and Womersley, Lewis, *Expansion of Northampton: Consultant's Proposals for Designation* (London, 1966).

Wilson, Hugh and Womersley, Lewis, *Northampton, Bedford, North Bucks Study* (London, 1966).

Wilson, Hugh and Womersley, Lewis, *Northampton Master Plan* (London, 1966).

Wilson, Hugh and Womersley, Lewis, *Manchester Education Precinct; The final Report of the Planning Consultants* (Manchester, 1967).

Wilson, Hugh and Womersley, Lewis, *Cheltenham Study—Final Report* (Cheltenham, 1973).

Wilson, Hugh and Womersley, Lewis, *Change or Decay: Liverpool Inner Area Study* (London, 1977).

Wilson, Hugh and Womersley, Lewis, with Kirkpatrick, Scott Wilson and Partners, *Oxford Central Area Study* (London, 1968).

Wilson, Hugh and Womersley, Lewis, with Kirkpatrick, Scott Wilson and Partners, *Teesside Survey & Plan: Final Report of the Steering Committee* (London, 1969–71).

de Wolfe, Ivor [Hubert de Cronin Hastings], *Italian Townscape* (London, 1963).

de Wolfe, Ivor [Hubert de Cronin Hastings], *Civilia: The End of Sub Urban Man, a Challenge to Semidetsia* (London, 1971).

Wood, A. A. *City of Norwich Central Area Appraisal* ([Norwich,] 1966).

Worpole, Ken, *Here Comes the Sun, Architecture and Public Space in Twentieth Century European Culture* (London, 2000).

Woudsta, Jan, 'Reviewing the Corbusian Landscape: Arcadia or No Man's Land?', *Garden History*, 28.1 (2000), pp. 135–51.

Yelling, Jim, 'The Development of Residential Urban Renewal Policies in England: Planning for Modernization in the 1960s', *Planning Perspectives,* 14 (1999) pp. 1–18.

Young, Ken and Garside, Patricia, *Metropolitan London: Politics and Urban Change, 1837–1981* (London, 1981).

Young, Michael, *The Chipped White Cups of Dover* (London, 1960).

Young, Michael and Willmott, Peter, *Family and Kinship in East London* (London, 1957).

Zimmerman, Claire, ed., *Neo-Avant-Garde and Postmodern and Beyond* (London and New Haven, 2011).

Zweig, Ferdinand, *The Worker in Affluent Society* (London, 1961).

Index